Strategies to Enhance Literacy and Learning in Middle School Content Area Classrooms

Strategies to Enhance Literacy and Learning in Middle School Content Area Classrooms

THIRD EDITION

Judith L. Irvin

Florida State University

Douglas R. Buehl

Metropolitan School District, Madison, Wisconsin

Barbara J. Radcliffe

Florida State University

Boston • New York • San Francisco
Mexico City • Montreal • Toronto • London • Madrid • Munich • Paris
Hong Kong • Singapore • Tokyo • Cape Town • Sydney

Executive Editor: Aurora Martínez Ramos
Series Editorial Assistant: Lynda Giles
Executive Marketing Manager: Krista Clark
Composition and Prepress Buyer: Linda Cox
Manufacturing Buyer: Linda Morris
Manufacturing Manager: Megan Cochran
Cover Coordinator: Joel Gendron
Editorial-Production Coordinator: Mary Beth Finch
Editorial-Production Service: Stratford Publishing Services
Electronic Composition: Stratford Publishing Services

For related titles and support materials, visit our online catalog at www.ablongman.com.

Between the time Web site information is gathered and then published, it is not unusual for some sites to have closed. Also, the transcription of URLs can result in unintended typographical errors. The publisher would appreciate notification where these errors occur so that they may be corrected in subsequent editions.

Library of Congress Cataloging-in-Publication Data

Irvin, Judith L.,
    Strategies to enhance literacy and learning in middle school content area classrooms/
Judith L. Irvin, Douglas R. Buehl, Barbara J. Radcliffe. — 3rd ed.
        p. cm.
    Rev. ed. of: Reading and the middle school student. 2nd ed. 1997.
    ISBN 0-205-36061-0
        1. Reading (Elementary)—United States. 2. Reading (Middle school)—United States.
3. Content area reading—United States. I. Buehl, Douglas R. II. Radcliffe, Barbara J. III.
Irvin, Judith L., 1947-Reading and the middle school student. IV. Title.

    LB1573.I73 2006
    428.4071′2-dc22

                                                                                    2006045527

All photos are by Douglas R. Buehl except for the photo on page 128 by Frank Siteman and the photo on page 147 by T. Lindfors/Lindfors Photography.

Printed in the United States of America

10   9   8   7   6   5   4   3   2   1   11   10   09   08   07   06

Contents

7   *Using Prior Knowledge*   124

Preface

Strategies to Enhance Literacy and Learning in Middle School Content Area Classrooms is a book for prospective and practicing teachers, administrators, reading specialists, English language learner teachers, and literacy coaches concerned with improving the literacy abilities of middle school students. The last decade has seen tremendous interest in improving adolescent literacy. Also, current research and theory in reading education, learning theory, and brain-based research have contributed to what educators know about the most exciting ways for students to improve their literacy abilities. The powerful and exciting implications for instruction that result from this renewed interest, the fine and growing research base, and a commitment to adolescent literacy motivated us to write this book. Teachers deserve to receive the benefits of research and theory in a readable, usable form. Additionally, middle school students deserve instruction chosen because it is research-based and known to facilitate improved literacy learning.

Prospective middle school teachers will appreciate the discussion of the basic processes of literacy instruction and motivational techniques, student work, and step-by-step approaches to instruction. Numerous strategies are recommended for the instruction of understanding text, vocabulary, comprehension, and study skills. Veteran teachers will find the discussion of recent research findings useful to update their knowledge in such areas as developmental tasks of adolescence, motivation, struggling readers, and strategic learning. This book serves as a handy reference for learning strategies in all content-area instruction.

New to This Edition

This edition has been heavily updated to reflect current research in the field and includes many new features, including a wealth of practical strategies for fostering literacy in all subject areas for middle grade students. Each chapter addresses specific strategies that can be used by middle school teachers with English language learners. The book focuses on the integration of classroom implementation of literacy with content area instruction. It also includes new issues and trends in adolescent literacy, such as policy and position statements and federal action.

We would like to thank Lori N. Elliott of Georgia State University, Sharon A. Fesster of Newberry College, Joyce A. Minor of Morehaed State University, and Linda Thistlethwaite of Western Illinois University for reviewing earlier versions of this text.

We have a long-standing interest in and considerable experience with middle school students, teachers, and schools. Writing this book is our way of sharing what we know and how we feel about helping middle school students read and write better. We hope you enjoy reading and using this book.

JLI
DRB
BJR

1

Adolescent Literacy

Talking Points

- Why do you think middle schools have traditionally not offered reading support for all their students?
- What actions need to be taken to address the neglect of adolescent literacy?
- What is the classroom teacher's role in developing young adolescents who are effective readers and learners?

As students file into Ms. Dawson's sixth grade world cultures class, Eric trips and spills the contents of his bookbag all over the floor, scattering papers everywhere. After getting everyone settled down and Eric soothed, she begins her lesson on Argentina with a video clip about the history of the tango. She knew her students would be interested that the dance was created in the barrios of Buenos Aires but did not become "acceptable" until a debut in Paris. It is now the national dance and unique to Argentina. She also knew that many of her students needed help visualizing what they would be reading about and suspected that most of them lacked prior knowledge of South American cultures. After examining the pictures, maps, and other visual material in the book, it was time to read and create a chapter map to use tomorrow in a discussion comparing Argentina with Chile. As she moves around the room, she assesses her students as they begin reading the text.

Craig is an academically motivated student who excels in challenging math and science classes. But he is a slow reader, and he says that he misses a lot when he reads. His mother is concerned that his reading lags behind his other academic skills and reports that he almost never reads unless required to as classwork. He has a hard time determining what is important and what is not, so the chapter map is difficult for him to construct. Ms. Dawson spends time with him pointing out the headings and graphic signals.

Eric is new to the school, enrolling during the semester from a large urban district in another state. He participates in sports, but does not do well in classes and feels that school has little to offer people like him. He doesn't even try to read, props his head in his hand, and proceeds to fall asleep. Why should he try? He's not sure how long he will be going to this school anyway. When Ms. Dawson comes to Eric, she encourages him to begin the reading, hands him a cloze graphic organizer to complete the chapter map, and gives him some help to guide his reading.

Brittany likes school—that is, she likes going to school and socializing with her friends. She thinks that her classes are BORING, and that she will never use any of this "stuff." She liked the tango video and wondered what Christmas must be like when schools got out for summer vacation just one week before the holiday. Brittany liked it better when the teachers went around the room reading the text out loud. She was proud of her ability to read fluently and fast, prounouncing every word correctly. When she reads silently, however, she does not "get it." Ms. Dawson reminds her to use sticky notes to code the text, which helps her focus on main ideas and comprehend the text.

Qi is an earnest student whose parents do not speak English. As a refugee she finds that a great deal of the information that is common knowledge to her classmates is unknown to her. It takes her a long time to complete her classwork, and she is constantly encountering new words that she does not know. In courses like math she does quite well, but in many others, despite her strong work ethic, she is just getting by. Ms. Dawson encourages her to think about how Argentina is like or different from her home country by using a Venn diagram before working on the chapter map.

Tenille has received special education support since third grade for a learning disability in reading. She finds much of her class work beyond her ability to read independently, and it takes her a long time to complete assignments. Tenille's teachers let her take the work to her resource class to complete it. Ms. Dawson reminds Tenille to use a template of a chapter map and fill in the major headings first.

This classroom, like middle school classrooms across the nation, represents a diverse group of young adolescents who exhibit a multiplicity of literacy strengths and needs. Middle school teachers have no trouble identifying the Craigs, Erics, Brittanys, Qis, and Tenilles in their classes. Without question, developing the literacy skills of middle school students is a complex undertaking. In this chapter, we discuss current thinking about adolescent literacy, including a position statement published by the International Reading Association and recent policy statements; outline school-wide approaches to literacy learning; and provide a purpose and overview of the book.

The Neglect of Adolescent Literacy

"I am beginning to wonder whether there is a political and public mindset that literacy learning is critical only in early childhood. The faulty and misguided assumption, 'If young children learn to read early on, they will read to learn throughout their lives,' results in more harm than good"(Vacca, 1998, p. 606).

This insightful observation by Richard Vacca, past president of the International Reading Association (IRA) and for several decades a leader in adolescent literacy, underscores what he termed the "benign neglect" of addressing the needs of readers in our nation's middle and high schools. Or, as Carol Santa (1999), another past president of the IRA concluded: "Adolescents are being shortchanged" (p. 1).

National attention for funding programs and research in the last two decades has focused on the needs of beginning or early readers. The national mantra in literacy that "every child will learn to read by third grade," while targeting the crucial role of building a strong foundation in reading, unfortunately has communicated a misconception that learning to read is a short-term goal that can be accomplished during elementary school instruction. As the National Council of Teachers of English (NCTE) explained, in its Position Statement on Adolescent Literacy: "Reading is not a technical skill acquired once and for all in the primary grades, but rather a developmental process. A reader's competence continues to grow through engagement with various types of texts and wide reading for various purposes over a lifetime" (NCTE, 2004, p. 1).

The focus on young children has resulted in the needs of older readers being largely unmet (Vacca, 1998; Vacca & Alvermann, 1998). Systematic reading instruction is infrequently offered beyond grade five in many of the school districts of our nation. Where reading is offered in middle school, it is often provided only for those students who score significantly below average on nationally normed achievement tests (Irvin, 1998; Santa, 1998). The RAND Reading Study Group, commissioned by the U.S. Department of Education to delineate the research on reading comprehension, bluntly summarized the results of this neglect of the reading development of older students: "Research has shown that many children who read at the third-grade level in grade 3 will not automatically become proficient comprehenders in later grades. Therefore, teachers must teach comprehension explicitly, beginning in the primary grades and continuing through high school" (Snow, 2002, p. xii).

Middle school teachers are well aware that much more needs to be done with the literacy development of their students. Imagine you were to eavesdrop on the daily chat in the teachers' lounge as your colleagues savor a hard-earned cup of coffee and share reflections about teaching in today's middle schools. What might you hear?

Glen is a life science teacher who has taught two decades and worries that he has had to "water down" his curriculum over the years. More students are failing this required science course, which has administration concerned. Glen relies much less on the textbook than he used to, because the text is relatively difficult and he has found that many of his students do not read it anyway. He emphasizes lab work, but also delivers key components of the curriculum through teacher presentations and notes students are expected to copy from the chalkboard.

Susan is a pre-algebra teacher and a veteran educator. She has been using a text that follows the National Council of Teachers of Mathematics standards, but is concerned about "how much reading is in the book." Susan hopes that this curricular direction is the right one, but sometimes she wonders if the old math approach was better.

Marci is a language arts teacher who is starting her third year of teaching. She conscientiously plans for a very interactive classroom; she wants her students involved in learning, and she works hard to motivate them. Most students engage actively in her lessons, but she must constantly battle with "students who don't want to do any work." Sometimes she wonders if her curriculum is too interactive,

given the amount of time she expends managing the behavior of some easily distracted individuals.

Randall is a social studies teacher. He likes the recently adopted geography textbook because of its strong multicultural emphasis, but many students still say it's hard and do not do the assignments. "How am I supposed to teach geography to students who can't read?" he wonders. He incorporates current events as a motivational way to make connections to geography. Students are required each week to locate a newspaper article that relates to some element of the curriculum, but sometimes nearly half his students neglect to complete this assignment. He has taught seventeen years.

Tina has many low-achieving students in her health classes, several of whom are receiving special education services. She strongly feels that they are capable of handling more challenging tasks, although they repeatedly assure her that they cannot. She is constantly looking for ideas and materials that will help them become more skilled. Frequently, lessons she plans do not go as well as she'd like and she's not sure how to use materials that she knows the kids will find difficult. Beginning this year, Tina is team teaching this course with a special education teacher, as the school attempts to transition to offering a more differentiated curriculum. She has taught health and physical education for ten years.

Middle school teachers can readily identify with the literacy issues with which Glen, Susan, Marci, Randall, and Tina are grappling: students who experience daily difficulties learning from text materials, students who regularly refuse to do required reading out of class, students who are virtually unable to read middle school materials, students who are still learning the rudiments of the English language, students who read but fail to comprehend the most important information, students who are bored or uninterested with much of what they read. "How do you plan successful lessons," teachers ask, "when these literacy frustrations are a daily reality in our classrooms?"

A New Focus on Adolescent Literacy

In recent years, a number of influential organizations have focused their attention on adolescent readers. The International Reading Association (IRA) formed the Commission on Adolescent Literacy (ALC) in 1997, to examine the state of adolescent literacy in the United States. The ALC undertook several initatives to confront the "crisis" in adolescent literacy. In major cities across the country, the ALC sponsored institutes and conference sessions that highlighted the challenges faced by secondary educators and shared exemplary reading programs and practices. To increase public support for secondary literacy programs, the ALC sponsored numerous publications, including the influential *Position Statement on Adolescent Literacy* (Moore, Bean, Birdyshaw, & Rycik, 1999). This position statement advocated seven principles for adolescent literacy:

1. Adolescents deserve access to a wide variety of reading material that they can and want to read.
2. Adolescents deserve instruction that builds both the skill and desire to read increasingly complex materials.
3. Adolescents deserve assessment that shows them their strengths as well as their needs and that guides their teachers to design instruction that will best help them grow as readers.
4. Adolescents deserve expert teachers who model and provide explicit instruction in reading comprehension and study strategies across the curriculum.
5. Adolescents deserve reading specialists who assist individual students having difficulty learning how to read.
6. Adolescents deserve teachers who understand the complexities of individual adolescent readers, respect their differences, and respond to their characteristics.
7. Adolescents deserve homes, communities, and a nation that will support their efforts to achieve advanced levels of literacy and provide the support necessary for them to succeed.

Another national organization that has mobilized to meet the crisis in adolescent literacy is the Alliance for Excellent Education (AEE). AEE has published critical documents that articulate an agenda for adolescent literacy by providing

guidance to school and district leadership, as well as policy makers, about the best ways to enhance literacy achievement of middle and high school students.

In *Every Child a Graduate: A Framework for an Excellent Education for all Middle and High School Students*, Joftus (2002) presented data that confirmed that graduation rates are appallingly low, especially for minority, urban youth. AEE proposed that this problem can be addressed through four initiatives: Adolescent Literacy Initiative, Teacher and Principal Quality Initiative, College Preparation Initiative, and Small Learning Communities Initiative. Through the Adolescent Literacy Initiative, AEE recommended that every high-needs middle and high school employ a literacy specialist "who trains teachers across subject areas to improve the reading and writing of all students" (p. 3).

In *Adolescents and Literacy: Reading for the 21st Century*, Kamil (2004) reviewed key literature and presented critical issues in adolescent literacy, including the developmental nature of reading and content learning, the differing needs of English language learners, the role that technology can play in helping students become better readers and learners, the importance of professional development for teachers, and the infrastructure for reading in middle and high schools. Kamil concluded that "there is a strong body of research-based knowledge that is available about adolescent literacy . . . [and that] policy makers should use [this] research . . . as a foundation for change in secondary schools" (p. 29).

In *Reading Next: A Vision for Action and Research in Middle and High School Literacy*, Biancarosa and Snow (2004) created a framework for reform efforts that focuses on comprehension and proposes fifteen key elements of effective adolescent literacy programs that are bifurcated into instructional and infrastructure improvements (p. 4–5) (See Table 1.1).

In *The Literacy Coach: A Key to Teaching and Learning in Secondary Schools*, Sturtevant (2004) presented the rationale for a literacy coach who collaborates with teachers on the literacy development of their students as they teach their various

TABLE 1.1   *Elements of a Literacy Program*

Instructional Improvement	
1. *Direct, explicit comprehension instruction,* which is instruction in the strategies and processes that proficient readers use to understand what they read, including summarizing, keeping track of one's own understanding, and a host of other practices.	6. *Diverse texts,* which are texts at a variety of difficulty levels and on a variety of topics.
2. *Effective instructional principles embedded in content,* including language arts teachers using content-area texts and content-area teachers providing instruction and practice in reading and writing skills specific to their subject areas.	7. *Intensive writing,* including instruction connected to the kinds of writing tasks students will have to perform well in high school and beyond.
3. *Motivation and self-directed learning,* which includes building motivation to read and learn, providing students with the instruction and supports needed for independent learning tasks they will face after graduation.	8. *A technology component,* which includes technology as a tool for and a topic of literacy instruction.
4. *Text-based collaborative learning,* which involves students interacting with one another around a variety of texts.	9. *Ongoing formative assessment of students,* which is informal, often daily assessment of how students are progressing under current instructional practices.
5. *Strategic tutoring,* which provides students with intense individualized reading, writing, and content instruction as needed.	
Infrastructure Improvement	
10. *Extended time for literacy,* which includes approximately two to four hours of literacy instruction and practice that takes place in language arts and content-area classes.	13. *Teacher teams,* which are interdisciplinary teams that meet regularly to discuss students and align instruction.
11. *Professional development* that is both long-term and ongoing.	14. *Leadership,* which can come from principals and teachers who have a solid understanding of how to teach reading and writing to the full array of students present in schools.
12. *Ongoing summative assessment of students and programs,* which is more formal and provides data that are reported for accountability and research purposes.	15. *A comprehensive and coordinated literacy program,* which is interdisciplinary and interdepartmental and may even coordinate with out-of-school organizations and the local community.

Source: From Biancarosa & Snow, 2004.

content subjects. The literacy coach initiative is especially important because reading specialists have been rarely found in secondary schools, and content area teachers generally do not feel competent or adequately prepared to meet the literacy needs of their students (Bintz, 1997; O'Brien & Stewart, 1992; O'Brien, Stewart, & Moje, 1995; Ratekin, Simpson, Alvermann, & Dishner, 1998). Yet, it is unrealistic to expect language arts teachers, who have been prepared to teach writing, literature, and grammar, to shoulder sole responsibility for reading instruction in content fields such as science, math, social studies, and technology. New federal and state initiatives are encouraging the training of literacy coaches to collaborate with teachers, especially those working with students not meeting acceptable levels of achievement.

In a historic endorsement of the literacy coach concept, five professional educational associations—the IRA, the National Council of Teachers of English, the National Council of Teachers of Mathematics, the National Science Teachers Association, and the National Council for the Social Studies—joined in a task force to formulate national *Standards for Literacy Coaches* (International Reading Association, 2006). These influential standards emphasize the need for literacy coaches to work with middle and high school teachers across the curriculum.

The federal government is beginning to respond to accelerating pressure to address adolescent literacy. In August 2005, the United States Department of Education announced the Striving Readers program, which was created to improve the literacy skills of teenage students. Two integral aspects of the Striving Readers program include school-level strategies that increase reading achievement of all students and provide professional development in literacy for teachers across the curriculum and interventions targeted for those students struggling most in reading. All of these national efforts have focused attention on the literacy and learning needs of young adolescents.

Impact of Federal and State Mandates on Adolescent Literacy

Teachers in many states are engaged in aligning their curriculum to state and national standards in their content fields. In addition, a number of states have coupled student performance on statewide assessments with these content standards. Some of these assessments take the form of high stakes tests, such as grade-level promotion tests. On these assessments, students are usually asked to demonstrate more than knowledge within a content area; they are also compelled to display their ability to read and understand content materials and to reason through written responses.

No Child Left Behind has challenged the nation's schools to ensure that students meet academic standards. The NCLB requirements for middle schools include three main areas: teacher quality, testing, and adequate yearly progress. In the area of teacher quality, NCLB treats middle schools like elementary schools on some occasions and like high schools on others. The requirements for teacher quality are less defined and shift depending on the structure of the middle school. If the state considers a K–8 school as elementary, then the teachers must meet the teacher quality requirements of the elementary level; however, if the state deems a K–8 structure as a "school within a school," then NCLB holds the middle school teachers to the secondary school standards of teacher quality. These challenges require some teachers to have full certification in their content fields. NCLB ultimately scrutinizes the practice of all teachers as student achievement becomes more closely monitored and more public.

Perhaps the most significant aspect of NCLB for teachers is the accountability for Academic Yearly Progress, or AYP, which is the measure by which schools and districts are held accountable. Each state is responsible for developing an AYP definition that all schools must meet. In addition, each state is required to establish measurable, annual objectives that each student must meet by the year 2014. The ensuing assessments must also take into account the yearly progress of subgroups of students that include economically disadvantaged, racial and ethnic groups, students with disabilities, and second-language learners. Thus, the demand that schools assess and reach predetermined targets of achievement for all students will put pressure on teachers to ensure that all students are achieving at expected levels. For students to perform better academically, teachers must integrate literacy learning strategies into all subject areas. As states develop standards and align curriculum, assessments will continue to play a pivotal role in the academic lives of students, teachers, and administrators.

School-wide Approaches to Improving Adolescent Literacy

Learning to read is a lifelong process. It is impossible for a student to attain reading maturity in the few years of elementary school immersed in beginning reading instruction. Middle school students are expected to read increasingly difficult texts and increasingly more expository versus narrative material. Textbooks for middle school courses often require students to understand abstract concepts that assume a significant degree of background knowledge on the part of the reader. Middle school students are also expected to do more with what they read, to read increasingly longer text segments, to take notes, and complete homework assignments based on what they read. Young adolescents cannot be expected to accomplish all of these feats on their own. They need guidance and instruction.

Middle school teachers often feel frustrated by the contention between what they consider as their subject matter and competing claims on their time, energy, and expertise to help students with the process of learning. Teachers do not expect, of course, that their students will learn everything they will ever need to know about their subject area in those years leading up to high school; they want to develop students who will become lifelong learners, who will continue to integrate new knowledge into their understanding of various subject disciplines.

The idea that "each teacher who makes reading assignments is responsible to the direction and supervision of the reading and study activities that are involved" was first published by the National Committee on Reading (National Society for the Study of Education, 1925, p. 71). The theme that all teachers are responsible for their students' reading performance can be traced in workshops, reports, conferences, and educational literature year after year since 1925.

During the 1970s, issues connected with secondary reading gained increasing prominence (e.g., Herber, 1970). Secondary schools were encouraged to broaden their perspectives on adolescent literacy beyond offering some sort of a "fix-it" class for "remedial" readers. "Teaching reading in the content areas" became a theme of staff development initiatives and the foundation for reading programs that targeted the development of the literacy needs of all adolescent learners. Middle school teachers of science, math, music, art, physical education, and other disciplines became familiar with the slogan "Every teacher a teacher of reading." Many states mandated secondary reading coursework for all teachers as part of their university and recertification requirements.

Yet, despite these consistent references to the need to teach reading in the middle school, relatively little action has been taken over the years. When teaching reading is everyone's responsibility, few seem to actually do it. O'Brien, Stewart, and Moje (1995) suggested that content literacy is difficult to infuse into the secondary school because it challenges the deeply embedded "values, beliefs, and practices that secondary teachers, students, and other members of the school culture hold" (p. 443) and involves rethinking curriculum, pedagogy, and school culture.

A school-wide approach to adolescent literacy becomes necessary if all teachers are to be expected to assume their roles in literacy instruction within their curricula areas. Buehl and Stumpf (2002) identified three essential components for a total school commitment.

1. Classroom reading comprehension instruction that emphasizes teaching strategies that assist all readers, both in the effective learning of course content as well as reinforcing their growth as proficient readers
2. Targeted reading instruction by trained reading teachers that recognizes the developmental needs of struggling readers and is coordinated with the general school literacy program
3. Support for learning in content classes, such as tutoring assistance and strategy support, which is offered within a class, during study periods, or during times outside the school day

These three essential components were visually represented as a three-legged stool (see Figure 1.1). Each leg was envisioned as a vital aspect of a comprehensive middle school literacy program. Clearly, this visual representation was meant to convey that if any of the three necessary components was missing or inadequate, the stool (namely an effective adolescent literacy program) would topple.

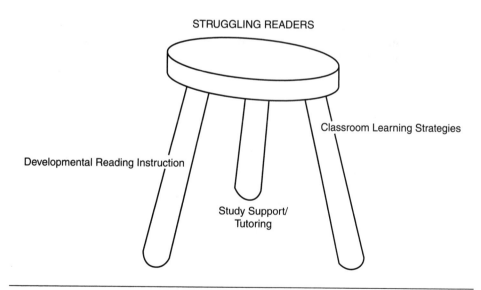

STRUGGLING READERS

Classroom Learning Strategies

Developmental Reading Instruction

Study Support/
Tutoring

FIGURE 1.1 *Struggling Readers*

Growing as Teachers of Literacy

Professional development that is long-term, job embedded, and focuses on the literacy learning process and strategies to improve reading and learning content is important for all middle school teachers as they continue to refine their abilities to work with a diverse range of readers daily in their classrooms (Fisher, 2001). Ideally, this professional growth is initiated and supported by district or school personnel, but educational settings are not always ideal. Nothing prevents individual teachers or small groups of teachers, however, from trying some of the strategies that have been supported by research and from sharing these new methods with each other. If one social studies teacher and one science teacher explore how to integrate reading and writing instruction in one cooperatively planned unit, professional growth would occur and students would ultimately benefit. If one reading teacher taught students a strategy for reading a life science book and shared that strategy with the science teacher, professional growth would occur and students would ultimately benefit. If one language arts and one social studies teacher worked together to read and write about a piece of literature, professional growth would occur and students would ultimately benefit. The possibilities for professional growth for teachers and for benefit to middle school students are limitless.

Purpose and Overview of the Book

This book is intended to assist middle school educators in applying current research and theory in the field of literacy to teaching and learning. "Literacy" as used throughout this book refers to any reading, writing, speaking, listening, viewing, or representing event, but the focus of this book is primarily on reading. Reading, however, is only one of the language systems and should be learned within the context of writing, speaking, listening, viewing, representing, and thinking. Although topics such as the writing process and higher order thinking are not specifically addressed in this book, most educators certainly recognize the necessity for integrating the instruction of all language systems with the development of thinking abilities.

In this chapter, we set the stage for improved literacy for middle school students by discussing national efforts to build an adolescent literacy agenda. In addition, we presented some ways that schools and districts can work collaboratively to create a literacy plan for everyone to follow. The foundational knowledge about literacy that many secondary school teachers lack since they were prepared mainly for teaching their content area is presented in Chapter 2 along with some common symptoms of ineffective learning. Motivating students to read and write better is a common concern for teachers. In Chapters 3 and 4, we present ways to create classroom environments that engage students in literacy and learning and discuss the special needs of struggling readers. In Chapter 5, we discuss ways that students can negotiate different types of text and present a method for evaluating textbooks. The current research in vocabulary acquisition is presented in Chapter 6 along with many strategies for helping students become independent word learners. Chapters 7–9 are filled with learning strategies to help students comprehend text. The book concludes with a discussion of assessment that guides instruction in Chapter 10.

Summary

Middle school provides an opportunity for educators to help students become proficient readers and writers before entering high school. Students who are confident in their ability to read and write hold the key to independent learning. What is necessary to enable students to achieve this goal? Teachers must understand their subject matter; understand the physical, emotional, social, and intellectual needs of students; and understand the nature of learning and the teaching of language and content. Beyond this, those making administrative decisions must understand how to organize the learning environment for the teaching of reading and writing in middle schools. Finally, educators must find ways to capitalize on young adolescents' natural desire to use language in the way it was intended—as a means of communication.

Extending Learning

Reviewing the Talking Points

Answer the questions now that you have read the chapter and compare your prereading and postreading responses.

Revisiting the Vignette

As the opening vignette indicated, students in today's middle schools represent a wide range of diversity in both ability and experience. The students in this vignette required teachers to address their strengths and their weaknesses on a variety of levels. This demand is part of the challenge of teaching in today's middle schools. Select one of the students in the opening vignette and discuss with a fellow teacher or classmate how you would address the needs of that student.

Terms to Remember and Use

adolescent literacy	explicit comprehension instruction	motivation
collaborative learning	NCLB	formative assessment
literacy initiatives	AYP	literacy coach

Write a series of sentences that meaningfully connect pairs of the above key terms. Your sentences should refer to ideas and concepts related to the literacy of middle school students.

Modifying Instruction for English Language Learners

Almost ten percent of the total student population (or more than 4.5 million students) in grades K–12 in the American school system are English language learners (ELLs) (National Center for Education Statistics, 2002). With over one million immigrants moving to the United States each year (Martin & Midgely, 1999), a growing number of ELLs arrive in the United States at different ages and developmental stages, bringing with them different backgrounds, school experiences, and literacy levels.

As native English-speaking students embrace the increased academic demands of middle school, their ELL counterparts encounter more challenges because of the English language barriers that they may or may not have overcome. Reading, one of the central aspects of most content areas and a fundamental skill necessary for advancement, becomes vital for these students' academic success. Moreover, the situation in the classroom for them is further complicated because

- English language learners come from diverse language backgrounds
- Some of their first languages are not based on the English alphabet
- Most educators, except for some bilingual ELL teachers, are monolingual and can only communicate with the diverse population of learners in English
- Mainstream teachers leave the university unprepared to teach using non-language-dependent ELL methodologies (Daniel, 2005).

More attention has been directed to ELLs as this population grows increasingly larger and their needs remain unmet. Mandatory placement and assessment requirements under the *No Child Left Behind Act* of 2002 require that ELLs have an education plan. Efforts to address ELL's academic and developmental needs are now included in some states' public education initiatives. Foundations also award grants to support research on special needs of ELLs and other literacy issues. For example, grants to the Center for Applied Linguistics (CAL) by the Carnegie Corporation of New York and the Rockefeller Foundation have enabled CAL to develop a language acquisition and academic literacy model—the Sheltered Instruction Observation Protocol (SIOP)—for middle and high school ELLs. These foundations also support another project, ExC-ELL (Expediting Comprehension for English Language Learners), which focuses on the special literacy needs of ELLs (deLeón, 2005). Although controversies continue around specific laws, mandates, policies, and research, ELLs deserve commitment and efforts to help them achieve their academic potential.

Beyond the Book

1. What challenges do you face with the diverse needs of your own student population?
2. Investigate the following Web sites for information on adolescent literacy.
   - Alliance for Excellent Education (www.all4ed.org)
   - International Reading Association (www.reading.org/resources/issues/positions_adolescent.html.
3. Investigate the following Web sites for more information on the *No Child Left Behind* legislation.
   - www.ed.gov/nclb
   - www.ed.gov/policy/elsec/leg/esea02
   - edworkforce.house.gov/issues/107th/education/nclb/nclb

References

Biancarosa, G., & Snow, C. E. (2004). *Reading Next: A Vision for Action and Research in Middle and High School Literacy*. Washington, DC: Alliance for Excellent Education.

Bintz, W. P. (1997). Exploring reading nightmares of middle and secondary school teachers. *Journal of Adult and Adolescent Literacy, 41*(1), 12–24.

Buehl, D., & Stumpf, S. (Eds.) (2002). *High School Reading Task Force Report, revised*. Madison, WI: Madison Metropolitan School District.

Daniel, M. (2005). Helping linguistic minorities read independently. *Academic Exchange Quarterly, 9*(2), 306–310.

deLeón, A. (2005). America's Literacy Challenge: Teaching Adolescents to Read to Learn. *Carnegie Results*. New York: Carnegie Corporation of New York. Retrieved from http://www.carnegie.org/results/10/page7.html.

Fisher, D. (2001). We're moving on up: Creating a schoolwide literacy effort in an urban high school. *Journal of Adolescent and Adult Literacy, 45*(2), 92–101.

Herber, H. (1970). *Teaching Reading in the Content Areas*. Englewood Cliffs, NJ: Prentice Hall.

International Reading Association. (2006). *Standards for Literacy Coaches*. Newark, DE: Author.

Irvin, J. L. (1998). *Reading and the Middle School Student: Strategies to Enhance Literacy*. Boston: Allyn and Bacon.

Joftus, S. (2002). *Every Child a Graduate: A Framework for an Excellent Education for All Middle and High School Students*. Washington, DC: Alliance for Excellent Education.

Kamil, M. L. (2004). *Adolescents and Literacy: Reading for the 21st Century*. Washington, DC: Alliance for Excellent Education.

Martin, P., & Midgely, E. (1999). Immigration to the United States. *Population Bulletin, 54*, 1–44. Washington, DC: Population Reference Bureau.

Moore, D. W., Bean, T. W., Birdyshaw, D., & Rycik, J. A. (1999). *Adolescent Literacy: A Position Statement*. Newark, DE: International Reading Association.

National Center for Education Statistics. (2002). *Public Schools, Students, Staff, and Graduate Counts by State: School Year 2000–2001* (NCES Publication. 2003-348). Washington, DC: Author.

National Council of Teachers of English (2004). *A Call to Action: What We Know About Adolescent Literacy and Ways to Support Teachers in Meeting Students' Needs*. Urbana, IL: Author.

National Society for the Study of Education (1925). *Report of the National Committee on Reading*. Twenty-fourth yearbook of the National Society for the Study of Education. Bloomington, IL: Public School Publishing.

O'Brien, D. G., Stewart, R. A., Moje, E. B. (1995). Why content literacy is difficult to infuse into the secondary school: Complexities of curriculum, pedagogy, and school culture. *Reading Research Quarterly, 30*(3), 442–463.

O'Brien, D. G., & Stewart, R. A. (1992). Resistance to Content Area Reading: Dimensions and Solutions. In E. K. Dishner, T. W. Bean, J. E. Readence, & D. W. Moore (Eds.), *Reading in Content Areas: Improving Classroom Instruction* (3rd ed., pp. 30–40). Dubuque, IA: Kendall/Hunt.

Ratekin, N., Simpson, M., Alvermann, E., & Dishner, E. (1998). Why teachers resist content reading instruction. *Journal of Reading, 41*(8), 604–609.

Santa, C. (1999). Adolescent literacy comes of age. *Reading Today, 17*(1), 1, 22.

Santa, C. (1998). Adolescents: The forgotten faction. *Reading Today, 15*(5), 16.

Snow, C. (2002). *Reading for Understanding: Toward an R&D Program in Reading Comprehension*. Santa Monica, CA: RAND.

Sturtevant, E. (2004). *The Literacy Coach: A Key to Teaching and Learning in Secondary Schools*. Washington, DC: Alliance for Excellent Education.

Vacca, R. T. (1998). Literacy issues in focus: Let's not marginalize adolescent literacy. *Journal of Adolescent and Adult Literacy, 41*(8), 604–609.

Vacca, R. T., & Alvermann, D. E. (1998). The crisis in adolescent literacy: Is it real or imagined? *Bulletin, 82*(600), 4–9.

2

Literacy Learning

Talking Points

- How can teachers tell when their students are not truly learning from their reading?
- What variables affect a reader's comprehension?
- How does brain research support an interactive model of literacy learning?
- How can teachers best develop readers and writers in their content areas?

Ms. Ranier knew that the topic "properties of a planet" was not one that would resonate with her seventh-grade students but it was covered by the state standards and an important part of the curriculum. So, she began with the traditional model of the nine orbs rotating around the sun and helped her students use mnemonic devices to name them all. She explained that meteors and other such things also orbit the sun; then she asked, "What are the qualities of a planet?" She wanted to make this study relevant to students. So, next she read a newspaper article about how UB_{313}, which is a land mass that is larger and brighter than Pluto, was just discovered, has a temperature of -248 degrees centigrade, and measures about 3,000 kilometers. Scientists are debating whether UB_{313} should be named as a new planet or whether Pluto should be stripped of the distinction. She asked again, "What are the properties of a planet?" and directed students to read the two pages from the textbook and answer the questions at the end of the section.

As she walked around the room she noticed several students engaged in "ping pong reading" (read the question, find the answer; read the question, find the answer) and wondered if they were really comprehending what they read. At the end of the class, she asked again "What are the properties of a planet?" Many students could read from their notes and cite the answers to the questions, but they had trouble applying their newfound knowledge to UB_{313}. Ms. Ranier concluded that she would help students construct a Venn diagram for tomorrow's class, comparing Mars with Pluto to help students engage more with the content of the text.

Then Ms. Ranier provided time for her students to tackle the reading assignment, to be completed for tomorrow's homework. On the surface, things began to proceed according to the lesson plan. Students were leaning over their textbooks, eyes focused on the print and pencils poised to write. But Ms. Ranier wondered what was happening on a cognitive level in the minds of her students. What kinds of thinking were the students engaged in? Were students merely "going through the motions" of getting work done to be handed in? Or, were they in the midst of something deeper and decidedly more exciting—students actively immersed in learning?

In this chapter, we present six metaphors for ineffective literacy learning that are frequently prevalent in middle school classrooms. Next, we discuss a model of interactive reading and learning. We then explain the thinking abilities that are essential to active learning and conclude the chapter by presenting current ideas on reading and writing connections as well as the move in some schools to more integrated literacy learning.

What Teachers See: Symptoms of Ineffective Learning

Reading is essential to learning in middle schools. Much of the curriculum in middle school must be accessed by students through print materials. As a result, students spend a significant amount of their study time learning through reading. Yet middle school teachers are well aware that many of their students are not successful learners of their course content. Conversations around the copy machine and in the teachers' lounge frequently focus on dissatisfaction with student performance. As teachers observe students interacting with print in their classrooms, they

witness a variety of student behaviors that suggest that successful learning is not taking place. These "symptoms" of ineffective learning are especially descriptive of students that Moore and Hinchman (2006) identified as adolescents who struggle with using reading to learn. Even students not ostensibly failing—students "getting by" in the classroom, perhaps the typical student in many instances—exhibit some of these behaviors. Very likely, some of these metaphors may describe many middle school learners.

What are some of the symptoms of ineffective literacy learning that occur daily in middle school classrooms? Metaphors can be especially valuable for describing what can go wrong with learning. Buehl (1993) detailed six metaphors for ineffective learning.

Metaphor #1: The Trip with No Scenery

The first metaphor compares reading with driving along a highly familiar route. For example, as commuters we travel daily to reach some destination. We drive or ride the bus to work; we make trips to the store; we visit friends or relatives. Often our minds settle into automatic pilot as we move along, lost in thought, listening to the radio, or busy with conversation. The trip itself becomes a blur, and we find that we paid virtually no attention to any of the scenery along the way. The point of the trip was to get somewhere, to arrive at our end point, not to partake in a sightseeing expedition.

Many students undertake a reading assignment as if they were traveling with a single, very limited objective in mind: to get finished. They do not read to experience ideas and information; they read to get done. Effort is focused on completing the required task, not on a thoughtful consideration of what an author is saying. The result is a very cursory motoring through the text, without an engagement with ideas and without periodic pauses to ponder what is being read. These students may almost defiantly inform their teachers, "Sure I read it, but I don't remember any of it."

A trip through text that takes in scenery involves a much different approach to reading. Certainly, students need to be peering out their mental windows to absorb as much as they can about what they are encountering. They need to vary their rate—slowing down, stopping, or even backtracking at times—when an especially important piece of "scenery" comes up. They may even need to take a second trip through the material, or consult a tour guide (a teacher or fellow student) for insight about what they are experiencing. And they need to internalize that the point of a trip through text is to gain as much scenery as possible, not to merely get done.

Successful readers actively monitor what they do when they read (Duke & Pearson, 2002). Unfortunately, many students rarely tune in that inner voice (which we will define as *metacognition* later in this chapter) that regulates what is happening during reading (Pressley, 2002). Struggling readers seem especially prone to scenery-free results from print. Some muddle through, perhaps hoping to learn through "osmosis," trusting that by casting their eyes over the text, somehow meaning will magically follow their gaze into their minds. Their eyes may be looking at the words, but their thinking is somewhere else. Comprehension, and as a result learning, is not occuring.

Metaphor #2: Ping Pong Reading

Some of the personal strategies that students employ to complete classroom assignments are not necessarily effective learning behaviors, but these routines may be very efficient ways of getting work done. Ping pong reading, a term coined by Pavlik (1979), is probably the most frequently observed ineffective learning behavior in middle school classrooms. Ping pong reading is usually witnessed when students are required to answer questions following a reading. Instead of starting with the text and carefully reading the entire passage before writing, ping pong readers go directly to the first question and then briskly skim along until the semantic and syntactic clues indicate that they have found the portion of the text that contains an answer. Some scurried writing and perhaps a bit of paraphrasing follows, and then they zip ahead to the second question, and continue skimming for answers. In this manner, students "ping pong" back and forth between the questions and the text, never involving themselves in more than a superficial sampling of what they are assigned to read.

Ping pong reading is, however, a very efficient strategy if the sole purpose is to answer questions that elicit literal, factual-based information. Students come to associate the point of the reading with answering questions, not interacting with a text to learn. Homework does indeed get finished, but the course content is not really understood or learned. Students who are habitual ping pong readers often remark that they have no difficulty completing homework, but they have trouble with tests, signaling that when they are accountable for remembering key material, they are unable to demonstrate mastery of the content.

Ping pong readers trust that the process of skimming for answers is somehow equivalent to studying and learning the material. Effective study, however, requires thinking about, organizing, or rehearsing information. Ping pong readers are able to extract isolated pieces of information from a text, but they lack the reflective mindset necessary to integrate information into something that makes sense. Skimming for answers does not amount to comprehension; as a result, homework may be satisfactorily completed but learning does not occur.

Metaphor #3: Mindless Routines

Much of what students are asked to accomplish in classrooms can be done with very little investment of mental energy, especially with assignments involving content texts. Pearson and Johnson (1978) demonstrated how students could successfully answer all the questions on a passage while obtaining virtually no sense of the content of the passage. Students confronted with a passage containing some nonsense nouns and verbs are still able to answer who, what, and why questions based on their knowledge of how language works and their ability to match a question with a grammatically similar segment of text. For many students, middle school texts present "nonsense" that can nevertheless be parceled out into small answers to specific questions, even when they understand very little about the reading. For example, when reading the following sentence, "The turgy wangle murrupted a burf," most students would realize that "turgy" describes "wangle" in some way and that a "burf" is what was "murrupted." Based on their knowledge of syntax alone, they could answer a series of literal questions (Who murrupted the burf? What did the wangle do to the burf? What action was taken by the wangle?), but they would not understand the meaning of the sentence.

Students can be very frank about the mindless rituals they are involved in during school. They may admit that they expend little effort to make sense out of reading assignments, holding out instead for the teacher to "explain" the material after they are finished. Teachers recognize these desires for mindless rituals when students lobby for more worksheets or literal-level exercises. The irony is that even though students may deride such activities as meaningless, they are comfortable with the ease with which such tasks can be accomplished.

Struggling readers sometimes appear the most eager to be assigned tasks that qualify as mindless rituals. These students may feel they are more likely to succeed with such activities. Mindless rituals reinforce an "assembly-line" mentality among such students, who often equate completing worksheet after worksheet with learning. Even teachers are pulled into the act, maintaining that struggling readers need these low-level tasks that help them "get the facts," even though such activities can be completed without comprehension, and once more, learning is not occuring.

Metaphor #4: Consumers and Extraterrestrials

Proficient learners approach reading assignments like enlightened consumers. Enlightened consumers enter a supermarket, for example, with a clear plan for shopping. They know what products they need to buy, they have a plan for what to do with the products when they get home, they have strategies for locating the products in the store, and they have strategies for determining which brands to purchase. If they encounter problems during shopping, they follow a series of alternatives to solve these problems. Finally, they leave the supermarket with the products they wanted.

Students who fall back on ineffective learning strategies are often confused by school tasks, such as reading a textbook assignment. Consider a fanciful analogy with extraterrestrial beings sent to earth to impersonate the natives. Although these beings have no idea what they are doing or why they are doing it, these aliens are able to imitate the consumers in the supermarket. They too walk the aisles, placing items in their shopping carts, but they have no clue as to what items to select. Thus, products are essentially snatched from the shelves at random, and when these bewildered beings arrive at the checkout counter, they have a hodge-podge conglomeration of meaningless items for which they have no determined use. They have deduced that the routines of shopping, like the routines of reading a textbook passage, must be what they are supposed to do. But they are only copying the overt behaviors; they have no way of knowing what thinking is also going on. In reality, they, like many of our students, have been faking it.

Struggling readers in particular find much of the learning in content classes an "alien enterprise." Such students follow a default approach to learning and memory. They wander aimlessly through print, missing out on the essence of the activity: that reading should be purposeful, that it should make sense, and that it should lead to becoming more knowledgeable and thoughtful about a topic. These students hopefully pluck out snippets of information from the text, but these isolated facts and ideas lack coherence and do not add up to any meaningful insights. They miss the point of the exercise. Brozo (1990) detailed a number of "mock participation" behaviors used by unsuccessful readers to disguise their ongoing difficulties with learning from text. Tactics such as changing the direction of the discussion, "apple polishing" (engaging in informal discussions or chats to avoid the content), and mock reading (book open, face buried in it, and head nodding) allow students to avoid frustrating experiences with print and sometimes go undetected by teachers. Even more compelling are those students who dutifully do all their work, but are not even aware they are faking it. They work hard pulling details from a text, but may achieve only fleeting comprehension, and after all their efforts, learning has still not occured.

Metaphor #5: Freeloading and First Down Punting

Teachers often comment about how much more thoroughly they understand their subject matter once they begin to teach it. Teaching necessitates a great deal of hard thinking about content priorities and how to organize these priorities for instruction. Conscientious teachers must interact vigorously with their content to establish what is essential for students to learn.

Many students depend nearly exclusively on their teachers for insights about their subjects. These students tend to approach learning passively, being primarily teacher directed rather than self-directed. Such students expect that the teacher will grapple with the essence of a discipline and will hand deliver prepackaged nuggets of knowledge and wisdom to them. By processing reading assignments passively and superficially, they hope to "freeload" off the teacher's intellectual labors, relying on the teacher to expand on "what the reading was really about" after they have closed their books.

Struggling readers are especially dependent on teachers to tell them what they need to know. Thomas (1979), Bristow (1985), and others referred to this condition as "learned helplessness." Students exhibiting learned helplessness feel defeated before they even start to read a passage, and they are generally convinced that their efforts will probably not prove successful even if they try. These students might be termed "first down punters," readers who come up to the line of scrimmage in their text and decide to "punt" on first down rather than run a play or two to see if anything might make sense. By bailing out early, they hope that the teacher will shortcut the process and move directly into telling them what is important. In short, students are relying on the teacher to do their thinking for them.

Students may employ a variety of effective strategies to manipulate the teacher into avoiding challenging reading assignments. Whining, complaining, doing the work incompetently, refusing to do the work at all, and misbehaving in class are all classic means of manuevering the teacher to "let students off the hook." Many teachers lose faith in assigning any material to be read, saying "It's too hard for my students." Comprehension is a result of thinking, and if students bypass constructing their own thinking about a text, learning is not likely to occur.

Metaphor #6: World Brains and School Brains

Finally, many students operate in school as if they possessed not one, but two brains. This two-brain metaphor does not correspond with the familiar right hemisphere–left hemisphere dichotomy. Instead, two brains might be labeled *the world brain* and *the school brain*. We might envision the world brain as appropriating most of the space in the student's skull. Stored in it is all of what this individual knows and understands about the world, all of life's experiences and personal explanations of what is and why things are. It is the world brain on which the student relies to make sense of the world. (Later on in this chapter we will define this store of personal knowledge as *schema*.)

The school brain is much smaller in capacity. The school brain is carefully insulated from the world brain—very little that enters it ever gets transferred into the brain that makes sense of things. The school brain has a minuscule storage capacity, but that is quite all right because information does not stay there very long. The most distinctive feature of the school brain is an ever-open chute, ready to dump today's lesson quickly and irrevocably into oblivion. Students use the school brain for short-term storage of the daily stuff of school; as soon as the test is over or a new chapter started, they flush out the backlog of old facts and stray information and ready themselves for another cycle of short-term learning. Nothing stays around very long in the school brain.

Obviously, student brains are not literally constructed like this! However, recent research on the brain confirms that students retain appallingly little of what was "learned." Sousa (1995) used the term "working memory" to describe material that is held in memory during instruction then subsequently jettisoned. This metaphor of two brains provides an explanation for the persistence of student misconceptions, many of which remain intact even after exposure to instruction that contradicts these naive or erroneous notions. Students who continue to believe that plants derive their food from the soil, even though they have just studied photosynthesis, illustrate the staying power of misconceptions. These students did not make the connection between what they were reading and how they thought things worked in the world.

In an extensive review of the research on misconceptions and misunderstandings, Harvard psychologist Howard Gardner (1991) concluded that a multitude of flawed interpretations, simplistic explanations, and stereotypic beliefs about how things are in the world remain comfortably intact even after explicit instruction to the contrary.

- We have seasons because the distance between the earth and the sun varies, causing warmer and cooler periods.
- You can get a cold from catching a chill.

- Wars are conflicts between good guys and bad guys.
- Talented writers have the knack to compose exactly what they want to say without editing.

As small children we constantly form theories and develop perfectly service-able explanations about what we see and experience in the world. These rudimentary "truths" become hardwired, and, Gardner (1991) noted, they are remarkably impervious to information that contradicts them. There lurks within the brains of all of us the "unschooled" mind of a five-year-old.

Certainly some of our students are very adept at perceiving the connections between what they already know and understand and what they are learning in our classrooms. They draw on their prior knowledge as they strive to integrate new information into their existing mental structures. They find that the new information does indeed help them to make more sense of their world, and they attend to the inconsistencies between what they think they know and new learning.

But for many students, school has seemingly little to do with the real world, and their failure to make connections basically insures that much of what they learn in school will be lost. If it is not clearly apparent that new learning directly contradicts the beliefs of many students, they may merely file the new learning into their "know this for the test" mental drawer, but totally overlook the profound implications for their own thinking and perceptions. As a result, much of our curricula gets relegated to the school brain. Comprehension involves reconfiguring how we understand things; when students do not engage in this kind of thinking, learning does not occur.

Middle school teachers will recognize many of the symptoms described here as ongoing phenomena in their classrooms. Some of the students who exhibit these characteristic behaviors are struggling readers, but even able students are tempted to take shortcuts through their daily workloads. An examination of the complexities of literacy learning throughout the middle school curriculum can provide teachers with direction for helping their students become active, purposeful, and strategic learners.

Interactive Reading and Learning

When *The National Reading Panel Report* was published (National Institute of Child Health and Human Development, 2000), the panel members named five components of the reading process: phoenemic awareness, phonics, fluency, vocabulary, and comprehension. Normally, children master phoenemic awareness and phonics during the primary grades and progressively become more fluent readers as they move on through the grades. Literacy instruction during the middle school years emphasizes a continuation of instruction for vocabulary acquisition and comprehension. Some terms are listed below that are normally associated with reading instruction (Harris & Hodges, 1995) followed by a more extensive description of the key literacy concepts of *schema*, *metacognition*, and *scaffolding*.

- **Comprehension**—the reconstruction of the intended meaning of a communication; accurately understanding what is written, said, or viewed
- **Fluency**—1. the clear, easy, written, or spoken expression of ideas; 2. freedom from word-identification problems that might hinder comprehension in silent reading or the expression of ideas in oral reading; automaticity; 3. the ability to produce words or larger language units in a limited time interval
- **Functional literacy**—a level of reading and writing sufficient for everyday life but not for completely autonomous activity
- **Phonemic awareness**—the awareness of sounds (phonemes) that make up spoken words
- **Phonics**—a way of teaching reading and spelling that stresses symbol-sound relationships, used especially in beginning instruction
- **Reading level**—an estimate of a student's current level of reading achievement as compared to some criterion or standard

Schema Theory

Meaningful learning occurs when a student relates new information to personal prior knowledge and experiences. That is, it is nearly impossible to learn new information that has no connection to what a learner already knows. *Schemata* comprise all of the information and all of the experience a reader has stored in memory. A particular schema, then, represents all of the associations that come to mind when a person reads about a certain subject.

For example, you have a schema for "cell phone." You have a mental picture of what does or does not characterize a cell phone. You also bring to that basic image many other associations. If you are a devoted user, your schema of a cell phone may be merged with positive feelings of limitless possibilities. If you have not yet joined the "wireless nation" or if you find yourself constantly annoyed by the cell phone users around you, feelings of being out of touch or irritation may accompany your understanding of this concept. Our schema determines the sum total of all our thoughts about and reactions toward a certain topic. Readers cannot separate their schema from what is read; thus, schema influences the interpretation and comprehension of texts.

Thelen (1986) likened schema to file folders in a file cabinet. Everyone has a unique and personal way of organizing cognitive structures (the cabinet). The schemata are the ideas contained within the file folders. Learners must be shown where and how new material fits into the existing structures. Because each reader has a uniquiely personal organization, it is important that teachers help students engage their schema to connect new information to what is already known. For this process to occur, students must be able to determine what is known and what is *not* known.

Students all come to school with bulging file folders on some topics and nearly empty folders on others. Sometimes their file folders are helpful in school and sometimes they are not. Sometimes, learning means the teacher's job is to hand students a new file folder, help them put a label on it, and work with them on selecting meaningful information to place inside. Other times, a teacher's job is to help students activate what they know by opening their file folders and reading what they have already stored in them. Even when students know something about a topic, they do not always think to use that information unless they engage in a pre-reading activity to activate that knowledge. When students know much about a topic, a teacher can be most helpful by helping students organize what they know before reading. This schema activation and organization is necessary to learn new information about any given topic.

Sousa (1995) described the limits of long-term retention of what is covered in daily classroom activities: "It seems that the learner's working memory asks just two questions to determine whether an item is saved or rejected. They are 'Does this make sense?' and 'Does this have meaning?'" (p. 16). Learning makes sense if it fits with the student's prior knowledge and experience, the individual's schema. Learning is meaningful if it has relevance to the student, if an individual can apply the new learning to some useful purpose or internalize it to shape personal perceptions, ideas, or beliefs. New learning that does not connect to students' schema or that does not seem to have anything important to do with their lives has an extremely low probability of being stored in long-term memory. "When students say, 'School is boring,' part of the comment reflects a common adolescent feeling. Yet there's more to it. Learners want school to be worthwhile and meaningful" (Jensen, 1998, p. 90).

Metacognition

Learning is often referred to as a cognitive event. It is that, but it is also a metacognitive event. *Cognition* refers to using the knowledge possessed; *metacognition* refers to a person's awareness and understanding of that knowledge. "Cognition refers to having the skills; metacognition refers to awareness of and conscious control over those skills" (Stewart & Tei, 1983, p. 36).

Students may thumb through a difficult text while thinking about tonight's basketball game; *knowing* they are not paying attention to the text is a metacognitive event. Strategic readers would take action—refocus and pay attention, close the book for later, or begin to take notes to organize their thoughts. Proficient readers who have developed metacognitive awareness do *something*; less proficient readers plow merrily (or not so merrily) along without stopping to assess, question, or correct the condition.

Proficient readers monitor their comprehension; in essence they watch themselves as they read and they consciously make adjustments when it is necessary. They apply strategies such as rereading, reading ahead, or searching their prior knowledge to make sure they understand. That is, they know when reading is making sense, and they know what to do when it is not. Effective listeners also know when speech does not make sense to them; they ask questions, take notes, and/or increase their concentration as they listen. Metacognition develops as a student matures, especially during adolescence, but it needs be taught and strengthened by explicit instruction and practice even at very early ages.

Scaffolding

Consider experiences that you have had in learning—in the home, on the job, mastering a skill. Much of the most important learning that we have achieved in life—whether it is baking pastries, fishing for brook trout, or throwing a pot on the wheel—has been in the role of apprentice to a master craftsman, an expert, an accomplished veteran. We learned by witnessing the expert engaged in an activity, and as we collaborated and received feedback on our performance, gradually moved from novice status to independence.

This apprentice learning model also has important implications for literacy learning. Pearson and Gallagher (1983) coined the phrase "gradual release of responsibility" to describe this dynamic in the classroom. Basing their model on the ideas of the Russian educational theorist Lev Vygotsky (1962), Pearson and Gallagher envisioned instruction that moved from explicit modeling and instruction by the teacher to guided practice and then to activities that incrementally positioned students into becoming independent learners. Instruction that supports students as they gradually become more accomplished readers and learners is called scaffolding.

A *scaffold* is a temporary structure that is constructed to help someone complete a task that would be very difficult otherwise. We use scaffolds frequently in

Teacher Regulated	Supported Practice (Scaffolding)	Student Regulated
	Zone of Proximal Development	
Future Development	Assisted Development	Actual Development
[What a student is not yet able to do]	[What a student can do with support]	[What a student can do without support]
Teacher Modeling and Think-Alouds	Classroom Literacy Strategies	Independent Learning

I Do/ You Watch   *I Do/ You Help* ➡ *You Do/ I Help* ➡ *You Do/ I Watch*

FIGURE 2.1 *Gradual Release of Responsibility*

Source: Parts of graphic adapted from Wilhelm, J., Baker, T., and Dube, J. (2001). *Strategic Reading: Guiding Students to Lifelong Literacy 6–12.* Portsmouth, NH: Heinemann Boynton Cook Publishers.

real life; we see scaffolds that are assembled to facilitate erecting or repairing a building; we see scaffolds used by painters to reach areas inaccessible without them; we see scaffolds dangling from high-rise offices that allow window-washers to undertake a task unimaginable without such a device. But when the job is completed, scaffolds are dismantled; they are temporary structures.

Likewise, classroom lessons that represent scaffolding are temporary lessons, constructed to help students as they embark into unfamiliar thinking, but designed to fade away as students become gradually comfortable with the learning and are able to work without this type of teacher guidance. Much of classroom instruction needs to take place in the central area of the gradual release model. During this stage students experiment with the processes the teacher has modeled, as they converse with the teacher and with other classmates to clarify their thinking and practice their new routines. "Teaching in the zone" relies on scaffolding, the support built into a lesson to guide student learning and prompt effective thinking.

Wilhelm, Baker, and Dube (2001) noted that while the gradual release model is frequently common practice with elementary teachers, it is rarely a reality in middle and high school classrooms. Students needing modeling, guided practice with feedback, and scaffolded lessons are instead assigned tasks that many may not be able to complete independently. Struggling readers in particular need scaffolded lessons that remind them what effective thinkers do during learning and guide them through texts that are challenging. In this book, we present teachers with a host of literacy strategies that can be used to scaffold instruction, especially for struggling readers.

Literacy Practices of Strong Readers

Literacy is a complex, socially embedded process. It involves much more than merely pronouncing words and answering comprehension questions. The triangle chart shown in Figure 2.2 was developed by the National Literacy Project™ and shows the relationship between the text, the reader, and the context for learning. The National Literacy Project™ is a nonprofit organization dedicated to improving literacy for intermediate, middle, and high school students.

The Learner

Students come to a learning context with minds full of information on particular topics; with vocabularies that may (or may not) be a match for classroom discourse; with attitudes about reading, writing, and school in general; with varying degress of motivation to learn; and with particular purposes for reading and learning. In addition, they are in the midst of working on the important developmental tasks of adolescence. It is the interaction between what is in the head and what is on the page within a particular context that causes students to comprehend what they read. Additionally, with large classes of students with varied levels of expertise and experiences, teachers face a greater diversity of learners in their classrooms. Not all

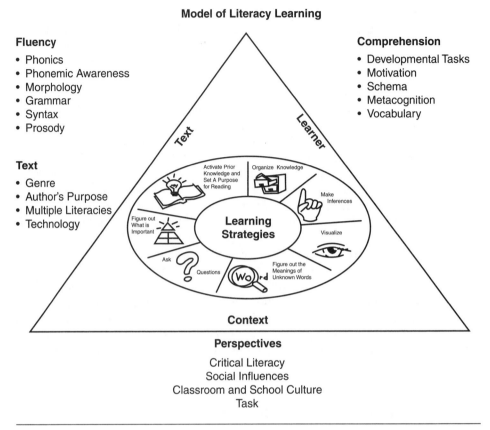

FIGURE 2.2 *Model of Literacy Learning*

Source: National Literacy Project™

students have learned prerequisite information in the same way, and in all likelihood their range of content knowledge has a random quality. That is, though students have theoretically covered a consistent body of information based on curriculum guides and standards, it is safe to assume that not all teachers have taught the same amount of information or taught in the same manner. Therefore, student experiences are varied when represented in heterogeneously grouped classes.

Schema is the lens through which learners see and interpret the information they encounter. Metacognition is how they evaluate what they are learning and integrate the new information into existing information. Certainly, a person's broader culture and ethnic identification are key components of schema. A teacher's understanding of the collective prior knowledge (schema) and ways of connecting with that schema (metacognition) are essential to constructing meaningful learning activities for students (scaffolding).

The Text

Imagine going to the mailbox and getting two letters addressed to you—one from a friend and one from a lawyer you do not know. These two letters look different even before you open them. You prepare yourself to read these two letters differently. Likewise, poetry is read differently from an insurance policy and a short story is read differently from a science passage. Students are exposed to a variety of text forms in middle school, from textbooks to novels, from newspaper articles to original source documents, from library reference sources to Internet sites. Thus, students need to be flexible in their reading strategies as they move from one text form to another.

Because textbooks predominate in middle school, special attention must be paid to teaching students to be effective users of them. From a student perspective, textbooks are massive compilations of facts in history, in science, in math, and on and on. Students often overlook the critical element of this material—text structure—which is how the information is connected or interrelated. Some textbooks do an outstanding job of forecasting cause-effect relationships, comparisons, problem-solution dynamics, and other significant ways of organizing information. Inconsiderate textbooks, however, force students to grapple with what might be important, with the result that students may miss the connections between facts that allow them to construct main ideas and make generalizations from their learning. Teaching students to use text structure enhances their comprehension and improves their learning in content classes.

An entire chapter is devoted to the Demands of Text (Chapter 5) and how to develop student flexibility in approaching different forms of text. The content, format, concepts presented, and organization are all factors that make a text easy or difficult to understand. In addition, sensitivity to different forms of text can enhance comprehension. The multiple literacies of adolescents and the role that technology plays in the changing demands on literacy are also discussed in subsequent chapters.

The Context

The context sets the purpose for reading. Proficient readers not only approach types of text differently, they also vary their reading according to their purpose. For example, if you encounter a difficult word in a novel you are reading for fun, you may guess at the meaning and then skip it and continue reading. An unknown word in a science textbook, however, could be an important concept that you need to understand before reading on. You may need to look it up in a glossary or ask someone. Purpose for reading also dictates how attentive you are to details or how much work you put into remembering what you read. Where (a classroom? a bus seat? a snug corner of a bed?) and when (first hour? last period? midnight?) the selection is read are additional factors that affect the reading process.

Reading/Writing Connections

Involving students in expressing their understandings through writing is a necessary facet of reading and learning. For too long, educators have treated reading and writing as separate subjects; instead, Shanahan (1990) suggested that we should teach "reading for learning and writing for communication" (p. 10).

Middle school teachers tend to take writing skills for granted, yet they expect their students to undertake a considerable amount of writing in their classes. Lab reports in science, answers to questions from textbooks, essays, reports, exams— all mandate student writing proficiency. Teachers are increasingly recognizing that writing is an important way to help students formulate ideas about what they are learning and sharpen their thinking. Initiatives such as the writing process, writing workshop, writing across the curriculum, and the six traits writing model have encouraged middle school teachers to integrate more writing into their classroom routines. Through a variety of formal and informal writing tasks, including learning logs, reflections, responses to reading, position papers, dramatic re-creations, writing from different perspectives, and the like, students use writing to deepen and refine their understanding of course content.

Most students "read a text once without pausing to reflect, rarely refer to any other sources for relevant information, and rarely consider what they already know as they develop plans for dealing with the subject matter addressed in a text" (Pearson & Tierney, 1984, p. 11). Numerous research studies and theoretical assertions in the 1980s and 1990s have led most educators to believe in the "mirror metaphor"—that both reading and writing are acts of composing meaning. The reader begins with text and uses language to create meaning. A writer begins with meaning and uses language to create text (Birnbaum & Emig, 1983).

Research has indicated that good writers are often (but not always) good readers. Similarly, good readers are often good writers (Stotsky, 1983). Knowledge of one process appears to reinforce knowledge of the other, and students "derive learning benefits across reading and writing when they understand that connections exist" (Shanahan, 1990, p. 4). The six traits writing model, in particular, offers middle school teachers an excellent framework for guiding student writing in their classes (Spandel & Culham, 1997). Content teachers are often frustrated with the quality of student writing they receive in assignments, yet they are uncertain how to communicate their expectations to students in an instructive way. The six traits model provides trait rubrics that allow teachers to provide specific feedback on ideas, organization, voice, word choice, sentence fluency, and conventions.

- **Ideas** refers to the content of the piece, the statement of a clear purpose for the writing, the inclusion of sufficient details to develop main ideas, and the establishment of the writer's viewpoint on the material.
- **Organization** involves the structure of the writing, how the ideas are connected and discussed.
- **Voice** brings the personality, the attitude, the perspective of the writer to the reader.
- **Word choice** refers to the language employed to convey the message, such as the use of strong verbs, precise adjectives and nouns, and the avoidance of clichés.
- **Sentence fluency** refers to the rhythm and flow of the writing.

- **Conventions** are those factors that lead to ease of communication, such as correct spelling, proper observance of grammatical rules, and attention to paragraph form as well as presentation factors, such as handwriting, neatness, and layout.

Adolescents are in a transitional stage as they develop as readers and writers, and middle school teachers play a pivotal role in helping their students use writing as a primary means of learning and knowing. As Spandel and Stiggins (1997) observed, students "will have to devise a personal process that fits them and that fits each new situation, inventing for themselves everything from topic to editorial requirements. They must learn to identify worthy topics, find and use good sources of information (not only the Internet but also experience, books, films, interviews—the works), organize findings, frame the results to fit the audience, self-assess, revise, edit, format, and then present their writings to a current employer, a prospective employer, a board of directors, a congressional committee, a group of students, members of the public, a team of specialists, reluctant voters, wary consumers—whoever, wherever, whenever" (p. 4).

Summary

Students moving from elementary school to middle school must adjust to an often departmentalized and content-focused school organization. Many teachers forsake reading and writing instruction for content. Yet, the adolescent years represent a productive opportunity to help students make the transition to the heavily expository-based reading of the middle school.

To make this transition, students must learn to become strategic and independent readers. They must learn the strategies that good readers use before, during, and after reading. An effective reading program must be integrated with an effective writing program. When teachers understand the demands of text, how to create an optimum context for learning, and how to help students connect their prior knowledge to new information, students tend to engage more actively in learning. Teachers must understand and apply the features of effective instruction to maximize learning for their students.

Extending Learning

Reviewing the Talking Points

Answer the questions now that you have read the chapter and compare your prereading and postreading responses.

Revisiting the Vignette

In the opening vignette, although Ms. Ranier tried to build background knowledge and create interest regarding the properties of planets, signs were evident that the instructional tasks assigned may have little value for meeting the intended objectives for some students. Students who have little ability to negotiate texts may exhibit work avoidance behaviors as a mask for their helpnessness.

1. What can be done to avoid each of the metaphors for ineffective learning?
2. How can a teacher determine if her students were actively engaged with the material they were assigned to read?
3. In what ways could assignments encourage a high level of involvement with texts?
4. How can teachers better ensure that writing is effectively integrated into content instruction?

Terms to Remember and Use

context	critical literacy	comprehension	student engagement
metacognition	schema	fluency	phonemic awareness
phonics	genre	scaffolding	gradual release of responsibility

Write a series of sentences that meaningfully connect pairs of the above key terms. Your sentences should refer to ideas and concepts related to the literacy of middle school students.

Modifying Instruction for English Language Learners

The six symptoms of ineffective learning can be easily observed with English language learners. Some symptoms may be more common among ELLs, and there are probably more that teachers may find with ELLs who come from particular cultures. For instance, ping pong reading is likely to be frequently used by ELLs who know the English alphabet but lack understanding of vocabulary. "Grabbing" the key words from questions and then trying to find answers by seeking similar words in the text, at least, engages them in an activity that resembles reading when there is nothing they can do without knowledge of the vocabulary. English language learners from countries where teachers "feed" information to students encounter higher risks of resorting to a freeloading approach in class. They may have been fed with "ready" knowledge rather than actively interacting with the text on their own.

When students get bored or frustrated, they may become disruptive and vent their frustration to draw the teacher's attention. This, however, would not usually happen to English language learners who have been socialized to be obedient and quiet in a very different culture. Additionally, the conflict between world brains and schools brains would more likely affect ELLs' learning when what they learn in school is discrepant with what their religion, culture, and family teach them. In these situations, some knowledge about students' background, the communities they are from, and their cultures would help teachers provide timely, effective assistance.

Considering the unique characteristics of ELLs, ways to teach native-English-speaking students to read may not work for students who are still learning English. Walqui (2000) proposed ten principles for developing effective teaching and learning contexts for immigrant adolescents, which can also be applied to middle school curriculum for improving ELLs' reading.

1. The culture of the classroom fosters the development of a community of learners, and all students are part of that community.
2. Good language teaching involves conceptual and academic development.

3. Students' experiential backgrounds provide a point of departure and an anchor in the exploration of new ideas.
4. Teaching and learning focus on substantive ideas that are organized cyclically.
5. New ideas and tasks are contextualized.
6. Academic strategies, sociocultural expectations, and academic norms are taught explicitly.
7. Tasks are relevant, meaningful, engaging, and varied.
8. Complex and flexible forms of collaboration maximize learners' opportunities to interact while making sense of language and content.
9. Students are given multiple opportunities to extend their understandings and apply their knowledge.
10. Authentic assessment is an integral part of teaching and learning.

Beyond the Book

- Interview a middle school student. Ask him or her to indicate how teachers organize the time in class when students are reading their texts. Ask them for specific activities that the teacher leads them through to make sure they are engaged with the text and task.
- Ask a middle school student to share the types of reading activities that he or she does apart from school reading. Make a list of the different types of reading that he or she does and ask him or her to rank them in order of preference.
- Interview a middle school teacher and ask him or her what he or she does to motivate and engage students with reading.
- Investigate the term *comprehension* on the Internet and determine the differences in how it is defined by various researchers.

References

Birnbaum, J., & Emig, J. (1983). Creating minds, created texts: Writing and reading. In R. P. Parker & F. A. Davis (Eds.), *Developing Literacy: Young Children's Use of Language* (pp. 87–104). Newark, DE: International Reading Association.

Bristow, P. (1985). Are poor readers passive readers? Some evidence, possible explanations, and potential solutions. *The Reading Teacher, 39*(3), 318–325.

Brozo, W. (1990). Hiding out in secondary content classrooms: Coping strategies of unsuccessful readers. *Journal of Reading, 33*(5), 324–328.

Buehl, D. (1993). Opening the door: Metaphors that connect with content teachers. *Wisconsin State Reading Association Journal, 37*(2), 31–38.

Duke, N., & Pearson, P. D. (2002). Effective practices for developing reading comprehension. In A. Farstrup and S. Samuels, *What Research Has to Say about Reading Instruction*, 3rd Ed. (pp. 205–242) Newark, DE: International Reading Association.

Gardner, H. (1991). *The Unschooled Mind: How Children Think and How Schools Should Teach.* New York: HarperCollins Basic Books.

Harris, T. L., & Hodges, R. E. (Eds.) (1995). *The Literacy Dictionary.* Newark, DE: International Reading Association.

Jensen, E. (1998). *Teaching with the Brain in Mind.* Alexandria, VA: Association for Supervision and Curriculum Development.

Moore, D. W., & Hinchman, K. A. (2006) *Teaching Adolescents Who Struggle with Reading: Practical Strategies.* Boston: Pearson: Allyn and Bacon.

National Institute of Child Health and Human Development. (2000). *The National Reading Panel Report.* Washington, DC: Author.

Pavlik, R. (1979). Making an impact by reading in the content fields. *Curriculum Report, 8*(4), 13.

Pearson, P. D., & Gallagher, M. (1983). The instruction of reading comprehension, *Contemporary Educational Psychology, 8*(3), 5.

Pearson, P. D., & Johnson, D. (1978). *Teaching Reading Comprehension.* New York: Holt, Rinehart & Winston.

Pearson, P. D., & Tierney, R. J. (1984). *On Becoming a Thoughtful Reader: Learning to Read Like a Writer* (Technical Report No. 50). Champaign, IL: Center for the Study of Reading.

Pressley, M. (2002). Metacognition and self-regulated comprehension. In A. Farstrup and S. Samuels, *What Research Has to Say about Reading Instruction,* 3rd Ed. (pp. 291–309) Newark, DE: International Reading Association.

Shanahan, T. (1990). Reading and writing together. What does it really mean? In T. Shanahan (Ed.), *Reading and Writing Together: New Perspectives for the Classroom* (pp. 1–18). Norwood, MA: Christopher-Gordon Publishers.

Sousa, D. (1995). *How the Brain Learns.* Reston, VA: National Association of Secondary School Principals.

Spandel, V., & Culham, R. (1997). *The Student Friendly Guide to Writing with Traits.* Portland, OR: The Northwest Regional Educational Laboratory.

Spandel, V., & Stiggins, R. (1997). *Creating Writers: Linking Writing Assessment and Instruction.* New York: Longman.

Stewart, O., & Tei, O. (1983). Some implications of metacognition for reading instruction. *Journal of Reading, 27*(1), 36–43.

Stotsky, S. (1983). Research on reading/writing relationships: A synthesis and suggested directions. *Language Arts, 60*(5), 627–642.

Thelen, J. (1986). Vocabulary learning and meaningful instruction. *Journal of Reading, 29*(7), 603–609.

Thomas, A. (1979). Learned helplessness and expectancy factors: Implications for research in learning disabilities. *Review of Educational Research, 49*(2), 208–221.

Vygotsky, L. S. (1962). *Thought and Language.* Cambridge, MA: MIT Press.

Walqui, A. (2000). *Access and Engagement: Program Design and Instructional Approaches for Immigrant Students in Secondary Schools.* McHenry, IL, and Washington, DC: Delta Systems and Center for Applied Linguistics.

Wilhelm, J., Baker, T., & Dube, J. (2001). *Strategic Reading: Guiding Students to Lifelong Literacy 6–12.* Portsmouth, NH: Heinemann Boynton Cook Publishers.

3

Learning Environments That Motivate Students

Talking Points

- How does effective literacy teaching involve being both a mediator and a coach?
- How do student perceptions of their abilities affect their performance in classrooms?
- What factors motivate students to engage in learning?
- How can literacy strategies that involve discussion motivate students to learn?

Dorothy Booth was a new teacher in the district and spent the summer reading the Curriculum Guide for Language Arts teachers. The Cay *was a required reading for the seventh grade and she needed to figure out how to motivate her students to read this book. She knew that her students could not relate to the issues of World War II, but the themes in the book were relevant. Survival, friendship, and prejudice were all issues that her students face on a daily basis. The question was: How could she relate the experience of a young boy during the opening years of WWII to students today?*

On the day that she would introduce The Cay, *Jamie and Jamal entered the room bickering about something that happened during physical education class. She mediated between them and got them to put the incident behind them. Dorothy began class with the question: "If you were stranded on an island, do you think you could survive?" She put students into groups and had them use the think-pair-share strategy to answer this question. Students formulated their own answers, talked about them in their small groups, and then shared their responses as a class.*

Dorothy knew that the desert island theme would not resonate with students, but survival was a topic they could relate to. The next question she asked was: "What do people need to survive in our society today?" As she listed their ideas on the board, she planned on coming back to them as she discussed the themes of The Cay. *She then proceeded to help students build background knowledge about the motivation of the Germans, why resources such as oil would be important, and the vulnerable position of islands around the world was pertinent.*

Ms. Booth knew that her students did not have much knowledge of the issues surrounding World War II. Unless she did something to connect the themes in the book to the lives of students, she knew what she would see. Some students would barely skim the pages, others would complain, whine, or cajole the teacher for help. A few may cheat and copy a classmate's paper. Still others will merely sit and stare out the window. Inevitably, someone would be likely to act out or resort to disruptive behavior.

In this chapter, literacy strategies are connected to student motivation to engage in learning. A vision of the classroom teacher as mediator and as coach is described. Research on motivation and engagement is presented, providing a theoretical base for instruction as students become more independent learners. Use of classroom discussion to motivate students and assist them in elaborating their thinking is reviewed, and the literacy strategies of think-pair-share, the discussion web, directed reading sequence, and other cooperative strategies are explained and examples provided.

Classroom Negotiations: The Teacher as Mediator

If you gather together a group of middle school teachers and ask them to jot down what frustrates them most about teaching adolescents, you will see the phrase "lack of motivation" often. They will say, "They don't care," "They aren't willing to put forth any effort, especially when the work is challenging," "They are comfortable with mediocre performance," "They are only concerned with getting a passing grade; they are rarely excited about learning for its own sake," or "They are apathetic and unmotivated!"

Motivation is a key component to learning in middle school classrooms. Yet teachers are often disillusioned by adolescents' apparent lack of interest in academic tasks. "What can I do to get students to concentrate, to put more effort into schoolwork, and to take it seriously?" is the persistent question for teachers. Newmann (1989) observed that "the problem of disengagement is especially acute for middle and high school students. During adolescence, students begin to develop new patterns of social and sexual relations that absorb a great deal of their energy and attention. At the same time, they also need to master knowledge that they apparently consider foreign to their interest. These forces combine to make serious student effort in school both more important for learning and harder to achieve than in the early years" (p. 34).

Developmental changes during adolescence have a significant impact on student motivation in middle school. Adolescents are experiencing

- A reexamination of their beliefs about their abilities
- An increasing desire for control and autonomy
- An evolving self-concept
- Fear of failure, especially in front of their peers

Middle school is an intensely social environment, and academic performance in the classroom may compete with the reality of all that is happening in the hallways and beyond, as KeKe relates in Figure 3.1.

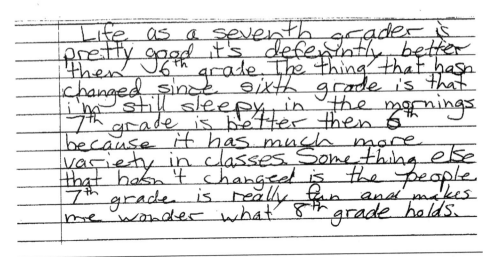

Life as a seventh grader is pretty good it's defenintly better then 6th grade. The thing that hasn't changed since sixth grade is that i'm still sleepy in the mornings 7th grade is better then 6th because it has much more variety in classes Something else that hasn't changed is the people 7th grade is really fun and makes me wonder what 8th grade holds.

FIGURE 3.1 *KeKe's Feelings about Seventh Grade*

Wigfield (1997) summarized scholarship on motivation by identifying two central questions students ask themselves: "Can I succeed?" and "Do I want to succeed and why?" First, motivation that is influenced by student perceptions about whether or not they can succeed involves students' beliefs about their abilities and competence in different areas as well as their expectations about how well they will handle a specific task. Second, even though students may perceive that they can be successful, they might lack motivation to engage in tasks because they lack interest in the tasks or they may feel that the task is not important or particularly useful to them personally.

Newmann (1989) identified five factors that are related to enhancing student engagement and motivation in school: competency, rewards, intrinsic interest, social support, and sense of ownership.

1. Adolescents have an especially powerful need to develop feelings of competency.
2. When students perceive that academic achievement will lead to rewards that they value, they are more willing to engage in hard work.
3. If students find material interesting or enjoy the way a topic is presented, they are more apt to expend effort in learning.
4. Because learning involves risk taking, adolescents in particular need to feel supported by teachers and their peers to overcome fears of failure and be regarded as accepted members of a community.
5. Adolescents need to have some influence on the nature of their learning; they need reasons to be personally invested in the work they are asked to do.

Marzano (1992) maintained that teachers must explicitly address student motivation as an integral part of lesson planning. Most important, adolescents need to perceive that the tasks they are asked to do have value. After reviewing the research on motivation, Marzano concluded that "when students are working on goals they themselves have set, they are more motivated and efficient, and they achieve more than they do when working to meet goals set by the teacher. . . . If educators expect students to be motivated to succeed at classroom tasks, they must somehow link those tasks to student goals" (p. 25).

Mediated Instruction and the Gradual Release of Responsibility

In Chapter 2, we described the gradual release of responsibility model for classroom instruction (Pearson & Gallagher, 1983). This model envisions much of classroom instruction falling into the zone of proximal development where lessons are scaffolded to support student learning. Scaffolded instruction can be viewed as teaching that is mediating (Vygotsky, 1962). The metaphor of mediated instruction assumes that teaching is a process of negotiating between students and unfamiliar content. This metaphor of the teacher as mediator is a powerful one. In this role, the teacher steps in as an intermediary to bridge the gaps between the new material and what the students already know.

Of course, teachers assume mediating roles many times during a school day. Teachers mediate between students who are having difficulty with each other. Teachers mediate between students and their parents to problem-solve various issues. Sometimes teachers even mediate between students and other teachers or school staff members. Teachers constantly find themselves in the middle of things, and to bring people together, teachers know that they have to go back and forth between sides to determine how difficulties or misunderstandings can be resolved. Teachers must also be in the middle of classroom learning.

Like labor mediators, teachers serve as go-betweens to bring about understanding in their classrooms. The art of teaching centers on forging connections between what students know and what they need to learn. Learning occurs when a student's accumulated wisdom about the world is related to a body of information that expands and deepens understanding. Mediated instruction actively addresses students' concerns about being successful or spending time on a task that does not seem interesting or valuable.

Through the gradual release model, Pearson and Gallagher (1983) argued that teaching is much more complicated than merely handing out materials and making assignments, with the expectation that meaningful connections will inexorably result. Very often students find that they do not know enough to make sense of a book, they do not see how they can link what they know to new material, or they discover that they are operating from a much different knowledge base than the author's. Some students will plug on, collecting facts that they really do not see any use for, in the hopes that somehow all this will come together. Others will proceed through the text at a superficial level, not worrying about whether things make sense but only trying to satisfy some assignment. Finally, many students will simply give up and reject making an effort to fit the new information with what they know. Students' motivatation to do their best is obviously flagging, and teachers bemoan their students' struggles to learn independently from their reading. At these points, it is time for the teacher to intervene to mediate between the student and the textbook in an effort to find a common ground for establishing an understanding.

Mediated Instruction and Prior Knowledge

Teachers who are mediators are ever conscious of the prior knowledge (referred to as *schema* in Chapter 2) that their students bring to learning. It is not enough to peruse reading scores on standardized tests to determine whether students are likely to encounter problems reading the course material. Students might demonstrate a general reading ability that allows them to handle reading demands on tests, but because they lack many of the critical concepts and vocabulary in a specific subject area, they still have difficulty understanding the textbook. For many struggling learners, limited background knowledge, not poor reading skills, underlies their problems with text.

As mediators, teachers work with their students to identify what elements of their personal knowledge would be most helpful in understanding new material. At times, the distance between new content and the students' knowledge can be too great to be spanned all at once, and more modest jumps need to be explored instead. At this point the textbook might need to be set aside, and alternative sources of information that more closely match what the students know should be substituted, such as a story or video. The role of mediator underscores the necessity

of interacting with students to determine who they are and what they know as the preliminary foundation for classroom learning.

As mediators, teachers attempt to bring the disparate parties (students and the text) together, but teachers know that ultimately, they cannot solve all the problems of understanding by themselves. Mediation in the classroom thus provides the motivation for a resolution—the understanding of challenging new material. To accomplish this end effectively, teachers need to be mentors who provide students with the learning tools that will help them to make these connections gradually more independently.

The gradual release model envisions teachers who are coaches as well as mediators. Like good coaches, effective literacy teachers realize that it is not enough to hover on the sidelines and issue commands. Successful coaches spend hours with their players developing skills to be used independently during a performance. Coaches know that it is not enough to tell players what to do; they need to show them. Coaches work as mentors alongside their players, modeling correct procedures and actions, providing feedback on their efforts, and supporting them as they gradually become more skilled and independent. Coaches who discover gaps in their players' skill development waste little time criticizing previous coaches for these shortcomings. Instead, they roll up their sleeves and undertake the necessary instruction themselves. If their players need to know something to be successful, these coaches do what needs to be done to help their players develop.

Like coaches, effective literacy teachers know that there is much more to teaching than standing in the background and blowing a whistle (Buehl, 1993). Struggling learners need explicit instruction in literacy strategies during the classroom routine. Teaching invariably involves being in the middle of things, in the aisles of the classroom, working alongside students as they attempt to learn. Teaching, like coaching, prepares students for independent performance, for a time when they can successfully learn with minimal assistance from others. Successful coaches are sometimes given the accolade that "they are teachers." Perhaps successful teachers deserve a similar compliment: "They are coaches."

Schoenbach, Braunger, Greenleaf, and Litman (2003) described this process of mentoring students as a reading apprenticeship. This approach to instruction involves classroom teachers meeting their content standards through supporting student learning by doing the following:

1. Engaging students in more reading
2. Making the teacher's discipline-based reading processes and knowledge visible to students
3. Making the students' reading processes, knowledge, and understandings visible to the teacher and to one another
4. Helping students gain insight into their own reading processes as a means of gaining strategic control over these processes
5. Helping students acquire a repertoire of problem-solving strategies for deepening comprehension of texts in various academic disciplines (p. 134)

Motivation and Engagement

Young children generally believe that "ability can be increased through effort, and high effort signifies high ability. During early and later adolescence, however, students often develop the notion of ability as a capacity, and begin to think of effort and ability as being inversely related. Therefore, they are capable of understanding that high effort, without success, is a sign of low ability" (Urdan, Midgley, & Wood, 1995, p. 15). When students come to believe that ability is a fixed trait, they become less likely to risk failure on a challenging task. In their thinking, if you try and fail at a task, you must be "dumb." Being perceived this way by peers is too much of a deterrent; it is safer to not try in the first place. The learning environment plays a critical role in determining how students view their own abilities. The challenge for teachers is to design instruction that supports students in expending the effort necessary to meet a curriculum that reflects the rigor of meaningful content learning (Resnick & Hall, 2000).

Motivation and engagement are intricately linked; it seems obvious that students must be motivated to engage in learning. After conducting a thorough review of the adolescent literacy research, Meltzer and Hamann (2004) concluded that there are three primary instructional practices guiding the facilitation of student-centered classrooms that promote student motivation to read, write, discuss, and strengthen literacy skills:

1. Making connections to students' lives, thereby connecting background knowledge to the text to be read
2. Creating responsive classrooms where students are acknowledged, have voice, and are given choices in learning tasks, reading assignments, and topics of inquiry that then strengthen their literacy skills

3. Having students interact with each other about text and with text in ways that stimulate questioning, predicting, visualizing, summarizing, and clarifying (pp. 13–14)

Making Connections to Students' Lives

Learning strategies that build background knowledge, activate knowledge, and assist students in organizing knowledge have been prevalent in the literature and in practice for many years. (Chapter 7 is entirely devoted to connecting and building students' prior knowledge.) When using strategies such as the Predicting and Confirming Actitivity, KWL, Concept Mapping, and Anticipation Guides, middle school teachers soon realize that when students can personally connect to the information in a discussion, video, or text, they not only enhance their literacy abilities, but also tend to learn and remember more content as well. "Helping students to make these connections is key because student engagement is determined by personal purpose for reading" (Meltzer & Hamann, 2004, p. 16).

Making connections with self and text is especially important for English language learners (ELLs). This means, of course, that teachers need to make an effort to know what their culturally diverse students know and understand. To assist ELL students in engaging with and understanding content, teachers much build bridges between what students know and the new information the teacher wishes to teach. "If building understanding is a matter of weaving new information into pre-existing structures of meaning, then it becomes indispensable for teachers to help English learners see these connections, through a variety of activities" (Walqui, 2002).

Creating Safe and Responsive Classrooms

The developmental tasks of adolescence such as autonomy—establishing a positive self-esteem and a personal identity—are important life work. Teachers who understand the developmental tasks of adolescents and design instruction that teaches content, enhances literacy, and accommodates these tasks naturally connect with students and engage them in learning tasks. Authentic tasks, formative assessments with meaningful feedback, and choice in reading material and projects all meet the students' literacy and developmental needs.

Safety and inclusion are significant considerations in middle schools. For those without adequate literacy habits and skills, it is often scary to reveal this to others and to begin the hard work of addressing the issues (Meltzer & Hamann, 2004). Teacher judgments of students often determine whether an individual continues to try or gives up in despair. This is particularly true of ELLs who might already feel inadequate because of their limited language skills.

Having Students Interact with Each Other and with Text

The evidence that motivation and engagement result from collaborative learning is clear (Biancarosa & Snow, 2004; Langer, 1999). When students work together to question, predict, visualize, summarize, and clarify, they are more likely to be motivated to interact with text, but they learn literacy and content as well. "Text-based discussion and collaborative learning also emerge in the ELL literature as two key instructional approaches for engaging ELLs with content-area learning and literacy development" (Meltzer & Hamann, 2004, p. 33).

Changing the culture of an entire school is without question a daunting task and not within the control of an individual classroom teacher. Teachers who understand developmental and cultural factors that influence student motivation, however, can change their classroom environments and their ways of interacting with students. Declining motivation for academic endeavors is a result of developmental factors of the students and cultural factors of middle schools. Secondary educators can attempt to avert declining motivation by changing the nature of teacher-student interactions, restructuring the curriculum to be more relevant to adolescents, rethinking reward systems in their schools, reducing the amount of comparison based on ability between students, and creating a safe environment for students to learn from failure. Figure 3.2 illustrates how one teacher (Mrs. Arnold) was able to change a student's view of his own ability.

Using Classroom Discussion to Motivate Students

Teachers' working one-on-one with students is certainly desirable. Most teachers, however, do not have time during the school day to assist each student. A common form of communication in a middle school classroom is the classroom discussion,

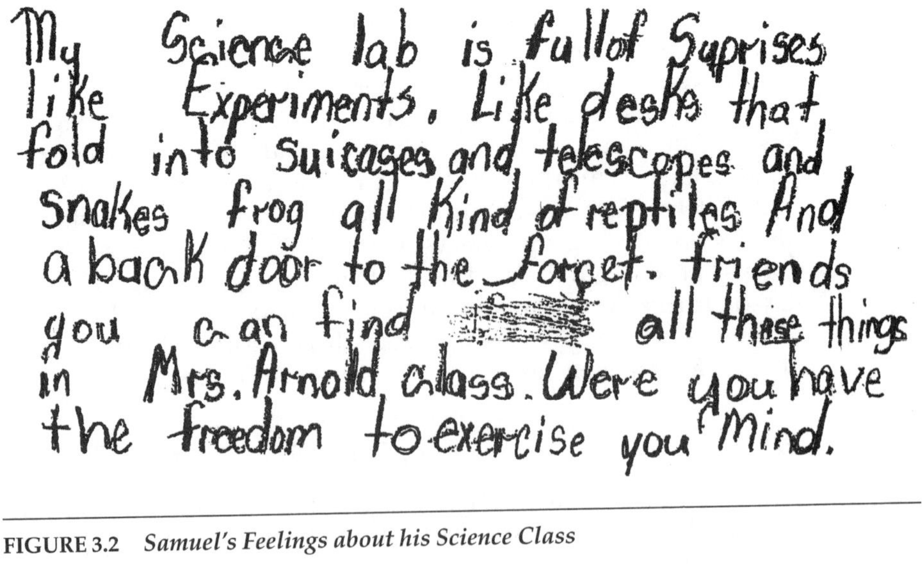

My Science lab is full of Suprises like Experiments. Like desks that fold into Suicases and telescopes and Snakes frog all Kind of reptiles And a back door to the forget. friends you can find all these things in Mrs. Arnold class. Were you have the freedom to exercise you Mind.

FIGURE 3.2   *Samuel's Feelings about his Science Class*

which can give students feedback and encourage them to reason at higher levels and elaborate on their initial thoughts. Classroom discussions can also validate students' ideas and efforts to solve problems.

Middle schools are very social settings. Students seem automatically programmed for interactive discourse, from the moment they hit the hallways before the first bell rings in the morning to the last telephone call before bedtime. They josh with each other, exchange juicy tidbits of gossip, console broken-hearted friends, and vent their viewpoints with alacrity. Middle schoolers find kid-talk very motivating, and they are more than eager to indulge in it.

Classroom discussions provide teachers with a vehicle for successfully channeling kid-talk into the curriculum. For years, researchers have noted the positive benefits of conducting classroom discussions. Sternberg (1987) stated that because "our ability to think originates outside ourselves, we must view class discussion as more than just a peripheral part of a thinking-skills program. Discussion is essential" (p. 459). This interchange of ideas facilitates the maturation of the adolescent from total egocentricism to a more balanced worldview.

Alvermann, Dillon, and O'Brien (1987) stated that "discussion is an integral part of the comprehension process" (p. 13) and "the use of recitation and lecture . . . cannot compete with discussion in offering opportunities for students to communicate their views to other students with different views" (p. 9). Guthrie, Schafer, Wang, and Afflerbach (1993) documented many benefits of classroom discussion such as increased time reading about related topics and a better understanding of science concepts. Furthermore, reading is placed in a social context. That is, discussion reduces the isolation that students sometimes feel when they are left alone to interact with text. Discussion often helps students to communicate, refine, and enrich their understanding of the assigned reading.

Alvermann, Dillon, & O'Brien (1987) maintained that discussion has the following three criteria:

1. Discussants should put forth multiple points of view and stand ready to change their minds about the matter under discussion
2. Students should interact with one another as well as with the teacher
3. The interaction should exceed the typical two or three word phrase units common to recitation lessons (p. 7)

Recitation might be visualized as a telephone switchboard operator—all lines run from the teacher to and from individual students; interaction between students is minimal. According to the preceding definition, recitation is not considered to be a "discussion."

Three types of classroom discussions are considered to be basic to the classroom environment:

1. Subject mastery discussions that extend student learning through talk about a topic—activating prior knowledge and building background information are

necessary in facilitating comprehension of any new topic of study (Chapter 7 contains a full description of using prior knowledge to comprehend text)

2. Issue-oriented discussions, which may depend on student needs and interests
3. Problem-solving discussions, which may grow out of a textbook assignment, lecture, or previous discussion or assignment

To have a successful classroom discussion, it is necessary to have the proper setting and climate. Students must feel free to express their opinions and recognize that what they say will be accepted. A physical arrangement that is conducive to discussion is one in which the chairs are arranged in a circle or horseshoe shape. The teacher must be an effective listener who instills respect for the opinions of others. Teachers should clarify, reflect feelings, resolve different points of view, interpose summaries, and redirect questions to students.

Discussions should be limited. The teacher should announce the length of the discussion ahead of time, along with the purpose. The teacher should also maintain the focus of the discussion and should respect the privacy of individual students by not insisting on direct participation, although it is often difficult to get all students to take part.

Classroom Talk That Is Accountable

It is not easy to create classrooms that are hubs of good talk—talk that deepens understanding of the curriculum, sharpens students' thinking, and sparks the exploration of new ideas. Teachers frequently find it a challenge to channel the natural convivial social talk of their students into the focused academic discourse that ignites learning. The University of Pittsburgh's Institute for Learning has extensively investigated strategies for embedding academic rigor into the curriculum. Lauren Resnick and her colleagues have been particularly interested in the central role of classroom talk as students collaborate in their learning. Resnick and her colleagues argue that classroom talk that truly engages learning is accountable on three levels. First, everyone accepts certain norms and practices that recognize and honor each other's legitimate participation in the talk of the classroom. Second, students connect classroom talk to the curriculum and realize their responsibilities to accurate and defensible information. Third, students employ principles of higher level thinking as they use evidence to formulate their arguments and clarify their ideas (Michaels, O'Connor, Hall, & Resnick, 2002).

Classroom talk can appear in a variety of guises, such as teacher-led whole-class discussions, cooperative group dialogues, partner shares, student presentations, peer conferences, and literature circles. But while the room might be brimming with talk, the classroom discourse might not be sensitive to and inclusive of all learners, it might stray from the content being considered, and it might be superficial, not achieving a deep and thoughtful processing of a topic. Creating a learning environment that establishes the expectations for productive classroom talk is a necessary first step. Any efforts that build community in a classroom, of course, contribute to the trust and acceptance that underlie encouraging and valuing the participation of all class members in the daily discourse fundamental to learning.

In particular, however, students need guidance in the behaviors associated with good talk. Good talk has a give-and-take quality; participants expect to take turns, there is a tacit understanding that no individual dominates the floor for an extended period, and it is a common norm that one listens intently when others talk. In a variety of ways, participants communicate that they care about what others say—they display nonverbal responses that reinforce that they are attending to the talk of others, they occasionally restate others' points and ask for clarification and elaboration, and they demonstrate serious consideration of others' arguments by sometimes respectfully challenging them or disagreeing with them.

Resnick and her colleagues emphasize the social basis of learning, which is dependent on a classroom environment that underscores the need for learners to rely upon each other to hone their understandings (Michaels et al., 2002). Such an environment is unlikely to develop without conscious modeling and feedback from the teacher. Students who are excited by the talk of a particular activity might have difficulty managing and balancing their enthusiasm; they might be impetuous in their responses, and they might overshadow or overwhelm others. In contrast, disengaged students or individuals who lack confidence might need frequent invitations and a variety of structures that integrate them into the talk as full participants.

For classroom talk to be truly worthwhile, however, it must also acknowledge "how we know what we say." Student statements need to connect directly to the material being studied. In other words, productive classroom talk needs to be purposefully intertwined into the curriculum. This second level, accountability to knowledge, stresses classroom talk that strives to represent information and ideas accurately. Students might be asked to refer back to a passage, for example, to ensure that what they are saying is consistent with what experts or the author would maintain (Michaels et al., 2002).

Although part of this dynamic reinforces learning through the checking and rechecking of "the facts," students also bring in knowledge that cannot be affirmed by classroom materials. Students will share information that they believe is relevant from a wide variety of sources and personal experiences. Although such references are an essential component of good talk, they can also be problematic, especially if students are unclear about their sources, if the information is secondhand or misinterpreted, or if the statements are more opinion than factual.

As a result, classroom talk cannot have an "anything goes" ethos. While students are expected to base their responses on good information and are encouraged to offer additional insights, they need to be constantly aware of whether acceptable support is available to back up their assertions. Opinion statements need special attention; an "it's just my opinion" justification effectively shuts down discussion. Acceptable statements are those that can be linked to agreed-upon sources for verification.

Finally, at a third level, classroom talk develops learners who are insightful and critical thinkers. As students begin to inventory what they know, they are poised to generalize, draw conclusions, and search for implications. When students construct arguable observations about the material, they must be prompted to adhere to acceptable lines of reasoning to support their thinking. They may marshal evidence, consider analogies, or suggest hypotheticals as they make a case. They might need to refine their ideas further as they respond to questioning, and they might find it necessary to qualify their positions when presented with challenges.

Teaching students the elements of good classroom talk can make a variety of classroom learning arrangements—from large group discussions to paired sharing—more productive and successful. Students become comfortable airing their ideas in front of others, and they become more willing to risk participation in public classroom discourse. In addition, students come to recognize the benefits of social interactions while learning as they continue to evolve their understandings of the curriculum. However, classroom talk that is accountable must be modeled and taught by the teacher; most students do not arrive at the classroom prepared to engage in such discourse.

During a classroom discussion, teachers often talk to the same four or five people who always have their hands raised. The other students might realize that they do not need to listen or participate in any way. Some timid students might become frustrated that they are never heard in class, and others might lapse into boredom and tune out the entire proceedings. The next section describes a variety of classroom strategies that can facilitate discussion from the entire class.

Think-Pair-Share

Think-pair-share (McTighe & Lyman, 1988) is a strategy that encourages full participation from all students without putting any individual on the spot. The teacher provides students with a prompt that focuses their thinking, such as posing a question that requires abstract thought. Students ponder for a few moments and jot down a response. Then students pair and talk about their answers with a partner. Finally, as a class, they discuss their thoughts. This strategy allows every student an opportunity to answer, at least to a partner, and allows students time to think, respond, and try to make connections with the world they understand. For example, a think-pair-share activity could jump-start discussion on an issue such as the American colonists' disenchantment with England. The teacher might direct a question to the class, such as "Why do people sometimes become unhappy with their government?" Students would be granted a few minutes to write their own answers. After this reflection time, students would then pair up to share their initial responses and then, after discussion, would be granted an opportunity to revise or modify their responses.

Think-pair-share allows time for thought and reaction, as well as providing for a fuller, richer, and more thoughtful discussion. This strategy can be used to help students structure their thinking in different ways (Whitehead, 1998). Modifications such as summarize-pair-share, question-pair-share, predict-pair-share, and visualize-pair-share serve different learning objectives and help students to elaborate and refine their thinking.

Paired retellings, for example, offer a discussion format for students to practice their paraphrasing and summarizing skills. In groups of two or three, students read short sections and retell them to their partners or a group. Or students can listen to the teacher or fellow students read aloud and then summarize main points to a partner. Paired retellings are effective because students have the advantage of a peer or group to help them cope with challenging text, and students are prompted to monitor their comprehension constantly through retelling what they have read in their own words.

The Discussion Web

Another strategy that engages all students in discussion is the discussion web (Alvermann, 1991). The discussion web incorporates reading, writing, speaking, listening, and thinking into a cooperative learning format and offers students multiple opportunities to interact. In addition, students are provided with a graphic organizer, which helps them to structure their thinking and buttress their arguments during discussion. This strategy is best employed with reading material that develops opposing viewpoints. A piece of literature that elicits differing views on a character's actions would be an excellent choice for a discussion web activity in a language arts class.

Step 1. **Students read the assigned material.** When they have completed this stage, they are ready to began a second examination of the text.

Step 2. **Students work with partners, and each pair is provided with a discussion web graphic organizer.** A focusing question is then stated; students write the question in the box in the center of the web. Each set of partners then revisits the reading and attempts to locate information and arguments that would support a "yes" answer to the question and information and arguments that would support a "no" answer. They are instructed not to take sides at this point but instead to involve themselves in a fact-finding mission so that the most compelling information is marshaled for both sides of the ledger.

For example, students in a language arts class read an article about the impact of popular singer 50 Cent's music and other rappers on youth and society as a whole. For their discussion webs, students were given the following question: "Do you think that 50 Cent's popularity is hurting our society?" Students needed to reexamine the article to search for pertinent support for each position on this question, regardless of their personal beliefs, and to produce a discussion web as shown in Figure 3.3.

Step 3. **When each set of partners has finished compiling evidence for both sides of the question, they then join with a second pair of students.** This new cooperative group of four is given the charge of working toward consensus on the question. Which side seems more compelling: the "yes" arguments or the "no" arguments? As a dynamic of this stage of the activity, students will likely discover new arguments to add to their discussion webs, both from their new collaborators and from their joint discussion of the question.

Step 4. **Students share with the entire class.** Each group of four selects a spokesperson who is permitted to discuss one reason for their conclusion on the question. Allowing each group to present only one reason diminishes the likelihood that the last groups to report will have nothing new to add to the class dialogue on the issue.

The discussion web strategy clearly elicits student emotions on open-ended curriculum topics, but students are also engaged in a careful analysis of information so that their opinions have a basis in fact. Once again, first with partners, then in groups of four, and finally as part of the entire class, students have multiple opportunities to participate in the discussion.

Cooperative Literacy

Another strategic teaching method is cooperative literacy, which involves placing students into heterogeneous groups for sustained periods of four to eight weeks. These noncompetitive learning teams provide opportunities for teachers to make a transition from independent and whole-class activities to smaller, more intimate, and deeper discussion groups.

Cooperative learning is an effective way to facilitate student interaction and socialization and to improve learning. Cooperative arrangements can provide a literacy focus for classroom management that promotes both student collaboration

Do you think 50 Cent's popularity is hurting our society?

Yes

- 50 Cent is glorifying gun violence
- He makes songs out of "How to Rob" people
- 50 Cent has attacked women at his concerts
- He exploits women in his videos
- He uses his lyrics to insult other rappers
- He has been a suspect in several shooting crimes
- His lyrics hold power over young impressionable fans
- Sometimes he appears more as an activist than an entertainer

No

- He just wants to make a name for himself
- He wants people to know how tough he is through his music
- He's been shot nine times and just wants people to understand
- Provides a voice for those who know gun violence as normal
- He does not want young men to become victims of gun violence
- His lyrics are a way for young listeners to release their frustrations
- He always motivates his young son to stay in school and don't do drugs
- His lyrics are harmless trash talk

Conclusion

Some people think that 50 Cent's popularity is hurting our society but I disagree. 50 Cent is just being real. He is telling about his experiences and wants to get teens to talk about the real issues. His music is not for every person but it sends real messages to teens who can relate because they have a life like his. If people are worried they should just talk about it, not judge him. You don't have to copy him just think about what he is saying.

FIGURE 3.3   *Discussion Web*

and achievement and can be used with all subjects across the curriculum. The success of cooperative learning, however, might not be as dependent on the structure of the activity or the roles that students play as on the preparation students have received in the prerequisite behaviors that support cooperative learning. The use of techniques that promote positive social behavior will benefit the classroom climate by accentuating a caring environment in which students share in completing a task and help each other with their learning. The ability of students to talk to each other about content, share information, lend encouragement to the group, and participate in group routines and ventures are behaviors that require training, especially if students have had no prior experience with cooperative learning.

A cooperative management system in the classroom facilitates students' ability to relate to each other (Klemp, 1996). Students who experience collaboration and sharing are more likely to feel that they belong than those who are exposed only to more traditional individualized and competitive organizations, which often diminish motivation to participate. Providing a means for students to engage in discussion about the material can prove more productive when students are allowed to communicate through their own forms of student-generated language. This process may be even more important if the learner is an English language learner.

Some teachers enhance their literacy-based strategies by changing the social organization of their classes into pods, or learning teams. Teachers can then show the processes that proficient readers use: reading, clarifying or verifying, restating main ideas or thesis statements, and summarizing. The directed reading sequence provides the structure for students to engage in and practice effective reading behaviors.

Directed Reading Sequence

Cooperative learning replaces more traditional teaching methods that center on individualized or large-group instruction featuring independent seat work. Small-group activity in conjunction with cooperative learning can be an effective means of instruction for low-achieving students. Teachers can capitalize on the tendency of young adolescents to gravitate to more social situations by employing strategies that inspire cooperation. Because language proficiency increases in conjunction with adolescents' psychological and social development, teachers can take advantage of this natural stage of growth by organizing classrooms where students promote each other's literacy as they learn content area material.

Teachers are sometimes reluctant to use small groups for fear of chaos and loss of control of the class. Cooperative learning, however, not only improves learning from text, but also allows students to observe strategies used by peers in text-based encounters. The arrangement of students in learning teams or pods becomes the social organization of the class. These continuous groups are maintained for approximately five weeks and are then changed to give students the opportunity to work with a different group of students. This management approach, when used consistently, eases the transition to cooperative lessons.

To compensate for struggling readers' difficulties with independent reading, some teachers resort to row-by-row round-robin reading—each student takes a turn reading a portion of the text aloud to the rest of the class. Unfortunately, use of this strategy might actually impede comprehension; many teachers report that students rarely follow along and fewer listen, especially when struggling readers fumble their way through a challenging paragraph.

In the directed reading sequence (Klemp, 1997), the teacher facilitates reading of text selections with students in groups or pods. This strategy provides much interaction, and readers who have difficulty can gain assistance from more proficient members of their pods. It also involves elaboration, summarization, and retelling.

Step 1. **Selecting the text.** Before the assigned reading time, the teacher predetermines which sections of the text match the learner outcomes. The use of the word "section" refers to any portion of the text that accommodates a break in the reading. For expository writing or textbooks, sections might break at boldface subheadings or at various points when concept load increases. For works of literature or narrative, breaks might occur at prediction points, scene or setting changes, or plot deviations. The teacher may also have the students preview the text selection in advance, raising some questions that require students to determine whether the text is fiction or nonfiction, whether there are boldface headings that give an indication of the content, or whether they have questions of their own.

Step 2. **Reading the text.** At the teacher's direction, the class reads a section silently. At the end of the allotted time, each pod receives an envelope containing four or five cards. The cards indicate the roles for the directed reading sequence. The cards state and describe the roles of: paraphraser, verifier, squeezer, and writer. In the debriefing of the section that occurs after the reading, students in each pod assume one of these roles.

- The *paraphraser* retells what was in the selection.
- The *verifier* either verifies what the paraphraser said, corrects errors, or adds items that were omitted.
- The *squeezer* creates one very general sentence that captures the essence of the selection.
- When the pod agrees with that sentence, the *writer* writes that sentence on the pod's memory chart.

The teacher may direct pods to share their squeezed sentence to model some of the summarized sentences. This polling also allows the teacher to assess how much of the information the pods have obtained. Essentially, the pod develops a group memory of the reading through the creation of the sentences.

Step 3. **Changing roles.** For the next section, the teacher has more options. The teacher might determine that the concept load for that selection is somewhat demanding and might choose to have an oral reading, followed by a sustained silent reading. At the next use of the directed reading sequence, the roles change. The writers pass their cards (and their roles) to the next person (the verifiers). In turn, the verifiers pass their cards to the squeezers, who pass their cards to the paraphrasers, who pass their cards to the writers. Thus, the roles change so that each member of the pod assumes each of the roles. If the teacher decides that sections of text are superfluous to learning outcomes, students may be directed to skip them.

Step 4. **Extending the reading.** When the teacher has finished the directed reading sequence and has guided the students through completing their reading, the teacher might extend the activity. For instance, the teacher might wish to have the students create a study guide using student-generated questions that then can be circulated among the pods to further extend the learning.

The use of the directed reading sequence creates new options for the teacher in guiding and sustaining reading activities. For example, the teacher might weave in and out of oral reading, which gives students an opportunity to listen to fluent reading. Students who are unfamiliar with the conventions of written language benefit from this opportunity to hear fluent reading. The teacher may read sections of the text to the students while they listen. Or, students may follow along if they choose.

The teacher might direct the students to read a section silently or use a combination of both oral and silent reading if the selection is particularly demanding. As teachers begin to use more cooperative methods to enhance literacy for students, they may find that students who previously showed reluctance to participate in learning and who perhaps were a source of disruption in the class begin to adhere to accepted norms of behavior. The directed reading sequence increases proficiency in text language for all learners, including those for whom English is not a first language. Providing students the opportunity to join a community of learning might require nothing more than a structured opportunity to use one of the best learning resources available to them—each other.

Summary

One of the frustrating aspects of working with young adolescents is their apparent lack of interest in academic tasks. Student motivation and relevance of the content being studied must be considered while planning curriculum and instruction. Teachers who act as mediator and coach integrate literacy strategies into the curriculum to help students make personal connections to new material and perceive value in what they are learning. Student perceptions of their own intelligence are important as well. Task-focused learning, then, provides a rationale for helping students to become more independent learners. Strategies such as classroom discussion, think-pair-share, and the directed reading sequence motivate students to become active participants in the learning process.

Recent research in the area of motivation and engagement clearly indicates how educators can connect their subject matter to their students' lives. Careful attention must be given to the needs of students and how best to connect new information to what they already know. Current research on motivation and engagement of students reveals that three factors are important:

1. Making connections to students' lives
2. Creating safe and responsive classrooms
3. Having students interact with each other and with text

Extending Learning

Reviewing the Talking Points

Revisit the talking points at the beginning of this chapter. Answer the questions now that you have read the chapter, and compare your prereading and postreading responses.

Revisiting the Vignette

In the opening vignette, Ms. Booth planned to connect the setting of *The Cay* with the prior knowledge of her students. Students are often given assignments with little guidance. Think back to your own experiences as a middle school student. How did you prepare yourself to relate to the subject at hand? What did your teachers do to help you?

Terms to Remember and Use

student motivation	adolescence	strategic teaching	mediated instruction
student engagement	autonomy	self-esteem	authentic tasks
responsive classroom	think-pair-share	cooperative literacy	accountable talk

Write a series of sentences that meaningfully connect pairs of the above key terms. Your sentences should refer to ideas and concepts related to the literacy of middle school students.

Modifying Instruction for English Language Learners

When it comes to English language learners, teachers must understand that the language barriers for ELLs can cause vulnerability, frustration, anxiety, and sometimes hopelessness. To motivate ELLs, teachers can apply Meltzer and Hamann's (2004) three primary instructional practices to the ELLs' specific needs.

Creating safe and responsive classrooms presumes an environment in which students are most willing to learn. Motivational factors at this stage are:

1. Students' attitude toward subject matter, teacher, environment, peers, and self
2. Students' needs (Thanasoulas, 2002)

Specific strategies for attending these factors include the following:

- Display a warm and supportive attitude toward students and demonstrate enthusiasm about the subject and content to be taught.
- Provide various resources to facilitate students' learning activities. For example, a dictionary, visual aids, or reference books might be needed.
- Encourage students to use their native languages strategically to help their learning activities in English language. For instance, recalling the metacognitive skills that students developed when they first acquired language literacy would contribute to their second language development.
- Assist students in establishing realistic goals for learning activities. For example, in a language arts class when students are assigned a piece of reading, teachers are responsible for making ELL students realize that the objective is to grasp the main idea of the passage instead of articulating the accurate meaning of every single word.
- Give recognition to the effort that students make in accomplishing goals rather than punishing or rewarding on the basis of the final outcome.
- Use different grouping strategies for different tasks. Sometimes, ELLs can learn from modeling of strong readers; under other circumstances, they might feel more comfortable discussing with ELL students who are at the same English-language proficiency level or have similar language and cultural backgrounds. Individual students' personalities would be another consideration in grouping students for specific learning activities.
- Determine, through authentic assessment or by other means, individual ELL students' first-language literacy level, English-language proficiency level, interests, skills, and strengths. On the basis of this information, select study material and learning activities to meet students' learning needs.

Making connections to students' lives plays a pivotal role in maintaining student motivation. For middle school students, who are much more mature than young children, intrinsic motivation is important. To encourage intrinsic motivation, teachers should make students cognizant of how the curriculum can meet their needs and tell them about the benefits of their learning activities. The following strategies can help teachers to meet this challenge:

- Use learner concerns to organize content and to develop themes and teaching procedures (Thanasoulas, 2002). This strategy answers the question "Is the curriculum organized around 'big' questions?"—one of the key questions that Freeman and Freeman (2000) pose for meeting the needs of ELLs. The "big" questions that they mention involve those issues that are relevant to students' own lives. "How are we alike and how are we different?" is an example of a question around which teachers can select related literature to assist students in looking for answers. Similar questions that reflect ELLs' concerns may be "Where is my home?" or "What is my culture?" By providing opportunity for ELLs to explore such questions, teachers are helping them find their own identifies in this society of diversity, which is a major theme of education for immigration students.
- Involve students in selection of text. If this is impossible for classroom instruction, it should be granted at least for reading activities outside classroom. Only when students have a sense of ownership and responsibility of what they are reading are they likely to engage students in the learning process. This can also be viewed as a starting point of cultivating student autonomy.

- Create opportunities for ELLs to connect to their primary language acquisition processes and to facilitate learning by use of their primary languages. Quite a few studies have found either positive or neutral effects of first-language proficiency on second-language performance (Kamil, 2003). For example, Royer and Carlo (1991) found a positive correlation between L1 reading comprehension scores on later L2 reading comprehension scores in bilingual Spanish/English sixth graders, suggesting a positive transfer of reading skills.
- Connect instruction to students' prior knowledge as a result of previous classroom instruction, schooling in native country, or personal life experience. The prior knowledge will not necessarily be correct, but activation of such knowledge helps to engage students in the current learning process. Whenever appropriate, teachers can build new instruction on the basis of the concepts that students have already mastered and develop new knowledge. At other times, teachers can make learning happen by correcting particular misconceptions and misunderstanding.

Having students interact with each other and with text presumes other strategies that would be effective in motivating ELL students to learn.

- Provide authentic reading opportunities while reducing decontextized reading as much as possible. Freeman and Freeman (2000) asserted that "for bilingual learners, predictable whole stories, novels, plays, and poems, as well as complete pieces of nonfictions are more comprehensible than simplified texts and excerpts because the context is richer" (p. 3).
- Make learner reaction and involvement essential parts of the learning process, that is, problem solving, role-playing, and stimulation (Thanasoulas, 2002). If students view reading as a process during which their roles are only to receive information passively, the learning process cannot be successful. Teachers need to come up with various approaches that involve students in an interactive process in which they are expected to sympathize, feel, think, and comment. This goal can be realized through different means, such as group discussion.
- Use a group cooperation goal to maximize learner involvement and sharing (Thanasoulas, 2002). Some benefits of grouping ELLs and native English-speaking students in different ways have been discussed in previous paragraphs. Interaction among group members in reading activities also brings about multiple perspectives on the same issues. Further, collaborative activities contribute to ELLs' English proficiency development because language acquisition is a social activity (Smith, 1983), and students develop language in authentic social contexts as they help each other to make sense of content and concepts (Freeman & Freeman, 2000).

Beyond the Book

- Review the entire document by Meltzer and Hamann (2004) *Meeting the Developmental Literacy Needs of Adolescent English Language Learners through Content Area Learning*, which can be found on the Web site for the Center for Resource Management and Brown University (www.alliance.brown.edu/pubs/alit/adell _litdv1.pdf).
- Interview a middle school student about the types of tasks he or she is asked to perform with textbooks. Delve into the ways in which a student deals with his or her own tendencies to be motivated or how the student copes with a lack of motivation.
- Interview a middle school teacher in your own discipline. Ask him or her to describe ways in which he or she provides for student motivation and engagement.

- Conduct an Internet search on the writings of Jere Brophy. Discuss one of the articles found at the site concerning student motivation and learning.
- If you managed a company in which pay, time off, and the ability to remove employees were not part of the company's operating strategy, how would you organize the work force to keep it productive? Brainstorm and discuss your answers to determine whether there are common ideas for keeping the workers motivated to work.

References

Alvermann, D. (1991). The discussion web: A graphic aid for learning across the curriculum. *The Reading Teacher, 45*(2), 92–99.

Alvermann, D. E., Dillon, D. R., & O'Brien, D. G. (1987). *Using Discussion to Promote Reading Comprehension.* Newark, DE: International Reading Association.

Biancarosa, G., & Snow, C. (2004). *Reading Next: A Vision for Action and Research in Middle and High School Literacy.* New York: Carnegie Corporation of New York and Alliance for Excellent Education.

Buehl, D. (1993). Opening the door: Metaphors that connect with content teachers. *Wisconsin State Reading Association Journal, 37*(2), 31–38.

Freeman, D., & Freeman, Y. (2000). Meeting the needs of English language learners. *Talking Points, 12*(1), 2–7.

Guthrie, J. T., Schafer, W. D., Wang, Y. Y., & Afflerbach, P. (1993). *Influences of Instruction on Amount of Reading: An Empirical Exploration of Social, Cognitive, and Instructional Indicators* (Reading Research Report No. 3). College Park, MD: National Reading Research Center.

Kamil, M. (2003). *Adolescents and Literacy: Reading for the 21st Century.* Washington, DC: Alliance for Excellent Education.

Klemp, R. (1996). Cooperative literacy through cooperative discipline: A management system to support cooperative learning ventures in middle level classrooms. *Journal of New England League of Middle Schools, 9*(1), 18–23.

Klemp, R. (1997). Using directed reading sequence as an interactive strategy in content area reading. *Middle School Journal, 28*(5), 46–49.

Langer, J. (1999). *Guidelines for Teaching Middle and High School Students to Read and Write Well: Six Features of Effective Instruction.* National Research Center on English Learning and Achievement. Retrieved on April 28, 2004 from: http://cela.albany.edu.

Marzano, R. (1992). *A Different Kind of Classroom: Teaching with Dimensions of Learning.* Alexandria, VA: Association of Supervision and Curriculum Development.

McTighe, J., & Lyman, F. T. (1988). Cueing thinking in the classroom: The promise of theory-embedded tools. *Educational Leadership, 45*(7), 18–24.

Meltzer, J., & Hamann, E. T. (2004). *Meeting the Literacy Development Needs of Adolescent English Language Learners through Content Area Learning.* Providence, RI: Brown University.

Michaels, S., O'Connor, M., Hall, M. with Resnick, L. (2002) *Accountable Talk[SM]: Classroom Conversation That Works.* Pittsburgh, PA: University of Pittsburgh Institute for Learning.

Newmann, F. (1989). Student engagment and high school reform. *Educational Leadership, 46*(5), 34–36.

Pearson, P. D. & Gallagher, M. (1983). The instruction of reading comprehension. *Contemporary Educational Psychology, 8*(3), 317–344.

Resnick, L., & Hall, M. (2000). *Principles of Learning for Effort-based Education.* Pittsburgh, PA: University of Pittsburgh Institute for Learning.

Royer, J. M., & Carlo, M. S. (1991). Transfer of comprehension skills from native to second language. *Journal of Reading, 34*(6), 450–455.

Schoenbach, R., Braunger, J., Greenleaf, C., & Litman, C. (2003). Apprenticing adolescents to reading in subject-area classrooms. *Phi Delta Kappan. 85*(2), 133–138.

Smith, F. (1983). *Essays into Literacy: Selected Papers and Some Afterthoughts.* Portsmouth, NH: Heinemann.

Sternberg, R. J. (1987). Most vocabulary is learned from context. In M. G. McKeown & M. E. Curtis (Eds.), *The Nature of Vocabulary Acquisition* (pp. 457–465). Hillsdale, NJ: Lawrence Erlbaum Associates.

Thanasoulas, D. (2002). Motivation and motivating in the foreign language classroom. *ESL Articles.* Retrieved on May 1, 2005 from http://www.tefl.net/esl-articles/motivation-esl.htm.

Urdan, T., Midgley, C., & Wood, S. (1995). Special issues in reforming middle level schools. In A. Wigfield & J. S. Eccles (Eds.), *Middle Grades Schooling and Early Adolescent Development: Part II: Interventions, Practices, Beliefs, and Contexts* (pp. 9–37). Thousand Oaks, CA: Sage.

Vygotsky, L. S. (1962). *Thought and language.* Cambridge, MA: MIT Press.

Walqui, A. (2002). *Conceptual framework: Scaffolding Instruction for English Learners.* In *Quality Teaching for English Learners: Conceptual Framework,* (pp. 1–20). San Francisco: WestEd.

Whitehead, D. (1998). *Catch Them Thinking and Writing.* Arlington Heights, IL: Skylight.

Wigfield, A. (1997). Children's motivations for reading and reading engagement. In J. T. Guthrie and A. Wigfield, (Eds.). *Reading Engagement: Motivating Readers Through Integrated Instruction* (pp. 14–33). Newark: DE: International Reading Association.

4

Assisting Struggling Readers

Talking Points _____

- How extensive is reading underachievement in U.S. middle schools?
- What characteristics distinguish strong readers from struggling readers?
- How can classroom teachers scaffold instruction to benefit struggling readers?

Meagan loves her art class. The teacher is helping her experiment with different mediums. She especially likes creating new pieces with clay, although the collage she made for the exhibit on "freedom" is now hanging in the local airport. She hopes to be an art teacher herself one day. But, as she moves through the day, the reading and writing demands of all of her other classes sometimes get her down. In elementary school, she learned how to pronounce words and she always enjoyed reading out loud. In fact, she can read aloud without even thinking about what she is reading. But when she has to read silently, she just cannot concentrate and she rarely understands what she reads. When it comes to completing an assignment after reading, she is usually the last one to finish. She often thinks, "What's the point in trying?"

Jamal shares Meagan's frustration at reading his textbooks but for a different reason. He stumbles over most words when reading aloud. He is really embarrassed when his classmates provide words for him. When he really tries to read an assigned passage, he rarely understands much about it, because he just does not know too much about history or science. Some of his teachers consider Jamal a troublemaker, but what is he supposed to do during all of that time that everyone else is reading?

Nestor is another student who is often frustrated reading his textbook. He was a good student back home in Spain. But, since his family moved to the United States, he is struggling. He picks up English pretty quickly when it comes to talking to his friends, but when he tries to read a science or social studies text, there are just too many words he does not know. He uses his dictionary a lot, but it takes him a long time to read even a short passage. After all of that work, he sometimes cannot concentrate on what the passage means.

Middle school teachers are well acquainted with students who have stories similar to those of Meagan, Jamal, and Nestor. Although every student in the classroom is issued a hefty, expensive, multicolored textbook as a basis for the year's curriculum, teachers know that for many students, a serious mismatch is inevitable. "How are we supposed to teach social studies, or science, or *The Diary of Anne Frank* to students who cannot read these materials?" they ask. "How are we supposed to accommodate all the students who cannot read?"

Lyon (2002) clearly stated that "widespread illiteracy among our nation's children is not simply a disgrace, but rises to the level of a major public health problem" (p. 2). The need for a literate populace is critical to our success in a global economy and for providing opportunities for all of our citizens to reach their highest potential. Unfortunately, an increasing number of adults in the United States have not mastered basic literacy skills. Educators face numerous challenges in literacy learning, and it is undeniable that many, many students leave school unable to perform basic literacy tasks. But the problem of underachievement in reading and writing is complex and grows more so as students advance through the middle grades and into high school. Cultural pressures, students' attitudes about themselves as learners and about school in general, an increased demand for sophisticated literacy abilities, and the changing nature of the curriculum are all factors that influence success or failure in learning to read and write proficiently.

Recent research points to environmental factors within schools and classrooms, homes, and communities that contribute to underachievement and lack of motivation. In this chapter, the status of reading proficiency across the nation is examined, followed by a discussion of the literacy practices of strong readers. Some promising practices conclude this chapter.

The Status of Reading Proficiency in the United States

The literacy crisis is recognized by the *No Child Left Behind* legislation, with its emphasis on early development of reading skills. But many adolescents have already been left behind. Despite emphasis on early literacy programs over the past decade, 38 percent of America's fourth graders and 29 percent of America's eighth graders were still reading below the basic level on the 2005 National Assessment of Educational Progress (NAEP) tests, leading to fears that without intervention in the next few years, even more secondary school students will be left behind in coming years. Reading support is critical for adolescents who struggle to learn from a variety of texts. The 2005 results of the NAEP indicated that while fourth grade students showed improved reading scores, eighth grade students showed a slight decline from 1998 (Perie, Grigg, & Donahue, 2005).

According to the U.S. Department of Education, roughly 80 percent of high school dropouts are poor readers (Kaufman, Alt, & Chapman, 2001). Students who are poor readers have trouble in many of their subjects in school, drop out, and too often end up in the prison system or at the bottom of the social ladder. The Alliance for Excellent Education (AEE) warned that six million students in U.S. middle and

high schools are in "serious danger of being left behind" (Joftus, 2002). The nation's staggering dropout rate has a significant impact on the future for these students and our society as a whole. The national graduation rate for the public school class of 2000 was 69 percent. The rate for white students was 76 percent, for Asian students it was 79 percent, for African-American students it was 55 percent, for Hispanic students it was 53 percent, and for Native Americans it was 57 percent (Greene & Winters, 2002). Those without a high school diploma earn on average just over half the salary of the average worker.

The adolescent literacy crisis does not affect all schools equally. Young adults who read poorly are much more likely to be found in high-poverty, high-minority schools. It is not unusual for over 70 percent of eighth graders in high-poverty, high-minority middle schools to comprehend at below basic levels (Balfanz, Spiridakis, & Neild, 2002). At least in part because they did not receive the learning opportunities and support they required in the elementary grades, fewer than 50 percent of eighth graders from high-poverty, high-minority schools graduate from high schools within five years (Balfanz & Legters, 2001). In fact, many of these students never even make it as far as the tenth grade, partly because they find it difficult to read the required curriculum materials. Reading and writing are such fundamental skills in the everyday lives of U.S. citizens that they cannot be taken for granted. Certainly, many middle school teachers are frustrated in meeting this challenge in their classrooms.

Bintz (1997) described a number of "reading nightmares" of secondary teachers: students who experience daily difficulties learning from text materials, students who regularly refuse to do required reading out of class, students who are virtually unable to read their school materials, students who do read but who fail to comprehend the most important information, and students who are bored with or not interested in much of what they read. Most middle school teachers recognize many, if not all, of these students. Bintz identified several beliefs about adolescent literacy that underlie middle and high school teachers' frustrations about reading.

- Their students come to class with experiences and attitudes that lead the students to be passive readers, reluctant readers, or nonreaders.
- Inadequate teaching has contributed to the lack of reading achievement, but teachers feel ill-prepared to take on this challenge themselves.
- Teachers were trained and hired to teach a content, not literacy skills.
- Textbooks are part of the problem, but teachers feel that they are often stuck with a single text that does not accommodate the range of abilities in their classrooms and that students do not find engaging.
- Someone else is generally at fault: parents, elementary school teachers, and perhaps sometimes even their own colleagues—elementary school teachers are especially singled out as culprits for the reading woes of adolescent learners.

Helping Struggling Readers to Become Strong Readers

Developing competent, proficient readers who are capable of using reading for learning in all curricular areas is a worthy goal that all students can attain. With appropriate instruction, struggling readers can become stronger readers. It is important for middle school educators to recognize the literacy practices of strong readers so that they may guide and support struggling readers. Figure 4.1 compares the behaviors of struggling and strong readers (Buehl & Stumpf, 2002).

The literacy behaviors before, during, and after reading that differentiate struggling and strong readers should be recognized as falling on a continuum between two extremes. For example, students might range from being extremely resistent to reading tasks, to being somewhat reluctant, to generally being confident, to approaching nearly all reading tasks with a high degree of self-assurance. It is also important to emphasize that these literacy behaviors are contextual; that is, they are exercised with various types of texts for a host of different purposes. As a result, students might seem more like struggling readers with some texts in some classes (like science, for instance), and less like struggling readers with other texts in other classes (for example, when reading short stories in language arts). Acknowledging that nearly all adolescents have attained "basic literacy"—the ability to decode predictable words and answer literal-level questions on fairly simple passages—Moore and Hinchman (2006) underscored this need to understand literacy attainment as multidimensional: "It does not lie on one scale, nor is it all or nothing" (p. 13).

Understanding literacy practices of strong readers can redirect teachers' thinking about struggling readers' attitudes and characteristics and can provide direction for scaffolding classroom instruction to build struggling readers into strong readers. The gradual release of responsibility model, described in Chapter 1,

FIGURE 4.1   *Characteristics of Struggling and Strong Readers*

BEFORE READING		
Struggling Readers		*Strong Readers*
reluctantly approach or resist reading tasks	→	confidently approach reading tasks
possess limited background knowledge	→	activate their background knowledge on the subject before reading
inconsistently recall or use background knowledge	→	connect background knowledge to new learning
read without a clear purpose	→	know their purpose for reading
read without considering how to approach the material	→	make predictions and choose appropriate strategies
set minimal or no goals	→	set relevant, attainable goals
DURING READING		
Struggling Readers		*Strong Readers*
possess a limited attention span	→	focus their complete attention on reading
need guidance for reading tasks	→	are able to read independently
possess a limited vocabulary	→	possess an extensive vocabulary
do not consistently apply word attack skills	→	use appropriate decoding or word attack skills
read word-by-word, lack fluency	→	read fluently
do not monitor their comprehension	→	monitor their comprehension
a. do not perceive organizational structures	→	a. use text structure to assist comprehension
b. read everything at the same rate, often very slowly	→	b. adjust rate according to purpose
c. read to get done	→	c. read to learn; anticipate and predict meaning
d. give up when reading is difficult or uninteresting	→	d. persevere even with unfamiliar passages
e. get only pieces rather than integrating information	→	e. organize and integrate new information by searching for main ideas, inferring, synthesizing, etc.
f. do not ask relevant questions	→	f. raise related questions
g. often do not create mental images as they read	→	g. create visual and sensory images from text
h. do not realize and/or know what to do when they do not understand	→	h. use fix-up strategies when they do not understand (re-read, read aloud, etc.)
i. do not recognize important vocabulary	→	i. strive to understand new terms
j. do not use context clues	→	j. use context clues
k. use a limited number of strategies or repeat their mistakes	→	k. are flexible according to task

AFTER READING		
Struggling Readers		*Strong Readers*
forget or mix-up information	→	reflect on what they have read and add new information to their knowledge base
only look for "the answer" and give verbatim responses	→	summarize major ideas and recall supporting details, make inferences, draw conclusions, paraphrase
do not read outside of school	→	seek additional information from outside sources
feel success is unattainable, a result of luck	→	feel success is a result of effort
rely on the teacher for information	→	can independently gain information
express negative feelings about reading	→	express opinions about or pleasure in selections they have read
avoid reading at all costs	→	choose reading for the sheer joy of it

Source: Madison Metropolitan School District. Middle school reading task force report; revised. Buehl, D. & Stumpf, S. (2002). Reprinted with permission of the Madison Metropolitan School District.

envisions teachers helping students to become increasingly more competent as readers as the students learn the course content.

English language learners face an even greater risk of becoming struggling readers. The difficulties that ELLs usually experience are twofold: difficulty in literacy itself and English proficiency. English language learners bring different first-language literacy and English proficiency levels to class. Various combinations of these two variables further complicate teachers' tasks of improving ELL students' reading abilities. In addition, ELL students often lack confidence in approaching reading and writing tasks. Teachers need to give ELL students extra emotional support while providing appropriate technical assistance. Specific strategies that can be used include the following.

1. Encourage students to try different new strategies or techniques of their own, those taught by teachers, or ways shared among their fellow students. Help students to reflect on how they process information.
2. Demonstrate more tolerance and patience while explicitly expressing willingness to help when students make mistakes or fail to meet expectations.
3. Establish rapport with students. Understand more about individual ELL students through interaction with them, cooperation with their parents, and communication with communities where they come from. Information that would be very helpful includes the student's background, first-language literacy level, stage of English proficiency, learning style, and study habits. The more a teacher knows about his or her students, the more likely it is that the teacher can provide individualized, effective assistance for them.

Strategies for Struggling Readers

Balfanz, McPartland, and Shaw (2002) identified three types of struggling readers entering ninth grade.

1. Five to 10 percent of students who are in need of intensive and massive extra help who read at about the second or third grade level. These students need intensive interventions and extra time to improve their reading ability.
2. A larger group of students who can decode, but read with limited fluency and read at about the fifth or sixth grade level. These students have limited content knowledge, which would usually have been learned in middle school.
3. Students who are not fully prepared to succeed in standards-based courses in high school. They can read and comprehend but not at high levels and have not mastered intermediate-level skills and knowledge.

Although the percentages may vary across schools and districts, these researchers concluded that all but the very lowest (who require special remediation) can be helped to become significantly better readers. The implication of this research is that by having all content teachers take responsibility for helping students to become more literate in their content areas, 90 percent of struggling readers can be helped significantly. What is necessary, however, is a total school commitment to literacy improvement.

Most teachers recognize the common behaviors of struggling readers. These students wish to appear as readers, they pretend that they do not care about succeeding, and they often listen well or depend on friends who can help them. Brozo (1990) observed in high school classrooms and noticed the following coping strategies or mock participation employed by struggling readers: avoid eye contact with the teacher, engage in disruptive behavior, become a good listener, rely on a "with it" classmate or a good reader, seek help from friends, forget to bring books and other materials to class that might be needed for reading, use manipulative techniques in and out of class to gain teachers' positive perceptions.

Recognizing these behaviors, teachers can support struggling readers in the following ways: develop a personal rapport with the students, help them to take control of their own learning, encourage reading in their areas of interest and authentic responses to that reading, talk about text and how it is organized, and teach specific strategies for independent word learning through the use of context and recognition of meaningful word parts such as roots, prefixes, and suffixes.

Dean and Harper (2006) developed a cross-age literacy tutoring program (*Succeeding in Reading*) for English language learners and native English speakers. In their training manuals, they have grouped strategies into the instructional framework of before reading, during reading, and after reading to assist struggling readers at each step of completing assignments. These steps and the skills that students need for mastery are listed in Table 4.1.

Struggling readers need to engage in the behaviors that strong readers use to comprehend text. Proficient readers have learned to engage in these strategies automatically and naturally. Struggling readers need to have these strategies taught to them

TABLE 4.1 *Before, During, and After Reading Strategies*

Steps of the Reading Process	What Good Readers Do	Specific Skills to Practice
Before reading	PAS • Preview the text • Access your prior knowledge • Set your purpose	• Figure out the genre (e.g., poetry, novel, essay, short story, informational text). • Examine text features (columns, chapter sections, headings, subheadings, bulleted lists). • Examine pictures, captions, charts, graphs, maps, and illustrations. • Identify the topic. • Think about and write down what you already know about the topic. • Determine why you are reading the text and set yourself up to read accordingly. • Analyze text structure (how the text is developed—comparison/contrast, cause/effect, description, etc.). • Ask questions that the text may answer.
During reading	VIP • Visualize what you are reading about • Interact with the text • Predict what will come next	• Try to make mental pictures of what you are reading. • Use highlighters or sticky notes to mark important parts of the text. • Use highlighters or sticky notes to write down questions or observations about the text. • Ask questions about the text. • Clarify the meaning of words you do not know. • Make an educated guess about what is coming next in the text.
After reading	POW • Practice • Organize your ideas about the passage • Write about what you read	• Reread parts of the text that you did not understand. • Read difficult sections aloud. • Make a chart or graphic organizer with the important information in the text. • Write a summary about what you have read. • Write a reaction to what you have read.

Source: Dean, N. & Harper, C. (2006). *Succeeding in Reading: Buddy Reading Guide.* Gainesville, FL: Maupin House.

explicitly, and they often need more support, more scaffolding, and more structure to engage in these behaviors. Strategy instruction must begin with simple text and clear directions if students are to be able to embrace the strategies as their own. Newspapers can be used to help students engage in these strategies. Newspaper articles are relatively short, generally interesting, and often easier for students to comprehend.

Interactive Reading Guides

As described in Chapter 3, collaborative group activities, such as cooperative literacy and the directed reading sequence, can especially benefit struggling readers. *The Interactive Reading Guide* (Wood, 1988) is another cooperative reading strategy that can assist struggling learners' move towards a productive reading of text materials. The interactive reading guide is a variation of the study guide; in essence, the teacher prepares the reading material ahead of time so that students have a blueprint for tackling a demanding passage successfully. An interactive guide involves students working with partners or in small groups to figure out the essential ideas in their reading.

Step 1. **Teachers first preview a reading assignment to determine the major information to be learned and to locate possible pitfalls for understanding.** Teachers need to be sensitive to text features that could trip up struggling readers. As part of this preview, the teacher is especially alert for salient features of the text that students might overlook, such as visual information portrayed in pictures, charts, and graphs.

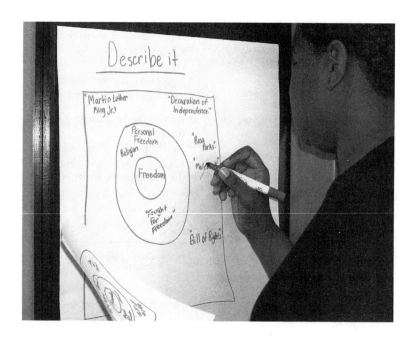

During this preview phase, teachers need to determine whether there might be an occasional mismatch between students and the text. Does the author assume knowledge that some students might lack? Does the author introduce ideas and vocabulary without providing sufficient explanation or examples? Does the author use language or a sentence style that will be tough reading for struggling readers?

Step 2. **Next, the teacher constructs an interactive reading guide for students to complete with partners or in cooperative groups.** This guide should be designed to help students decide where to focus their attention during reading and to support their learning when the material becomes challenging. Questions in the guide should compel students to think carefully about the material and to make meaningful connections and draw conclusions. Such questions motivate students to problem solve with each other to ascertain the appropriate responses rather than merely searching for answers (Ping Pong reading, as described in Chapter 2).

When constructing the guide, the teacher should break the passage into segments. Some segments might be designated to be read aloud by individuals to their groups, some segments to be read silently by each student, and remaining portions that are less important to be skimmed. In places teachers may wish to use the guide to provide additional background information or to encourage students to brainstorm what they already know about the topic. An example of an interactive reading guide for a biology text designed for cooperative groups of three students (adapted from Buehl, 2001) is shown in Figure 4.2.

Step 3. **Organize the class into cooperative groups; struggling readers should be included in groups that contain strong readers as well**. The students then work as a team to complete the interactive reading guide and agree on the best response for each item. When completed, interactive reading guides can serve as organized notes on the text material for classroom discussions and follow-up activities. They also make excellent study guides for examinations.

Interactive reading guides can make it possible for students to learn from text materials that might be too difficult for independent reading. As a part of this activity, students are conditioned to read materials at differential rates, for varying purposes, because they are directed to read some sections carefully and to skim others. In addition, students are able to use each other as resources as they tackle a challenging reading assignment, and they discuss the material as they read rather than afterward. Interactive reading guides are especially effective for supporting the learning of struggling readers.

Summary

Many students still lack the reading ability to be successful in middle school. In addition, as students move through the elementary, middle, and high school

Water Clarity and Sediments (pages 11–12)

1. This article will talk about factors that influence the health of streams and rivers. <u>Entire group:</u> Make a list of things you already know that can affect how healthy a stream might be for fish and other animals.

2. Look at the drawing of the fish at the top of the page. "Stream troublemakers are mentioned." <u>Entire group:</u> predict what two examples of "stream troublemakers" might be.

3. A key word in this article is "clarity." <u>Student A:</u> Read paragraph 1 out loud to your group. <u>Rest of group:</u> Decide what "water clarity" means and write your group's definition.

    Imagine you are a fish. Decide what would be the best type of water for you, according to paragraph 1.

4. Paragraph 2 talks about the color of a stream. <u>Entire group:</u> Silently skim this paragraph. Locate two things that can change the color of water in a stream.

5. Paragraph 3 is the main point of your article. <u>Student B:</u> Read paragraph 3 out loud to your group. <u>Rest of group:</u> Summarize what effect algae and sediments have on water.

6. The next section describes algae. <u>Entire group:</u> Silently read paragraph 4. Look for the following key ideas on algae:

    • What kinds of streams are most likely to have algae?

    • What exactly is algae?

    • What color is water that has a lot of algae?

    • Where in your community might you find algae?

7. <u>Student C:</u> Read paragraph 5 out loud to your group. <u>Rest of group:</u> Decide what kinds of things could become sediment in a stream.

    Which of these kinds of sediment might be a problem in your community?

8. <u>Entire group:</u> Silently read paragraph 6. Look for ways in which sediment gets into streams. Summarize what these ways are and write them here.

9. <u>Entire group:</u> Silently skim paragraphs 7, 8, and 9. Imagine you are a fish. Decide which source of sediment sounds the worst to you? Explain why.

10. Sediment and algae make water cloudy. Cloudy water causes trouble for fish. The next paragraphs tell five reasons why. <u>Student A:</u> Silently read paragraphs 10 and 11. <u>Student B:</u> Silently read paragraphs 12 and 13. <u>Student C:</u> Silently read paragraph 14. Then share the five reasons why cloudy water is bad for fish and write them in your own words.

FIGURE 4.2   *Biology Interactive Reading Guide*

grades, numerous students fall farther and farther behind because they do not get continued and sustained instruction in reading (or instruction that is appropriate) and because the demands increase dramatically for comprehending, analyzing, synthesizing, and evaluating text.

Understanding the practices of strong readers can help teachers to feel more confident in helping students acquire those practices. The causes of underachievement are many and complex but can be reversed if teachers help students develop strategies for learning from and remembering text. Procedures such as the interactive reading guide hold promise for meeting the needs of struggling readers.

Chapters 5–10 offer additional strategies that benefit all readers, but particularly struggling readers.

Extending Learning

Reviewing the Talking Points

Revisit the talking points at the beginning of this chapter. Answer the questions now that you have read the chapter, and compare your prereading and postreading responses.

Revisiting the Vignette

In the opening vignette, three students are typecast as struggling readers who feel disengaged from the books they are asked to read. Meagan is more of a passive student, while Jamal is characterized as a bit of a troublemaker. Nestor is just frustrated with his lack of facility with the English language. Think about the students in your class or students who were in your classes in middle school and determine whether there are any similarities. Discuss what you think the teacher in this vignette might do to lend support and assistance to these students to prevent them from eventually dropping out of school. What do the teachers need to do for these students, and also, what do the students themselves need to do?

Terms to Remember and Use

interactive guide	comprehending	analyzing	synthesizing
evaluation	NAEP	engagement	fluency
intensive intervention	mock participation	authentic responses	reading guide

Write a series of sentences that meaningfully connect pairs of the above key terms. Your sentences should refer to ideas and concepts related to the literacy of middle school students.

Modifying Instruction for English Language Learners

The *Predicting-Connecting with Text-Summarizing* strategy (Minnesota Writing Project Demonstration Lesson, 2004) is effective with English language learners using narrative text. This strategy can be used in a language arts class during which students first look at the cover and back of a book, make some predictions based on the pictures, and complete an anticipation guide. The teacher teaches three substrategies one at a time, and has students practice them as a group, in pairs, and individually using various chapters throughout the book.

1. Probable passage. Pick out ten important words from a chapter and put them into a table that includes characters, setting, problem, outcome, and some unknown but important words. Students are then required to write a summary statement using as many of the ten words as possible and share their statements with the whole class.
2. Double journal entry (text-to-self connections). Students are asked to make a T-chart, write down at least three quotes from the chapter that resonate with them and write their own responses next to them, and then share in pairs or in groups of four.

3. <u>Somebody wanted but so</u>. "Somebody-wanted-but-so" is written at the top of a page. Students then create a summary by picking out words and putting them under each of those topics. Then students use the words to write complete sentences about the content in the chapter. This strategies helps ELL students who have trouble picking out the main ideas in a chapter.

Beyond the Book

- Look up the NAEP Web site and explore the trends in reading performance over the past decade. What do you notice about the various groups?
- Interview a colleague about his or her own reading strategies. Determine if he or she can actually make a list of the various behaviors he or she uses when accessing an informational text selection. Categorize those into before, during, and after reading strategies.
- Go to the Web site for the Alliance for Excellence in Education (all4ed.org). Based upon the information on that Web site, determine what your school can do to create a literacy plan for all students, including the struggling readers.
- Create an interactive reading guide for a content piece from your own textbook. Share the results with a member of your class and determine how successful it was.
- Go to the NCES (National Center for Educational Statistics). Find the NAEP trends for your state. Explore the aspects of the text and go to the links that describe what skills are necessary to perform at grade level on NAEP assessments. Discuss how teachers play a role in reinforcing those skills in their instructional delivery.
- Discuss these issues.
  1. Why might there be a higher percentage of struggling students in schools that have a lower socioeconomic status and higher minority representation?
  2. Why might the interactive reading guide prove to be successful with struggling readers?
  3. How can an examination of the strategies of strong readers be useful in assisting readers who have not mastered those strategies?

References

Balfanz, R., & Legters, N. (2001, January). *How Many Central City High Schools Have a Severe Dropout Problem, Where Are They Located, and Who Attends Them? Initial estimates using the common core of data*. Paper presented at Dropouts in America: How Severe Is the Problem? What Do We Know about Intervention and Prevention? Conference at the Harvard Civil Rights Project and Achieve, Inc. Cambridge, MA. Retrieved online at www.civilrightsproject.harvard.edu.

Balfanz, R., McPartland, & Shaw, A. (2002, April). *Re-conceptualizing Extra Help for High School Students in a High Standards Era*. Washington, DC: Office of Vocational and Adult Education, U.S. Department of Education.

Balfanz, R., Spiridakis, K., & Neild, R. C. (2002, November). *Will Converting High-Poverty Middle Schools to K-8 Schools Facilitate Achievement Gains?* A Research Brief for the School District of Philadelphia. Philadelphia: Philadelphia Education Fund.

Bintz, W. (1997). Exploring reading nightmares of middle and secondary school teachers. *Journal of Adolescent & Adult Literacy, 41*(1), 12–24.

Brozo, W. G. (1990). Hiding out in secondary content classrooms: Coping strategies of unsuccessful readers. *Journal of Reading, 33*(5), 324–328.

Buehl, D. (2001). *Classroom Strategies for Interactive Learning* (2nd ed). Newark, DE: International Reading Association.

Buehl, D., & Stumpf, S. (2002). *Madison Metropolitan School District: Middle School Reading Task Force Report*, Revised. Madison, WI: Madison Metropolitan School District.

Dean, N. & Harper, C. (2006). *Succeeding in Reading: Buddy Reading Guide*. Gainesville, FL: Maupin House.

Greene, J. P. & Winters M. A. (2002, November). *Public School Graduation Rates in the United States.* Civic Report for Center for Civic Innovation at the Manhattan Institute.

Joftus, S. (2002). *Every Child a Graduate: A Framework for an Excellent Education for All Middle and High School Students*. Washington, DC: Alliance for Excellent Education.

Kaufman, P., Alt, M. N., & Chapman, C. (2001). *Dropout Rates in the United States: 2000.* U.S. Department of Education. Retrieved from http://nces.ed.gov/pubsearch/pubsinfo.asp?pubid=2002114.

Lyon, G. R. (2002, February). The right to read and the responsibility to teach. *Plain talk: The Newsletter for the Center for Development and Learning, 7*(3), 1–24. Retrieved from http://www.cdl.org/pdf/Feb02PTlyon.pdf.

Minnesota Writing Project Demonstration Lesson. (2004). Retrieved from http://mwp.cla.umn.edu/resources/demos/2004demos/bertrand.pdf.

Moore, D. & Hinchman, K. (2006). *Teaching Adolescents Who Struggle with Reading: Practical Strategies.* Boston: Allyn and Bacon.

Perie, M., Grigg, W. S., & Donahue, P. L. (2005). *The Nation's Report Card: Reading 2005.* Washington, DC: National Center for Education Statistics.

Wood, K. (1988). Guiding students through informational text. *The Reading Teacher, 41*(9), 912–920.

5

The Demands of Text

_____

- Why do so many students find textbooks difficult to read?
- How can teaching text structure improve reading comprehension?
- What features should teachers look for when selecting texts that are appropriate for their students?
- How are electronic texts changing the nature of reading in middle school classrooms?

Sasha moved from class to class lugging her bulging backpack and making frequent trips to her locker. She started the day with her literature anthology—they were currently studying poetry and she enjoyed learning about the meter of poetry and how to read it. Next, she tackled her math textbook that had examples, some explanations, and problems to solve. Her assignment in social studies was to interpret the charts and graphs to reach a conclusion about the resources available to the South during the Civil War. At lunchtime, she practiced reading the play her group was to perform next month for their parents. After lunch, her teacher assigned a lab report to read and she was to use the model given to her to write up her experience. Finally, her music teacher explained the "libretto" or text of an opera.

The demands of middle school reading include negotiating various types of texts and tasks. The daily required reading dose can loom as a formidable undertaking for young adolescents; a social studies textbook, a science textbook, a mathematics textbook, a foreign language textbook, a language arts anthology, a health textbook—the standard issue for classes in a typical middle school. But adolescents have to adjust to more than the staggering weight of their bulging backpacks: The reading demands in middle school are markedly different from what students experienced in elementary school.

As readers, of course, young adolescents do read an amazing variety of texts: popular magazines, Web sites, sports pages, e-mails, ads for fashionable clothing, computer game protocols, song lyrics, comic books, movie schedules, and CD covers. "School reading," however, generally addresses only two kinds of text: narrative and expository. Beginning readers first learn to read through stories. Reading and listening to stories continues through the middle school years as adolescents refine their understanding of narrative elements such as plot, characterization, and setting. A different text genre, however, becomes prevalent in middle school as well—the content-area textbook. The awareness of how expository textbooks are structured begins later than for narrative text and develops as students acquire more abstract levels of thinking. A major task for middle school educators is to assist students in developing a schema for expository text so that they can successfully read, use, and understand textbooks.

In this chapter, the changes in reading material that students face as they grow older are described, two types of text (narrative and expository) are compared, and suggestions are given for helping students to become more sensitive to these text structures. Then the difficulties students have with content-area textbooks are explained. Last, the use and evaluation of textbooks is discussed and a textbook evaluation guide is presented.

The Transition to Informational Text

Reading instruction during the elementary grades is based predominantly on a reading series, publisher-selected collections of children's literature that are generally written in narrative style. Narrative text follows a story form and is recognized by an identifiable plot, a setting, a group of characters, and a sequence of events. Frequently, the vocabulary in these texts is controlled to be age-appropriate in difficulty. In the middle grades, the transition to informational texts is met with varying degrees of success. The expository text of content textbooks is factual rather than fictional and is organized around a hierarchical pattern of main ideas and background details. Teachers generally expect that their students will make this rather sophisticated transition without much explicit instruction on how to read this kind of material. Instead, in the middle grades and into high school, teachers emphasize teaching only their content; students must make the necessary adjustments on their own. With the exception of the literature that is taught in language arts classes, students read almost exclusively expository material. But who takes the responsibility for teaching students how to read these texts?

In addition to the demands of reading textbooks to learn course content, students are increasingly asked to perform on high-stakes state tests by reading and answering questions using expository text. Although instruction in reading usually occurs with narrative text, 60 to 80 percent of the items on state tests are informational. There appears to be a mismatch between the material that we use for reading instruction and what is used on performance measures.

Middle school teachers might assume that the responsibility for teaching reading should fall on language arts teachers. But language arts teachers focus their instruction primarily on fiction and narrative literature—novels, short stories, biographies, and poetry. Therefore, although middle school students are expected to read extensively from expository texts, no one, it seems, teaches them how to read and understand these texts.

Students frequently report that they can bypass learning through reading in some classes. Although teachers distribute textbooks, many of them may have little confidence in their students' abilities to learn from these texts. Instead of teaching students successful strategies for learning from expository texts, content teachers may instead deliver critical course content through lecture and class presentations, video, or other means. Students soon realize that listening to the teacher will substitute for carefully reading the textbook. The life science or physical science student, for example, might never have to develop the sophisticated reading skills necessary to access information from the textbook; they trust that the teacher will give them what they need to know. Although various promising strategies for helping adolescents to learn successfully from their textbooks are constantly appearing in the professional literature, many teachers just tell students what is in their textbooks, meaning that students do not have to read these materials for themselves.

Attaining independence in reading narrative literature in elementary grades does not prepare students to read the expository material independently in their science, social studies, or mathematics texts. Students need to learn to adapt reading comprehension strategies to a variety of reading materials. Ideally, students should receive a gradual introduction to reading expository text beginning in the elementary grades and transition into more sophisticated texts in middle and high school. Becoming an independent learner is a lifelong process. For this reason, continued and systematic reading comprehension instruction during middle and high school is imperative.

Kinds of Text

Young children think in stories that grow out of their everyday lives. Stories compose children's literary exposure and thinking until about third grade, when more informational texts are introduced. As students progress through the grades, they must become more sensitive to a variety of text genres and adapt their thinking accordingly. The RAND Reading Study Group concluded: "The texts that children read in today's schools are substantially more diverse than those used several decades ago. Thirty years ago, children were assigned specific readings that were crafted for instructional purposes, or they were exposed to a select group of books in the narrative, descriptive, expository, and persuasive genres. . . . We now live in a world that is experiencing an explosion of alternative texts that vary in content,

readability levels, and genre. They incorporate multimedia and electronic options and pertain to a variety of cultures and groups. This variety makes it much more difficult for teachers to select appropriate texts for individual readers" (Snow, 2002, p. 24).

When students recognize and use text features to comprehend, they are more likely to remember what they read. Teaching students to use headings, titles, sub-headings, graphic clues, and signal words when previewing text helps students to use text features to comprehend text and is particularly helpful to second-language learners (Chen & Graves, 1998). Another major difference between narrative and expository text is that pictures, often found in narrative text, are typically replaced by tables, graphs, and diagrams.

Most teachers do not devote much time to helping students become aware of textual features. Awareness of text structure is an important metacognitive skill that should be made a part of learning to read and write. Although adults are generally proficient in reading a variety of text genres, such as persuasion, advertising, and technical reading, two types of text are most commonly found in school settings: narrative and expository.

Narrative Text

Narrative text is usually encountered in stories such as those that are commonly found in literature anthologies or in longer fictional works, such as plays or novels. Narrative text usually has the following elements: setting, sequence, characterization, and plot. In general, middle school students have less trouble with this type of text because it usually has a clearly defined structure, and they have had a great deal of experience reading the story form. Middle school readers know that they will meet characters within a certain period and setting and that a series of events will unfold, followed by some sort of resolution. Because students are familiar with

the structure of narrative text, they tend to have less difficulty reading it than content area textbooks.

Story grammars have been developed to heighten student awareness of the structure of stories and facilitate the identification of the predictable aspects of a story. One way to help them understand the structure of a story is to provide students with a story grammar before the reading. Then, as students read a story with a partner or within a cooperative group, they decide how to complete the elements in their story grammar diagrams. Story grammar diagrams help students to track key elements of the story and perceive the inherent structure of narrative texts. They can be especially useful with stories that are confusing or told in a nonsequential fashion. Figure 5.1 is a story grammar applicable to a middle school setting. This diagram may be modified to fit different purposes. Students can fill in the different parts of the diagram as a teacher reads a story to them or it can then be used as a springboard for discussion. Students can be asked to read the story first and then reexamine their understanding by clarifying the details that are appropriate for completing the story grammar diagram.

Story frames can help students to understand the structure of stories through writing or to understand the relationships between people and events. The story frame and relationships chart shown in Figures 5.2 and 5.3 respectively, can be used in a variety of ways, such as a story starter or a summary for an existing story.

Expository Text

Textbooks in content areas such as social studies and science demand more complex reading than story form and are written in a variety of text structures. These materials require increasingly abstract thinking that can perceive relationships

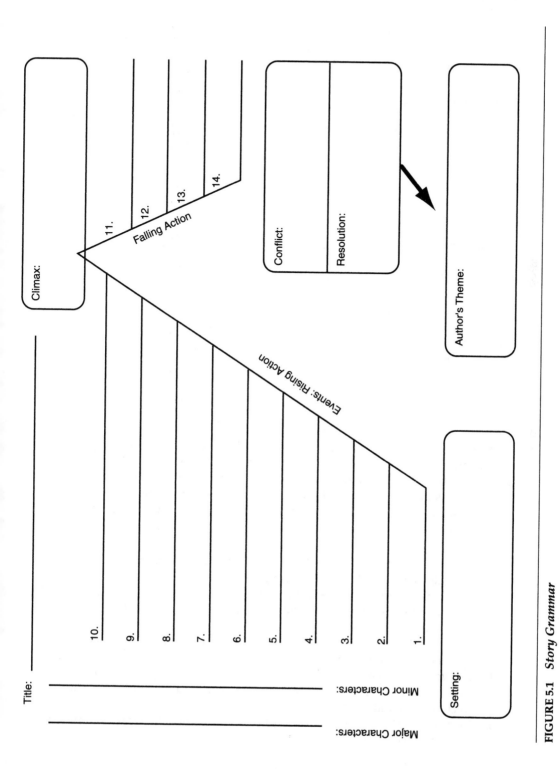

FIGURE 5.1 Story Grammar

Source: Classroom Strategies for Interactive Learning, 2nd edition by D. Buehl. Copyright © 2001 by the International Reading Association. Reprinted with permission of the International Reading Association.

Story Frame

The story takes place _____ .

_____
is a character in the story who _____ .

_____
is another character in the story who _____ .

_____
A problem occurs when _____ .

_____
After that, _____

_____
and _____
The problem is solved when _____

_____
The story ends with _____

_____ .

FIGURE 5.2 *Story Frame*

Source: From *Responses to Literature: Grades K–8* by J. M. Macon, D. Bewell, & M. E. Vogt. Copyright ©
1991 by the International Reading Association, Inc. Reprinted with permission of the International
Reading Association.

such as comparison and contrast and cause and effect. This type of text provides
an explanation of concepts in consort with much factual information; a reader
must identify a hierarchy of ideas in expository text. Research in the area of expository text has helped educators to understand the ways in which these types of
materials are organized. Following is a list of the six most common organizational
structures of informational text.

1. *Cause and effect patterns* show the relationship between results and the ideas
   or events that made the results occur (see Figure 5.4).
2. *Problem and solution patterns* identify at least one problem, offer one or more
   solutions to the problem, and explain or predict outcomes of the solutions
   (see Figure 5.5).
3. *Compare and contrast patterns* point out similarities and differences between
   two concepts or ideas (see Figure 5.6).
4. *Sequence or chronological order* (or goal-action-outcome) patterns show events
   or ideas in the order in which they happened or present steps in the order in
   which they should be followed (see Figure 5.7).
5. *Description patterns* explain a concept or idea and usually offer examples of
   the concept (see Figure 5.8).

Somebody	Wanted	But	So

FIGURE 5.3 *Plot Relationships Chart*

Source: From *Responses to Literature: Grades K–8*, by J. M. Macon, D. Bewell, & M. E. Vogt. Copyright © 1991 by the International Reading Association, Inc. Reprinted with permission of the International Reading Association.

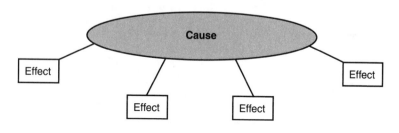

FIGURE 5.4 *Cause and Effect* Cause and effect patterns show the relationship between results and the ideas or events that made the results occur.

6. *Proposition and support patterns* present an argument, theory, or hypothesis, which is then supported by facts, data, examples, or expert verification (see Figure 5.9).

Expository texts are not necessarily neatly laid out in one of these structures, and sometimes a passage may switch from one to the other. But if students can begin to recognize text structure, they can use it to help them understand the ideas that are being presented.

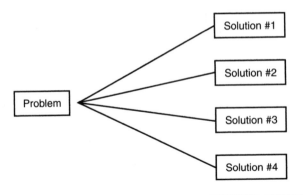

FIGURE 5.5 *Problem and Solution* Problem-solution patterns identify at least one problem, offer one or more solutions to the problem, and explain or predict outcomes of the solutions.

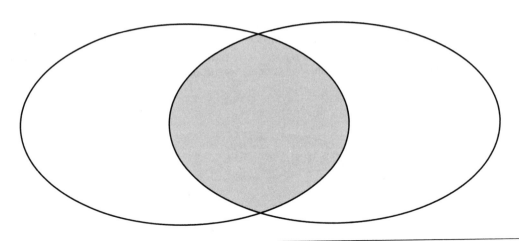

FIGURE 5.6 *Compare and Contrast* Compare-and-contrast diagrams point out similarities and differences between two concepts or ideas.

Helping Students to Understand Text Structure

One way proficient readers understand and use text structure is through the use of signal or transition words. Signal words do just that. They signal relationships between words and ideas. Common lists of signal words are presented in Figure 5.10.

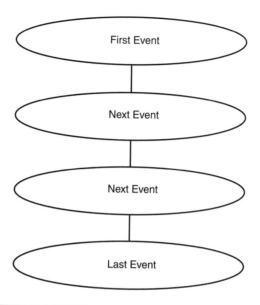

FIGURE 5.7 *Sequence or Chronological Order* Sequence or chronological-order diagrams show events or ideas in the order in which they happened.

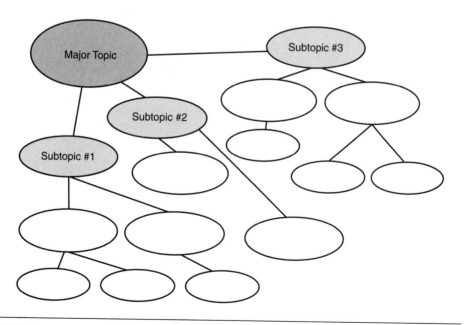

FIGURE 5.8 *Topic or Concept Map*

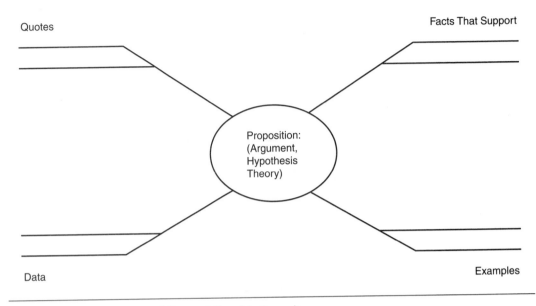

FIGURE 5.9   *Proposition and Support Graphic Organizer*

Cause and effect	Compare and contrast	Description	Problem and solution	Sequence	Proposition support
because since consequently this led to . . . so if . . . then nevertheless accordingly because of as a result of in order to may be due to for this reason not only . . . but	different from same as similar to as opposed to instead of although however compared with as well as either . . . or but on the other hand unless	for instance for example such as to illustrate in addition most importantly in addition another furthermore first, second . . .	Problem the question is a solution one answer is need to should change	not long after next then initially before after finally preceding following on (date) over the years today when	for example data suggest granted that indicate therefore supports in conclusion

FIGURE 5.10   *Signal or Transition Words*

One way to encourage students to recognize signal words while reading and to use signal words in writing is through the use of paragraph frames. These frames are an excellent way to teach students how to use signal words and text structure to understand content area reading material. Figures 5.11 and 5.12 provide examples of paragraph frames designed by Nichols (1980, p. 229).

At the end of _____ what happened was that _____ _____. Previous to this _____ _____

Before this _____
The entire chain of events had begun for a number of reasons including _____

Some prominent incidents that helped to trigger the conflict were _____

FIGURE 5.11   *Time Order*

Source: From "Using Paragraph Frames to Help Remedial High School Students with Written Assignments," by J. N. Nichols, *Journal of Reading,* 23(3) 1980, 228–231. Reprinted with permission of J. N. Nichols and the International Reading Association.

_____ in several ways. First of all _____ _____ while _____

Secondly, _____
while _____
So it should be evident that _____

FIGURE 5.12   *Compare-Contrast*

Source: From "Using Paragraph Frames to Help Remedial High School Students with Written Assignments," by J. N. Nichols, *Journal of Reading,* 23(3) 1980, 228–231. Reprinted with permission of J. N. Nichols and the International Reading Association.

Using graphic organizers can help students to "see" the structure of the text, organize their thinking while reading, and present their knowledge after reading. A graphic organizer is a visual representation of key concepts that illustrates relationships using boxes, circles, arrows, and so forth. The following is a sequence for helping students use graphic organizers, which increase their awareness of text structure and improve comprehension (Irvin, 2001).

1. Students preview the material to be read, making a special note of the signal words that indicate the structure of the text and the type of thinking that will be required.
2. Students hypothesize which graphic organizer would be best to display the information and their understanding of the material.

3. Students read the text silently, taking notes.
4. Students work in cooperative groups to create a graphic organizer of their understanding of the text.
5. Students present the finished product to others in the class.

Students who are sensitive to text structure are likely to remember more of what they read. Previewing text and preparing to display information using graphic organizers has the potential of helping students understand and use text structure.

The last decade has yielded much research on text structure and how students can use this structure to comprehend text better and remember it longer. Some publishers have taken advantage of this research and thinking to produce textbooks that are more considerate than those available for previous generations. In the next section, guidelines for evaluating textbooks are presented.

Difficulty with Content-Area Textbooks

Try your luck with understanding the following passage:

> A postscript standard spooler usually runs on a piece of software connected to your network. The spooler's name appears when you access the chooser desk accessory. Standard spoolers let you take advantage of printer description files (APDs). The APD decides the printer configuration.

Huh? For many of us, a computer manual is an inscrutable document, to be deciphered only by techno-whizzes who are amply versed in the obscure terminology and have logged hours using the software. The rest of us had better consult the "resident expert" who can explain all this in English. Why do we as adults struggle with these types of texts? First, we probably lack the requisite knowledge, the schema that would help us to make sense of the information. We are not conversant with the key vocabulary, and we have an insufficient background in this field to comprehend such material adequately. Second, manuals and other technical materials are frustratingly notorious for their deficiencies in qualities that make print accessible to readers. The authors tend to miss opportunities to connect their messages to their readers. Third, we might lack experiences in effectively using texts such as computer manuals. Because they are difficult, we avoid them and never really get the hang of how to employ them effectively. We rely on knowledgeable colleagues, or we muddle along, making mistakes and underusing our software while the manual gathers dust, neglected on a crowded shelf.

Unfortunately, students frequently express the same sentiments about their textbooks. They might read stories or entire novels—narrative text—with little difficulty, but when they turn to their social studies or science book, they struggle with understanding. In fact, this negative experience can sour students' interests in social studies, math, or science.

Daniels and Zemelman (2004) argued that while some textbooks are clearly superior to others, textbooks in general present a number of significant problems to students.

1. Although textbooks are often huge and seem to contain everything you would need to know, they are basically superficial in their treatment of key ideas.
2. Textbooks are reference books that are hard to read because the information is so condensed and they do not encourage reader engagement with the text.
3. Many textbooks are badly designed; although they attempt to entice readers with splashy visual information, readers get lost in the colorful displays and cannot easily follow ideas.
4. Textbooks are authoritarian, in that a single textbook is often the basis for the curriculum of a course; alternative ways of thinking are not available.
5. In addition to being often factually incorrect and horribly expensive, textbooks are not really written for students; instead they are pieced together to meet content standards so that they will be marketable across the country.

Yet textbooks remain a reality for middle school students. The purpose of reading a content-area textbook is to acquire new information and to construct new understandings about the world we live in. Obviously, textbooks that are flawed or "inconsiderate" can present students with problems in their learning. In addition, students may have difficulty reading expository text for the following reasons:

1. Students lack the content or strategic knowledge to understand the text
2. They have uneven and sometimes insufficient classroom experiences with reading in the content areas (Armbruster, 1984)
3. They are unclear about the task to be performed as a result of their reading

Content and Strategic Knowledge

A reader at any age has difficulty understanding text about an unfamiliar topic. To learn anything new, this information must be connected in some way with existing prior knowledge (or schema). Developing and activating students' background knowledge are imperative before students attempt to read a content textbook. Students who have difficulty with textbooks may lack relevant prior knowledge, have the knowledge but fail to access it, or have knowledge or beliefs that interfere with acquiring new information. In initially teaching students how to comprehend expository text within a discipline or in working with struggling readers, it is preferable to begin with highly familiar passages as a starting point.

Teachers can assume that many students enter middle school not knowing how to read a content textbook effectively, meaning that teachers need to integrate reading comprehension instruction into their classroom routines. In Chapter 2, we referred to this instruction as *scaffolding*, supporting students through activities that guide their learning and help them to become comfortable with a wide variety of content texts and organizational structures. Often, content teachers focus only on the "stuff" of their curriculum, on the learning of information, concepts, and generalizations, rather than with helping students develop strategies for acquiring new knowledge from the textbooks in their discipline.

The ability to use the structure of text to guide understanding correlates highly with memory of information and comprehension of course content. That is, "students who have processed the text strategically using their knowledge of expository text structures will recall the text better" (Richgels, McGee, Lomax, & Sheard, 1987, p. 179). Developing and activating content knowledge and teaching students to use strategies to learn from textbooks are keys to helping students become more successful learners of the course curriculum. Prereading and prewriting strategies (see Chapter 7) help students to access, evaluate, and use their prior knowledge during reading. Using text structures to comprehend text takes a certain degree of abstract thinking. Given the developing nature of cognition during adolescence, this is an opportune time to deliver instruction in text structure. Obviously, the more students construct maps, frames, or graphic organizers, the better they will comprehend and the more they will learn about the structure of text.

Classroom Experiences with Textbooks

Teachers sometimes use textbooks as the curriculum and religiously assign students to read all parts of all the chapters so that the curriculum is "covered." Others tend to use textbooks only as a reference or designate students to read only short selections. Some teachers depend heavily on textbooks but resort to round-robin reading, a highly questionable practice that asks each student to read a paragraph as the rest of the class supposedly follows along. In lieu of teaching students to read their content materials effectively, some teachers decide to forgo any reading assignments, electing instead to expose course content through lecture, class presentations, video, and other means.

In addition, textbook reading is usually fragmented by teacher questioning or activities. For many students, Ping Pong reading (described in Chapter 2) is their primary experience with textbook material. In math classes, students often skip the reading and attempt to do homework problems by scouting the sample items and hoping the teacher will work out similar problems on the chalkboard. Students are rarely taught how to detect text structures and recognize the hierarchy of ideas in content-area textbooks. If more time and attention were given to helping students to become successful readers of expository text, they would be better able to apply this lifelong skill to new texts.

Textbooks and other content materials need to be viewed as providing students with experiences reading the discourse of an academic discipline. The term "discourse" is used to describe the talk we engage in with various individuals and groups. Discourse involves an accepted use of language, often a specific pool of vocabulary, as well as an actual way of interacting. Discourse also assumes a common knowledge base, a shared set of experiences and beliefs. Each of us is comfortable employing a wide array of discourses. The specific discourse that we choose depends on who is receiving our talk and the conditions of our interaction. People who share a specific discourse are referred to by researchers as "discourse communities" (Gee, 2000). Doctors, for example, are a discourse community, a group of people who share a common vocabulary, experiences, outlook, and mien. Lawyers, accountants, pharmacists, civil engineers—all exhibit the qualities of discourse communities. If you are a member, you know how to talk, read, and write within your field.

Teachers belong to the discourse community of people who are versed in the fields they teach. Some teachers are members of the science discourse community; others are members of communities of discourse in history, literature, foreign language or music. Teachers know how to talk the talk of their disciplines. For students to learn within a discipline, they too must gain membership in that discourse community. They need to develop confidence in reading and expressing themselves in the language of that discipline; they need to become comfortable using the vocabulary of social studies, of life science, of mathematics. Novice learners within a discipline—our students—require multiple opportunities to explore hearing, reading, and communicating an academic discourse. Students who are denied the instruction that helps them to access the academic discourse of the various content disciplines that they are studying will be seriously limited in the extent to which they can successfully learn in those classrooms.

The Task.   Many students are not aware that texts are to be read at different rates for different purposes. Novels, for example, are usually read at a fairly rapid pace to maintain the storyline. Textbooks, however, often need to be read more methodically to gain new information, draw conclusions, and make generalizations about the material. Reading to write a report requires a different type of reading and note-taking than does reading to answer questions on a test or reading to participate in a group discussion. These study skills and more are discussed in depth in Chapter 9. The two strategies that we present next can help students with identifying and using the structure of texts and becoming more successful while reading them.

PIC: A Text Previewing Guide.   Previewing is an essential part of the process of identifying and using text structure to comprehend text. Also, thinking about the purpose for reading and focusing on the most important ideas helps readers to focus their reading. PIC, which is an acronym for **P**urpose, **I**deas, and **C**onnect, provides students with a strategy for previewing a new text before reading. *PIC: A Text Previewing Guide* was developed by Irvin (2001) for social studies teachers, but it can be used successfully with any content-area material.

Step 1. **Purpose for reading.** Make sure students know what they will do with the information after reading. (What is the assignment or purpose for reading? How will students use the information?) Have them peruse the organizational features of the text to be assigned, noting special features such as summaries or guiding questions. Alert students to use the table of contents, glossary, and index of the book to locate information.

Step 2. **Important ideas.** Students should flip through the assignment, noting the headings that indicate the major points in the reading. They should try to understand how this passage fits within the larger chapter or unit. Students should also read the key vocabulary in boldface type or italics to see whether the concepts are familiar to them. These are probably the most important ideas in the text.

Step 3. **Connect to what you know.** Students need to think about what they know about the topic before starting to read. Encourage them to wonder about the topic, asking, "What would I like to find out?" Finally, students should identify questions they want answered about the topic. They can use a chart like the one in Figure 5.13 to organize their ideas.

What I know about the topic	What I wonder about the topic	Questions I would like to have answered

FIGURE 5.13   *K-W-Q Chart*

The PIC previewing strategy can be used in conjunction with the next strategy, Double S: Signal Words That Indicate Structure, as well as with the graphic organizers presented in this chapter.

Double S: Signal Words That Indicate Structure.   Noticing the signal or transition words, identifying the structure of the text, and preparing for a specific type of text are necessary to understand the content and can go a long way to helping students to become more independent readers of expository text. In time, they will use these clues intuitively as they read text (Irvin, 2001).

Step 1.   **Survey the text.** Have students survey the text and list all the types of reading they will have to perform, such as documents, charts, diagrams, maps, a short story, or expository text. Usually, the expository text of a social studies textbook explains or informs the reader. But, if primary source material, such as a diary, is included, this will have to be read differently. The primary source probably supports or expands major points presented in the text.

Step 2.   **Identify the signal words.** Use a blank transparency and have students circle transition words in the text. Some students prefer to highlight photocopied pages of text or attach sticky notes to help them locate the transition words. Or they might simply generate a list. Whatever the vehicle, students need to identify the signal words that are present in the text.

Step 3.   **Identify the structure of the text.** Individually or in a small group, students should discuss what they think the main structure of the text may be (cause and effect, compare and contrast, description, problem and solution, sequence or chronological order, and proposition and support). They should ask themselves, "What kind of thinking will be necessary to understand the information in the text?" and "How could I best display the information after reading using a graphic organizer?"

Step 4.   **Predict the main idea of the passage.** Using what they know about the signal words and the structure of the text, students should write a sentence stating what they think the main idea of the passage may be.

Step 5.   **Read the text.**

Step 6.   **Revisit the main idea prediction.** After reading, students should go back to their predictions of the main idea of the passage. They may then use a graphic organizer to display the information, write a summary, or in some other way organize what they have read.

These two strategies are by no means the only previewing strategies that may be useful to students, but they contain the steps that help guide students to notice and use the clues presented in text that aid in comprehension. These previewing strategies become difficult for students if the textbook is inconsiderate or difficult to read. Choosing the right textbook for students is an essential part of a teacher's job.

Using and Evaluating Textbooks

Textbooks have a powerful influence on education in the United States. Students spend much of their classroom and homework time using textbooks. In many cases, the textbook has become the curriculum. Despite the predominance of textbooks in classrooms, how they are used varies greatly and the amount of actual reading of the textbook is questionable. Textbooks are read silently or orally, or often are just looked at (such as graphs, maps, or pictures).

Some teachers depend heavily on round-robin reading, especially when students have difficulty reading the text. This type of reading is frequently interrupted by teacher questions and discussion. Students tend to depend on the teacher, however, not the textbook, as the primary source of information. The textbook continues to provide the impetus for questions and discussion in most content-area classrooms. (Chapters 7, 8, and 9 present numerous strategies for reading and using the textbook meaningfully.)

Students spend a great deal of time answering questions related to the text. Most questions that originate from the textbook focus on details, definitions, and other facts that can be assessed objectively. Well-designed questions follow the structure of the text (description, comparison and contrast, problem and solution, sequence, cause and effect, and proposition and support) and focus on the important points of the selection.

If students are having difficulty reading a textbook, it might be because they have not yet acquired proficiency in reading or, it might be because the textbook is organized in a way that is confusing or is just plain hard to read. Science textbooks, in particular, often contain an overabundance of unfamiliar words that are specialized or technical. The teacher, then, must make the determination of which textbooks are chosen and how they are to be used in the curriculum.

When selecting a textbook, teachers are usually provided with readability scores. A life science textbook might have a readability score at the 7.3 grade level, for example. A readability score is obtained from a formula that generally examines the length and complexity of sentences and the level of difficulty of the vocabulary. Although several formulas exist to determine a textbook's readability level, they tend to be similar in approach—the longer the sentences and the greater the number of multisyllabic words, the higher the score. Even though teachers tend to feel reassured by a readability score, there is nothing magical or profound in what these scores tell us. Complex sentence structures and long words frequently correlate with prose that is more difficult to read, but as teachers know, readability scores cannot and do not measure whether a textbook will be appropriate and accessible for their students. In addition, monosyllabic words and short, choppy sentences can produce text that is stilted and boring.

Text materials today are increasingly evaluated by using lexiles. The lexile measure is based on the examination of an entire work in terms of its semantic difficulty (vocabulary) and its syntactic complexity (sentence length). Lexile scores range from 200 (material for beginning readers) to 1700 lexiles (highly sophisticated material for mature readers). Middle school lexile scores fall between 650L for sixth grade to up to 1000L for eighth grade.

When comparing textbooks for possible adoption, teachers should extensively examine each choice to ascertain whether key features of considerate texts are present. A checklist, the User-Friendly Text Analysis (Buehl, 1997), is presented in Figure 5.14.

Summary

Helping students to use the text features, including headings, graphic signals, and transition or signal words, can improve their comprehension of narrative and expository text. A clear text structure (description, comparison and contrast, cause and effect, problem and solution, sequence, and proposition and support) and student questions that reflect that structure make a textbook easier to understand. Strategies presented in this chapter can help students read, use, and understand textbooks. Teachers, though, must assume the responsibility of evaluating and choosing textbooks that facilitate rather than impede student learning.

Extending Learning

Reviewing the Talking Points

Revisit the talking points at the beginning of this chapter. Answer the questions now that you have read the chapter and compare your prereading and postreading responses.

Revisiting the Vignette

Think back to your experiences with textbooks as a middle school student. Reflect on some of the textbooks you used and write down your thoughts about those texts that you felt were useful and those that you thought were difficult and unfriendly. Share your reflections with a classmate.

Terms to Remember and Use

signal words	narrative	expository	text structure
story grammar	cause and effect	graphic clues	proposition and support
graphic organizers	main idea		chronological
User-Friendly Text Analysis	text previewing guide		sequence

Write a series of sentences that meaningfully connect pairs of the above key terms. Your sentences should refer to ideas and concepts related to the literacy of middle school students.

Modifying Instruction for English Language Learners

Narrative text is often easier to understand than expository text because people have a natural inclination to follow stories. However, teachers should be aware that figurative language in literature can pose problems for English language learners. They do not have

FIGURE 5.14   *User-Friendly Text Analysis*

Determining the extent to which a textbook is user-friendly involves analysis of a number of factors. The following steps will help you decide whether a specific textbook is a "match" for your students. Use a three-point rating system when evaluating each factor (1 = low, 2 = average, 3 = high).

Layout Factors

A student's first response to a new textbook is to "eyeball" it to see how inviting it appears. Does it look like a book that might be interesting to read, or does it appear dense, forbidding, and foreign? To start your analysis, page through the text and try to look at it from a student's perspective.

- Is the book visually appealing?

    _____ colorful and visually attractive layout

    _____ avoids cluttered and over-crowded look

- Do the text passages look packed and dense?

    _____ font size (small, medium, or large)

    _____ adequate white space between lines of print

    _____ visuals interspersed throughout print sections

    _____ adequate white space (unprinted areas, such as margins) so pages do not appear congested

- Do pages convey information in a variety of forms?

    _____ text passages alternate with pictures, graphics, pull quotes, marginal notes, etc.?

Language Factors

Examine the language factors that influence the readability difficulty of a text. Initially, use a readability formula (a popular formula such as the Fry will do, or locate a lexile score) to estimate complexities of sentence structure and vocabulary load. A readability formula will give you a grade level score, but these formulas are too simplistic to really ascertain how a book might work with a particular group of students. Other language factors are more critical in your examination. Spend some extended time reading sections of the book.

- How sophisticated is the prose at the sentence level?

    _____ infrequent use of long and complex sentences

    _____ infrequent use of short simple sentences

    _____ proximity of subjects and verbs to each other

    _____ proximity of subjects and verbs to beginnings of sentences

    _____ complexity of punctuation

- How smoothly does the language flow at the paragraph level?

    _____ use of a variety of sentence constructions, simple as well as compound and complex

    _____ use of transition sentences

    _____ use of connective language, such as prepositions

    _____ use of signal words such as second, next, however, then

    _____ use of a noun after this, some, one, these, etc.

    _____ clarity of it and other pronouns

- How does the book "talk" to the student?

    _____ use of "you" to involve students in the text

    _____ use of active voice for most of the writing

    _____ use of strong and descriptive verbs

    _____ use of a fluid and engaging writing style

_____ stimulation of mental imagery vs. dry, choppy, fact-laden prose

_____ inclusion of narrative as well as expository prose

Prior Knowledge Factors

Consider ways the textbook attempts to make connections to your students. A text is more user friendly when it anticipates what will be confusing or novel to the readers. Some texts appear very "distant" from the students and merely present information. Others attempt to bridge this distance by eliciting student experiences that will help readers understand the new material.

- Does the book relate new material to student experiences?

_____ activates student experiences and knowledge to link new information with previous knowledge

_____ relates to events in student's lifetime

_____ relates to events in student's environment

_____ introduces chapters with examples from student's experiences

_____ provides explicit applications of new learning to the student's lives

Organization Factors

Examine the textbook to see how clearly it is organized for learning. Texts that help students differentiate key concepts from background detail are more user-friendly than those that may overwhelm with a preponderance of facts.

- Does the book focus student attention on main ideas?

_____ outlines a clear chapter structure (i.e., cause and effect, problem and solution, concept and definition, compare and contrast, sequence, proposition and support)

_____ provides headings that are descriptive phrases rather than just nouns

_____ focuses on main ideas through explicit topic sentences

_____ selects sufficient details to develop main ideas

_____ avoids superfluous details (fact overloading)

_____ provides questions that ask students to respond to major concepts, not specific details

_____ tells "why" rather than merely lists "what" (provides reasons for information rather than just presents information)

Study Aid Factors

Finally, inventory the study aids that the textbook offers to facilitate learning.

- What prereading features help students pinpoint important concepts?

_____ outlines main themes and concepts in introductions

_____ establishes purposes for reading

_____ highlights key vocabulary

- What study aids assist students during reading?

_____ offers sufficient visual aids (pictures, illustrations, maps, etc.) that contribute to understanding the material

_____ offers graphic representations of material (concept maps, matrixes, charts, etc.)

_____ directs student attention in the text to interpreting visual and graphic information

_____ uses color coding for differentiating

_____ offers vocabulary aids (pronunciation cues, clear and understandable definitions, examples, analogies, etc.)

_____ includes marginal notes that highlight key ideas

_____ includes links to relevant web sites and CD-ROM connections available with the text

_____ reviews main themes and concepts in summaries (at end of sections and chapters)

the same cultural backgrounds and linguistic experiences as native English-speaking students do and they might miss much of the essence of what they read when slang, metaphors, idioms, and allusions are used. Teachers can check students' knowledge about these usages of language and explicitly explain their meanings whenever possible, which will help students increase their repertoires of these expressions. ELLs will learn new information about the English language and develop their prior knowledge, which will help them to learn more content across curriculum.

Different ways or styles of writing in other cultures might interfere with ELLs' understanding of text written in a western or American way. For instance, topic sentences cannot always be identified in some types of text in Chinese culture. Students who have learned Chinese language in school for some time could have difficulty following the topic sentence/examples/support/elaboration pattern when they read and write. It is most helpful to teach expository text from least to most complex. In addition, teachers can connect instructions about expository text to the content of other subjects.

Beyond the Book

- Interview a middle school student. Determine whether he or she has an understanding of how to make effective use of textbooks to aid in students' comprehension of the text material.
- Observe a middle school core content classroom. As you observe, determine how the teacher facilitates understanding of the text. Does he or she allow time to explore the structure of the text? Does he or she point out certain text features for the students? Is he or she able to make effective use of the various text structures by calling out cause and effect, problem and solution, and so on?
- Contact a textbook publisher and speak with a member of the editorial staff. Ask this person to explain how the publisher makes a determination of the various aspects of text structure and what considerations are given to usability. Share your findings with your classmates.
- Select a portion of a middle school subject-area textbook. Use one of the strategies listed in this chapter to determine the usability of the text, the basis of the structure, and the graphic information made available for students.
- Use the same portion of the text as in the previous question to make a chart of the signal words that appear in that selection. On the basis of your analysis, decide which text structure description is most compatible.
- On the basis of your description of the text structure in the previous question, determine how you would strategically teach this portion of text.
- Analyze another chapter from a textbook to determine whether the graphic clues and signals effectively promote students' understanding of the content of the text.

References

Armbruster, B. (1984). The problem of "inconsiderate text." In G. Duffey, L. Roehler, & J. Mason, (Eds.). *Comprehension Instruction: Perspectives and Suggestions* (pp. 202–217). New York: Longman.

Buehl, D. (1997). User friendly textbooks: Select those that aid meaning. *Wisconsin Education Association Council News and Views, 32*(9), 17.

Chen, H. S., & Graves, M. F. (1998). Previewing challenging reading selections for ESL students. *Journal of Adolescent and Adult Literacy, 41*(7), 570–571.

Daniels, H., & Zemelman, S. (2004). *Subjects Matter: Every Teacher's Guide to Content-Area Reading.* Portsmouth, NH: Heinemann.

Gee, J. P. (2000). Discourse and sociocultural studies in reading. In Kamil, M. L., Mosenthal, P. B., Pearson, P. D. & Barr, R. (Eds.), *Handbook of Reading Research, Volume III.* (pp. 195–207). Mahwah, NJ: Lawrence Erlbaum Associates.

Irvin, J.L. (2001). *Reading Strategies in the Social Studies Classroom.* Austin, TX: Holt, Rinehart & Winston.

Nichols, J. N. (1980). Using paragraph frames to help remedial high school students with written assignments. *Journal of Reading, 24*(3), 228–233.

Richgels, D. J., McGee, L. M., Lomax, R. G., & Sheard, C. (1987). Awareness of four text structures: Effects on recall of expository text. *Reading Research Quarterly, 22*(2), 177–196.

Simpson, M., & Nist, S. (2000). An update on strategic learning: It's more than textbook reading strategies. *Journal of Adolescent and Adult Literacy, 43*(6), 528–541.

Snow, C. (2002). *Reading for Understanding: Toward an R&D Program in Reading Comprehension.* Santa Monica, CA: RAND Corporation.

6

Vocabulary Knowledge

Talking Points _____

- Why is vocabulary learning so vital for reading comprehension?
- What factors are associated with effective vocabulary instruction?
- What literacy strategies can teachers employ to enhance vocabulary learning in their classrooms?

Mr. Gutierrez suggested to Lindsay that she tackle a book a little more difficult than the ones she had been reading for Sustained Silent Reading time. He also reminded her to use the strategies they had covered in class to figure out the meanings of unknown words. As she began reading, she encountered several words she did not know. But, she read on. The first word she encountered was "bifurcated." The context was "The pioneers settled where the river bifurcated." First, she thought—"Is this word important to understanding the story?" She decided it was. Then, she looked at the little words in the big word. She knew "bi" meant "two" such as in "bicycle." She guessed it had something to do with two rivers, but the sentence read "where the river bifurcated." That was singular. She guessed it meant that the river split in two. Just to make sure, she looked this word up in the dictionary. Her guess was right!

The next unknown word she encountered was "azure" as in "the azure sea." She reasoned that "azure" told her what color the sea was. She did not want to stop reading to figure it out and decided that the color of the sea was not important to understanding the story. It was taking some time to stop and think about these words, but Mr. Gutierrez said the best way to improve your vocabulary was to tackle increasingly complex text, use strategies for figuring out unknown words, and read, read, read.

If students are to become successful learners in middle school subjects, they must develop effective strategies for mastering the increased vocabulary loads of their content classes. Educators have long recognized the strong relationship between vocabulary knowledge and the ability to read and write proficiently. In fact, most educators intuitively know that people who do not know the meanings of many words probably have trouble with most learning tasks.

Although the vocabulary that students need for reading receives the most attention, people actually possess four vocabularies: listening, speaking, reading, and writing. The listening vocabulary is, of course, the earliest to develop and the largest. This vocabulary is made up of all the words a person hears and understands and is the foundation for learning other vocabularies. The second vocabulary to develop, the speaking vocabulary, includes all the words a person uses appropriately in everyday speech and includes words that they might never see in print, such as "wassup," "homey," or "dawg." The reading vocabulary consists of the words a person recognizes or can figure out in print, and the writing vocabulary encompasses those words a person can use appropriately in written communication. Although there is a normal sequence for the development of these vocabularies, they are recursive and one naturally builds on the other. For example, words that are learned during reading are reinforced by speaking, writing, and listening. New words that are encountered during listening can be added to speaking, writing, and reading vocabularies. A large store of words is, of course, essential for improving one's ability to think at increasingly abstract levels.

When children begin the process of learning to read, they understand the meanings of many words (listening vocabulary) but can recognize only a few in print. The focus of beginning reading instruction is to assist children in connecting the written symbol to the words they already use in listening and speaking. By about third or fourth grade, however, students "begin to encounter an increasing number of words whose printed forms they cannot recognize immediately and whose meanings are unknown" (Harris & Sipay, 1990, p. 511).

Research during the last few decades has resulted in new recommendations for effective vocabulary instruction. Educators now view vocabulary acquisition within the broader context of language and concept learning (Nagy & Scott, 2000). Vocabulary development is more than looking up words in a dictionary and writing sentences; rather, it involves the complex process of relating words to ideas and concepts. In fact, Laflamme (1997) found that direct instruction in vocabulary within the context of reading and writing improved students' scores on standardized tests. His findings support the general consensus in the field of literacy education that vocabulary should be taught and reinforced within the context of reading, writing, speaking, listening, and thinking. In this chapter, we discuss the importance of vocabulary knowledge, the various factors in vocabulary acquisition that researchers have identified, the issues related to vocabulary instruction, and guidelines for increasing vocabulary knowledge using researched and field-tested learning strategies.

The Importance of Vocabulary Knowledge

Vocabulary knowledge is strongly related to comprehension because understanding words enables readers to understand passages. Verbal aptitude underlies both word and passage comprehension and vocabulary knowledge may be related to a person's store of background information. Stahl (1990) reported that the "truth" of each of these hypotheses depends on "the particular contexts in which a word is found, the way the task of comprehension is defined, and the amount and types of knowledge a person has about a word" (p. 18). Whatever the reason, we know that the proportion of difficult words in a text is the single most powerful predictor of text difficulty, and a reader's general vocabulary knowledge is the single best predictor of how well that reader can understand text.

Nagy and Herman (1987) estimated that for students in grades four through twelve, a 4,500- to 5,400-word gap existed between low- versus high-achieving students. Others (Graves & Prenn, 1986; Graves & Slater, 1987) found huge individual differences between high- and low-ability students. Moats (2001) used the term "word poverty" to describe this disparity in vocabulary. The findings are clear: High-achieving students know more words than low-achieving students do.

Until about 1950, the focus of vocabulary research was directed toward four areas: vocabulary size at various ages, the relationship between vocabulary and intelligence, identifying the most useful words to know, and identifying a core of words that make text more understandable. In sum, most of the early research in vocabulary centered on choice of words to teach beginning readers and the implementation of readability formulas in the attempt to control text difficulty.

The last few decades have yielded much high-quality research in language comprehension and production. It is only within the context of this research base that researchers and practitioners can understand vocabulary acquisition and make viable recommendations for effective instructional practices. Beck and McKeown (1990) contended that those who are interested in vocabulary acquisition must first understand the relationship between words and ideas, the role of inference, and the organization of information. It seems that previous attempts to study vocabulary acquisition were fruitless until researchers were able to reach at least some level of understanding of the complexities of the mental processes that are involved in relating words to ideas.

Factors in Vocabulary Acquisition

Prior knowledge (especially prior knowledge about a topic), a student's use of context and morphology, and metacognitive abilities all work together to facilitate the development of an extensive vocabulary. On the basis of this research, the first step in making decisions about effective and efficient vocabulary instruction is an understanding of various factors in vocabulary acquisition. These factors include what it means to "know" a word, the role of morphology and context in incidental word learning, the usefulness of definitions, and the size and growth of vocabulary as a student matures.

Knowing Words

Consider the range of words a reader encounters during an hour immersed in, say, a news magazine. Most words will, of course, be commonplace, but in all likelihood,

some words will be less familiar and perhaps a few will be quite obscure. Paribakht and Wesche (1997) proposed a five-point scale of word knowledge:

1. Never saw the word
2. Heard it, but do not know what it means
3. Recognize it in context as having something to do with . . .
4. Know it well
5. Can use this word appropriately

It takes more than a simple, superficial knowledge of words to make a difference in reading comprehension. That is, readers do not need to know all the words in a text at the "established" level to comprehend what they are reading, but for instruction of specific words to make an impact on reading comprehension, the understanding must be beyond a superficial level. Nagy and Scott (2000) found that word learning is incremental. That is, an understanding of a word may improve as a reader encounters a word repeatedly and across new contexts.

Blachowicz (1986) suggested the use of knowledge rating before reading to help students analyze their levels of word knowledge (Figure 6.1). Before students read, the teacher presents a list of words related to the topic of study. Students then place a check mark along the continuum that reflects their level of knowledge of the word. The students analyze what they know about each word individually and then discuss which words are known or unknown and share information with each other. This activity leads naturally to the preteaching of vocabulary to be used later in the reading.

A related issue to knowing words is the importance of words in the text. Research suggests that students do not need to know all of the words in a text to

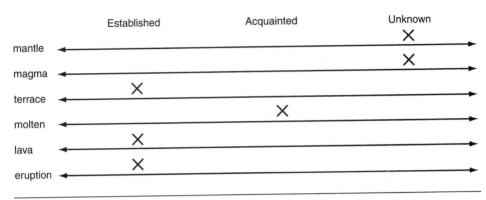

FIGURE 6.1   *Knowledge Rating of Words about Volcanoes*

understand it, especially with narrative text. Generally, students encounter text with 3 percent to 6 percent unfamiliar words. For example, reading the sentence "her mauve skirt fluttered in the wind as she fell over the precipice," a student might not know "mauve" and "precipice"; "precipice" is important to comprehension, but "mauve" is not. In sum, if the unfamiliar words are not important to the understanding of the text, students can tolerate a fairly large number of unknown words (about 15 percent) and still read with comprehension. It is therefore important to teach students to make good decisions when they encounter unknown words. Strong readers use multiple strategies; they may reread, skip words, think about what they are reading, sound words out, associate the word parts, or notice the syntax of words (the way the word functions in a sentence).

Morphology

Morphology involves gaining information about the meaning, pronunciation, and part of speech of new words from their prefixes, roots, and suffixes. It is clear that when students learn to chunk letters in a long word into meaningful morphemes this facilitates the processing of new words. However, structural analysis instruction of roots and affixes is often random and not connected with the context of text or the prior knowledge of the student. Students generally use morphology in three ways: to recognize words more efficiently, to remember the meanings and spellings of partially known words, and to figure out the meanings and pronunciations of new words. For example, a reader using morphology can confidently develop a working definition of a new word like "anthropocentric" by recognizing "anthropo-," which means *human* and "centric," which means *center*. Related words such as "anthropology" and "ethnocentrism" might come to mind, and the new word "anthropocentric" is understood as a belief that humans are the center of all activity. A list of the most common prefixes, roots, and suffixes is found in Figure 6.2.

Hill (1998) suggested using morphemes to extend students' knowledge of words through creating vocabulary trees in morphology journals. Students create

FIGURE 6.2 *Most Common Root Words, Prefixes, and Suffixes*

Root	Meaning	Examples
act	do	action, actor, react, transact, enact
aud	hear	audience, auditorium, audible, audition
cred	believe	credit, discredit, incredible, credulous
dic	speak	dictate, predict, contradict, verdict, diction
graph	write	autograph, paragraph, phonograph
loc	place	allocate, dislocate, locate, location
man	hand	manual, manufacture, manuscript
mot	move	demote, motion, motor, promote
ped	foot	pedal, pedestrian, pedestal
pop	people	population, popular, populace
port	carry	import, export, portable, porter, transport
sign	mark	insignia, signal, significant, signature
spec	see	inspect, respect, spectacle, spectator, suspect
tract	pull, drag	attract, detract, contract, subtract, traction
vid	see	evidence, video, provide, providence
volve	roll	evolve, involve, revolve, revolver, revolution

Prefixes	Meaning	Examples
ad	to	adapt, add, addict, adhere, admit
amphi	both, around	amphibian, amphitheater
an	not	anarchy, anesthesia, anorexia, anonymous
auto	self	automobile, automatic, autograph
co	together	coauthor, cognate, coincide, cooperate
de	opposite	deactivate, deform, degrade, deplete, descend
dis	opposite	disagree, disarm, discontinue, disgust
for	not	forbid, forget, forgo
il	not	illegal, illegible, illegitimate, illiterate, illogical
im	into	immediate, immerse, immigrate, implant
im	not	imbalance, immaculate, immature, impossible
in	not	inaccurate, inactive, inadvertent, incognito
ir	not	irregular, irreconcilable, irredeemable
mal	bad	maladjusted, malaise, malevolent
mis	bad	misbehave, misconduct, misfortune
pro	before	prognosis, progeny, program, prologue
pro	forward	proceed, produce, proficient, progress
re	again	redo, rewrite, reappear, repaint, relive
re	back	recall, recede, reflect, repay, retract
sub	under	subcontract, subject, submarine, submerge
trans	across	transatlantic, transcend, transcribe, transfer
un	not	unable, uncomfortable, uncertain, unhappy

Suffixes	Meaning	Examples
-ade	action or process	blockage, escapade, parade
-age	action or process	marriage, pilgrimage, voyage
-ant	one who	assistant, immigrant, merchant, servant

(continued)

Suffixes	Meaning	Examples
-cle	small	corpuscle, cubicle, particle
-dom	state or quality of	boredom, freedom, martyrdom, wisdom
-ent	one who	resident, regent, superintendent
-er	one who	painter, reader, writer
-ful	full of	careful, fearful, joyful, thoughtful
-ic	relating to	comic, history, poetic, public
-less	without	ageless, careless, thoughtless, tireless
-let	small	booklet, owlet, leaflet, starlet
-ly	resembling	fatherly, motherly
-ly	every	daily, weekly, monthly, yearly
-ment	action or process	development, embezzlement, government
-ment	state or quality of	amusement, amazement, predictament
-ment	product or thing	fragment, instrument, ornament
-or	one who	actor, auditor, doctor, donor

Source: From "Reaching Struggling Readers" by M. Hill, 1998, in K. Beers & B. Samuels (Eds.), *Into Focus: Understanding and Creating Middle School Readers.* Norwood, MA: Christopher-Gordon.

a page for each morpheme. Whenever they encounter a word with that part, they place it on their tree and note where they encountered the word.

While working with morphemic analysis, it is important to tell students that the conventions do not always work and that they must use their prior knowledge to check whether the word makes sense. For example, *-er* at the end of a word generally means "one who does something" such as a "reader" or a "writer." But is a "mother" one who "moths" or a "father" one who "faths"? When students learn to use morphology, context, syntax, and strategies for activating prior knowledge, they possess a powerful tool for expanding their vocabularies.

Context

Few would dispute the value of students' learning to use context to understand text and improve vocabulary growth. Researchers, however, have challenged some of the limited approaches of teaching context clues that were used extensively in the past. In naturally occurring text (such as a novel, in contrast to school materials such as textbooks that emphasize new vocabulary), context is relatively uninformative (Schatz & Baldwin, 1986). Most recent approaches to context clues encourage students to use their prior knowledge, their knowledge of syntax (how words are put together and function in a sentence), their knowledge of morphology and phonics if applicable, and their use of semantics (what makes sense). It is this attention to semantics, especially the larger context of the story or passage, that facilitates students' ability to make accurate inferences about word meanings.

Deriving the meaning of an unfamiliar word from context and learning the meaning of a word occurs at two different levels of comprehension. A single encounter with an unknown word might be enough to help a reader understand the text at hand but not enough for a thorough understanding of the word. The word remains at the "acquainted" level of understanding until another, more in-depth encounter moves it to a more "established" level.

The use of strategies to maximize the use of context, even if the context is lacking richness, is still useful instructional practice. When its use is paired with other strategies, such as morphemic analysis, it can be more effective than either approach in isolation.

Definitions

Used by itself, looking up words in a dictionary or committing definitions to memory does not lead to improved comprehension (Miller & Gildea, 1987; Scott & Nagy, 1997). This activity, a daily occurrence in hundreds of classrooms, leads to only a superficial understanding and rapid forgetting of words (McKeown, 1993). Using definitions as a way to learn new words is problematic because often a person must know a word to understand the definition and definitions do not always contain enough information for a reader to understand and be able to use a word. For example, a student who finds "forgive" as one of the definitions for the word *condone* might treat the words as interchangeable synonyms, leading to a sentence such as, "I asked my sister to condone me for losing her new sweater." This awkward sentence hardly captures the true meaning of *condone*. Miller and Gildea (1987) examined the types of errors students commonly make when they are asked to write a sentence from the definition of a new vocabulary word. They found that this substitution error based on partial understanding of a word was typical. They concluded that looking words up in the dictionary and writing sentences was "pedagogically useless" (p. 97).

The quality of the definition is important to being able to use the dictionary as an aid to understanding text (McKeown, 1993; Nist & Olejnik, 1995). It appears, then, that the dictionary or glossary can best be used as a verification of meaning, that is, after the reader has a hunch as to the meaning of a word (Scott & Nagy, 1997). Students need to learn how to combine the use of context, prior knowledge, syntax, and definitions to infer the meanings of unknown words.

Learning a word involves more than lifting its meaning from context or reading its meaning in a dictionary. Rather, word knowledge involves a complex process of integrating new words with ideas that exist in the schema of the reader. Dictionaries can contribute to understanding, especially for English language learners (Gonzalez, 1999).

Size and Growth of Vocabulary

Most children are capable of learning large numbers of new words each year. The question to ask is—Where and how do students learn these words? Nagy, Herman, and Anderson (1985) analyzed the number of words suggested in content-area textbook teacher's guides. They determined that only 290–460 of the 3,000 words that students learn each year can be directly attributed to instruction. Incidental learning of words from context while reading might be the major way in which students increase their vocabularies. Reading grade-level texts does produce a small but statistically reliable increase in word knowledge. Very few people have experienced systematic, intensive, and prolonged vocabulary instruction, yet many adults have acquired an extensive reading vocabulary. People learn words from a number of sources, but reading is possibly the single largest source of vocabulary growth, especially when students are reading text in which they encounter words that they do not know. When students read increasingly complex text and have the strategies for figuring out the meanings of unknown words, the likelihood of increasing their vocabularies is maximized.

Metalinguistic Awareness

Learning new words takes both skill and will. Struggling readers often lack the *skill* necessary to learn meanings for unknown words. Using the strategies that we suggest in this book and teacher and peer modeling, students can learn to use context, syntax, morphology, and prior knowledge in their reading and listening. Struggling, average, and even strong readers often lack the *will* to apply these strategies to increase their vocabularies; instead, they may merely skip unknown words and proceed on through the text. Nagy and Scott (2000) proposed that the facility to attend to words "depends on metalinguistic sophistication that continues to develop through high school" (p. 275). The following questions developed by Harmon (2000) can help students to become more sensitive to learning new words while reading.

- Do I know this word?
- Do I need to know this word to understand what I am reading?
- If I think this word is important, what do I already know about it?
- What does the word have to do with what I am reading? What is it referring to?
- How is it used in the sentence? Does it describe or show action?
- Do I see any word parts that make sense?
- Do I know enough about this word?
- Do I need more information?
- How can I find out more about this word? Should I ask someone or use the dictionary?

Teachers can assist students by guiding their decision making until effective strategies become automatic. Students need to understand what strong readers do when they encounter unknown words and realize that they are capable of making good decisions while they read (Guthrie & Wigfield, 1997). They must accept that vocabulary growth is an outgrowth of acquiring the *will* to learn new words.

Choosing Words for Instruction

Given that it is unlikely that students will learn a large number of words from direct instruction and given that instruction must be rich and extended, the words that

---

**Tier 1 Words—General Vocabulary Learned
Through Spoken Languages**

**Tier 2 Words—Vocabulary
Encountered in Written Texts**

**Tier 3 Words—Specialized
Vocabulary of Academic Discourses**

FIGURE 6.3   *Tiers of Vocabulary*

Adapted from Beck, I. L., McKeown, M. G., & Kucan, L. (2002). *Bringing Words to Life: Robust Vocabulary Instruction.* New York: Guilford Press.

teachers choose for instruction are important. Beck, McKeown, and Kucan (2002) recommended selecting words for vocabulary building by considering three levels of utility (see Figure 6.3). Tier 1 words are basic words that commonly appear in spoken language. Since they are heard frequently, in numerous contexts, and along with a great deal of nonverbal communication, tier 1 words rarely require explicit instruction in school. Tier 2 words represent the more sophisticated vocabulary of written texts. Mature language users use such words regularly, but students encounter them less frequently as listeners; as a result, these words are unknown to many learners. Due to their lack of redundancy in oral language, tier 2 words present challenges to students who meet them primarily in print. Tier 3 words appear only in isolated situations. These words tend to be limited to use in specific domains. Medical terms, legal terms, biology terms, and mathematics terms are all examples of tier 3 words. Tier 3 words are central to building knowledge and conceptual understanding within the various academic disciplines and should be integral to instruction of content, yet these words surface relatively rarely in general vocabulary usage.

Beck, McKeown, and Kucan advocated a focus on tier 2 words for general vocabulary instruction. Because these words are increasingly prominent in the written texts that students read as they move through school, adding them to one's vocabulary will have a high impact on reading comprehension. (*Redundancy, consort, sophisticated, domain,* and *explicit,* which were used in the previous paragraph, are examples of tier 2 words.) Tier 3 words must be taught as integral to learning a content discipline; these words are the vocabulary of academic discourse, as described in Chapter 5. Students use tier 3 words to express their understandings of core concepts in math, science, social studies, and other content areas and to communicate about them. (*Quadratic equation, preposition, feudalism,* and *xylem* are examples of tier 3 words.) Graves and Prenn (1986) classified the vocabulary students are learning into three additional categories: known concepts, synonyms/antonyms or multiple-meaning words, and unknown concepts. Each requires a higher investment of teacher and learner instructional time.

Known Concepts

The first type of word is one that might be in the student's oral vocabulary. Students merely need to decode the written symbol for this type of word. These words are generally mastered by the third or fourth grade, but struggling readers continue to have problems with this type of word. In addition, this category of words could include concepts that the student understands but has never connected with a particular term. For example, *aglet* might be an unfamiliar word, but when one is told that it is the term for the plastic tip on the end of a shoelace, a typical response might be "Oh! Is that what you call it?" No further explanation is necessary. Some words simply need to be labeled, others need to be associated with prior knowledge, and some concepts take extensive instruction in a discipline to understand them.

Synonyms/Antonyms or Multiple-Meaning Words

A second type of word is in neither the oral nor the reading vocabulary of the student but can be easily defined through the use of more familiar synonyms or antonyms. For example, although a student might not know the meaning of the word *altercation*, this word can easily be defined by the words *argument* or *quarrel*. Antonyms often help students to understand a word by explaining what it is not.

Another type of word that fits into this category is a multiple-meaning word such as *bank, run,* or *bay.* A student might know one meaning of a word but needs a new or second meaning explained. It is estimated that one third of commonly used words have multiple meanings. These multiple-meaning words are called *polysemous.* Teachers can reinforce different meanings of concepts across disciplines by using a simple figure such as the one in Figure 6.4. Words such as *negative, distance, function, age, product, relation, time, solution, process, space, element,* and *positive* are polysemous words that lend themselves to this type of word meaning expansion.

Polysemous words may be historically related. For example, students would recognize the word *coach* meaning a person who instructs a team; however, they might not know that a coach is also a term for a vehicle. The new meaning can be traced to what people in medieval England called the person who drove the team of horses pulling the coach. The term was later applied to tutors in college, leaders of crew teams, and even later to anyone who guided a team as hard to handle as eight spirited horses. Polysemous words may also have a specific meaning in a content area. For example, all students know the word *key* as the object that unlocks a door. However, *key* in a number of other contexts refers to something central or important, such as the key event in a novel. In geography, *key* has a specific meaning that is quite different from our everyday sense of the word; it refers to a reef or low island, as in the Florida Keys. In math, students are accustomed to checking their work with the "answer key," which is a listing of correct responses.

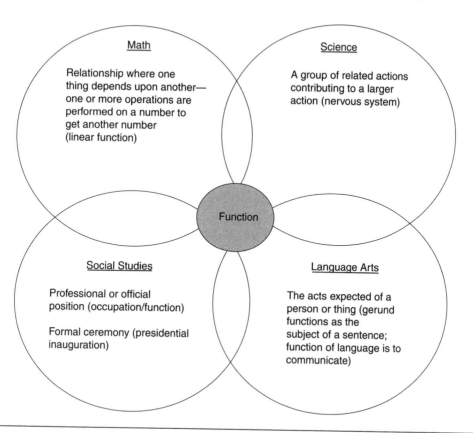

FIGURE 6.4   *Interdisciplinary Reinforcement of Polysemous Words*

In music, a "key change" refers to a switch in tonality, perhaps from C major to G major. Of course, in computer class, a key is a button on a keyboard.

Unknown Concepts

The third type of word is one for which the student has acquired no concept. This type of word is frequently a tier 3 word that is encountered in the content disciplines. The teacher must invest the time to develop the unknown concept through instruction before the word can be understood by the student. Words such as *cosine, fission,* and *acculturation* refer to difficult concepts that are more readily understood after examples have been given and prior knowledge has been built (Kibby, 1995). Extensive reading can certainly increase knowledge of tier 2 words, but direct instruction that engages students in using the word meaning, context, and prior knowledge is necessary for learning tier 3 words and for improving comprehension of content texts. It is for these words that are difficult to teach and commonly found in the content areas that rich, explicit instruction is most helpful.

Guidelines for Instruction

The English language is made up of a small number of words that occur very frequently and a large number of words that occur only infrequently (Nagy, Winsor, Osborn, & O'Flahavan, 1994). Students must use the strategies that they have learned to derive new word meanings, but more important, they must access their prior knowledge and engage their metacognitive thinking abilities to infer the meaning of the word or decide if it is important enough to stop and think about it. Sometimes the most useful strategy is to make a general guess at the word's meaning and move ahead with the reading. Although knowing a large number of words is certainly good, making expedient decisions about new words is better. Allen (1999) developed ten questions to assist teachers in making good decisions about vocabulary instruction.

1. Which words are most important to the understanding of the text?
2. How much prior knowledge will students have about this word or its related concept?
3. Is the word encountered frequently?
4. Does the word have multiple meanings (is it polysemous)?
5. Is the concept significant and does it therefore require preteaching?
6. Which words can be figured out from context?
7. Are there words that can be grouped together to enhance understanding of a concept?
8. What strategies could I employ to help students integrate the concept (and related words) into their lives?
9. How can I make repeated exposures to the word or concept productive and enjoyable?
10. How can I help students use the word or concept in meaningful ways in multiple contexts?

Help Students to Become Independent Word Learners

If wide reading is the most effective vehicle for large-scale vocabulary growth, then helping students make the most of learning words independently is imperative. A reader's ability to acquire word meanings by using context, morphology, syntax, and prior knowledge and the reader's monitoring of understanding of new vocabulary are the necessary ingredients for successful word learning. Teachers and fellow students sharing strategies that they used to figure out a meaning of a new word can help other students. The more opportunities students have to use strategies to predict the meanings of unknown words, the better they will become at using those strategies consistently when they read.

Encourage Active Involvement and Deep Processing of Words

What students do with newly learned words is more important than the number of words that they present. Teachers can help students to associate new words with what they already know through meaningful content or known synonyms. Students can learn how to make associations on their own to relate new words to their existing knowledge. Students need to process words meaningfully, connect them with their own life experiences, and apply them to future reading and writing tasks.

Provide Multiple Opportunities to Use Words

If words are to be retained, they must be used in meaningful ways in future reading and writing assignments. It seems logical that the introduction and use of new words should occur within a content area in which reinforcement can naturally occur. An obvious cause-and-effect relationship is at work here: The more students are exposed to a word that occurs in a meaningful context, the higher the chance of students using and understanding that word.

Help Students to Develop a Good Attitude about Learning Words

Some schools have adopted a word-a-day strategy to give vocabulary learning a high profile. For example, highly useful words such as those that commonly appear on SAT or ACT tests are targeted. Each day, a new word is included in the daily announcements, and teachers throughout the school write it on the chalkboard and try to use it as part of the daily discourse. A classroom variation is when a teacher develops a list of three to five words for the week. These words are written down and taped to the corner of the teacher's desk for easy referral. The teacher attempts to use each word five times during the week and informs the students what he or she is doing and why. ("I am trying to increase my vocabulary.") Other teachers have mystery words for the day or week. However the details of these types of activities work out, the clear message is that learning new words is a lifelong process.

Foster Extensive Reading Outside of Class

Wide reading facilitates large-scale vocabulary growth, as we have discussed repeatedly throughout this chapter. Teachers should encourage students to read outside of class. Having sustained silent reading times, giving students lists of books, conducting book talks, and using the library media center are all good ways of encouraging wide reading beyond the classroom walls. Of course, encouraging students to read increasingly complex texts with challenging vocabulary and giving them the tools to figure out the meanings of unknown words go a long way toward helping students to develop ownership of an increasing number of tier 2 words.

Evaluating vocabulary knowledge goes back to the notion of how well students know words and for what purposes they will use them. Simply asking students whether they know a word (yes or no) can be a fairly reliable indicator of word knowledge. Many teachers have found that asking students to evaluate a particular word as unknown, acquainted, or known is helpful in assessing word knowledge and is a basis for learning and remembering a word (Chase & Duffelmeyer, 1990). Personal interviews are probably the most accurate form of word-knowledge assessment, but they are also the most time consuming. The type of assessment a teacher chooses depends on the breadth and depth of the students' word knowledge and the purposes of the evaluation.

Vocabulary Strategies

The learning strategies that we present next are used widely in classrooms and are flexible enough to fit a variety of content. These strategies were chosen because they help students to become independent word learners; encourage active involvement by having students relate new words to previously learned concepts; provide multiple opportunities to use new words through reading, writing, speaking, and listening activities; and encourage students to use words in new contexts outside the classroom.

Possible Sentences

One of the most important aspects of assisting students in becoming independent vocabulary learners is helping them to use context effectively. The use of context

allows readers to make predictions about unknown words and to verify those predictions using syntactic and semantic clues. In a "possible sentences" activity (Moore & Moore, 1992), students receive a list of words or generate their own from an inductive vocabulary search or list-group-label activity (see the following strategy).

Step 1. **The teacher selects words that he or she thinks will be unfamiliar to students.** These are words that may be troublesome to students but are important for understanding the reading passage. Students generate sentences that link at least two of the words together in an effort to predict what the passage or story will be about. For expository text, students might use their sentences to predict the main idea or points in the passage. For narrative, students might wish to predict the storyline.

The following key terms could be provided as a possible sentences activity to world history students studying China: *dynasty, Mandate of Heaven, emperor, T'ang, civil service, nobility.* Students' predictions might lead to sentences such as "The Mandate of Heaven was a ceremony performed for the emperor." or "The nobility required civil service from their workers."

Step 2. **Students are now ready to read a passage to determine the accuracy of their predictions.** Their sentences may be modified either during or after the reading as a way of assessing comprehension of the new material. The sentences can then be combined to write a summary of the text. For example, students reading the textbook section on China might write the following.

- *The Chinese people supported each new emperor because of their belief in the Mandate of Heaven, which held that the leader was selected by heaven to rule.*
- *The T'ang dynasty of emperors developed the civil service system for government jobs. Officials were chosen by examination rather than because of membership in the nobility.*

Possible sentences activities can be used individually or in small groups. In a group format, students construct their own sentences and share with other members of the group. Students can give feedback as to whether the sentences are likely to work and can collectively review the sentences after the reading to determine how to fix sentences that need to be changed. Students can also use the dictionary or glossary to verify guesses.

Once the sentences have been verified, they can be shared with the entire class, providing a good means of reviewing the information. Additionally, the new vocabulary is continually reinforced. A final check of the listing will allow students to note which words they would label as *unknown, acquainted,* or *known.*

Possible sentences not only provide an opportunity for students to learn new words but also assist them in becoming independent word learners through the use of context clues. Students benefit from being actively involved in predicting and confirming word meanings. Finally, the proper role of the dictionary or glossary is emphasized throughout this activity, which is verifying guesses of word meaning.

List-Group-Label

Taba (1967) first developed the list-group-label strategy as part of her concept formation model. This strategy can also be used as a diagnostic instrument to find what students know about a subject and as an organizational tool to facilitate higher-level thinking. Because the strategy involves the categorization and labeling of words, list-group-label makes an excellent prereading strategy for a vocabulary development lesson as well.

Step 1. **The teacher elicits from students as many words as possible related to a particular subject.** A variety of stimuli may be used; the teacher can show a picture, read a story, show a film, present a lecture, or display artifacts or objects. Words may also be elicited by simply asking students to brainstorm what they know about a particular topic. The following sample list was gathered by asking students to generate meaningful terms from a textbook section on ancient China.

gunpowder	irrigation	emperor
peasant	deferential	meritocracy
mandarin	merchant	trade routes
public works	caravan	paddies
scholar	Buddhism	block printing
rice	porcelain	Confucianism
tea	silk	compass
fireworks	Asia	chopsticks

Step 2. **The teacher helps students to group related items by asking students which words could go together to form a group.** Students might note that items may belong to more than one group. After students determine appropriate categories, they group words accordingly.

Step 3. **After students have grouped related items, the teacher asks them to label each group of related words.** (See Figure 6.5.) Taba's model extends this initial phase of categorizing into interpretation of data. To encourage students to think at higher levels, they would be asked to compare observations of ancient Chinese civilization with what they know about life in China today. They could then be asked to identify similarities and differences. Next, the students would be asked to make generalizations about the similarities and differences noted. In the third phase, application of generalization, students would apply the generalization to a new situation and examine what would happen if the generalization were applied. To continue the example, after the list-group-label activity about China, the students might form the generalization that "China is radically different today in its form of government." The students then might be asked to apply this same statement to a new situation by considering the question "What governmental changes will possibly occur in China in the next 100 years?"

inventions

gunpowder
compass
block printing
fireworks

government

meritocracy
mandarin
public works
emperor

religion

scholar
Buddhism
deferential
Confucianism

trade

caravan
silk
porcelain
trade routes
merchant
tea

agriculture

peasant
paddies
rice
irrigation

FIGURE 6.5 *Grouped Words about Ancient China*

Educators have used the Taba model as a means of promoting concept development and higher-level thinking and developing vocabulary knowledge in students for four decades. This activity provides motivation through opportunity for success. Every student can participate by sharing with the class his or her perceptions. Students can then develop higher order thinking through categorizing, interpreting, and making generalizations. In addition, students learn words by grouping them logically and in a way that makes sense to the students. By examining examples of a concept and grouping them, students learn new vocabulary as they are exposed to the labels other students apply.

Inductive Vocabulary Search

The purpose of this strategy is to engage students in previewing text to generate a list of words. This search can be used with list-group-label or with possible sentences.

Step 1. **Ask students to preview the text selection to be used in the lesson.** During this preview, students should locate any words they feel are significant for any reason. Usually students are told they should look for words that they think might look important or words that they would expect to see on an exam. The words can be known words or unfamiliar words. Students should also be directed to notice the pictures, maps, diagrams, or other visual information and read the headings.

Step 2. **In a small group, students compile their lists of words.** When the allotted time is up, a member of the group shares his or her words with the entire class. The teacher may direct the students to put the words on charts or on overhead transparencies. Usually, a teacher will have a predetermined set of words that are content specific. If some of these content words are not being selected, you can simply ask a recorder to add the word. This way, the teacher can "seed" the charts.

Step 3. **As the words are shared, the teacher can suggest that students write down additional words, while pointing out aspects of the word.** The teacher can help students make connections to prior knowledge, use it in context, or provide an example of structural or morphological analyses as a means of modeling the way we learn new words. Students record notes next to the word to assist in their comprehension. For words that are not content specific but are unfamiliar, the teacher might wish to do the same type of word unpacking but might not have the students record the word. As each successive group presents its words, new words are added to each student's list. If words reappear, the student simply puts a check mark next to the word. Through this inductive vocabulary search, students create the listing of words and receive auditory, visual, and kinesthetic cues to help them remember the words. Once the lists have been presented, the teacher can move to a possible sentences activity.

Concept Maps

To learn content, students must understand the relationships between concepts. A concept map is a graphic organizer that helps students to see how the ideas relate to each other and can be used for study or for writing. The following is a sequence developed by Irvin (2001) for a passage on the topic of erosion.

Step 1. **Preview the passage.** Previewing can help a student to determine a possible structure for the map. In this case, students might notice that the major concept is *erosion* and the three subcategories—water, glaciers, and wind—are forces that cause erosion.

Step 2. **Sketch a concept map.** Students may look at the boldface type, headings, and general structure of the text and make their sketches. When students begin to sketch these concepts, they will quickly realize that the water section has the largest amount of text and the most terms to be defined. Putting *water* in the center can help students to display the ideas better.

Step 3. **Read the passage.**

Step 4. **Construct a concept map.** Using boxes, lines, arrows, bubbles, circles, or any other figure, have students display the ideas in the text in a concept map. Although Figure 6.6 looks somewhat complex, it simply represents the ideas presented in the text. If students understand the ideas presented in this concept map, they will most likely be able to use that information in writing a paper, taking a test, or discussing the topic with a friend.

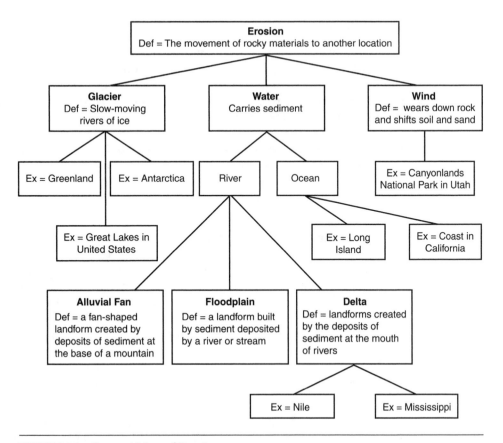

FIGURE 6.6 *Concept Map of Erosion*

Source: Irvin, J. L. (2001). *Reading Strategies for the Social Studies Classroom.* Austin, TX: Holt, Rinehart & Winston.

When first introducing the concept map to students, you might wish to create most of the map yourself, and after students use a prereading strategy and read the text, have them complete the map. The mapping strategy is most effective, however, if students create their own concept maps. Definitions and examples can be embedded within the maps to help remind students of the meaning of particular concepts.

Any combination and any organization of circles, bubbles, squares, triangles, lines, or arrows can be used to construct a concept map. Previewing helps students see the overall picture. Sketching gives students an idea of how the key concepts can best be displayed. Constructing the final map helps students to engage in understanding how the concepts relate to one another. Some teachers suggest sketching the ideas via sticky notes and then constructing the final concept map when the students are happy with the display.

Word Family Trees

The word family tree (Buehl, 1999) is another activity that encourages students to learn vocabulary as concepts rather than definitions. The word family tree is a graphic organizer that connects a key term to its origins, to related words that share a common root, to words that serve a similar function, and to situations in which one might expect the word to be used.

Step 1. **Provide students with a word family tree graphic organizer and introduce the concept by using a genealogical family tree as an analogy.** Family trees usually list an individual's ancestors, direct descendants, and other relatives, such as cousins, aunts, and uncles.

Step 2. **Select a group of target words for students to investigate.** These could be pivotal words in a short story, key terms in a unit of study, or general high-utility vocabulary words. For example, key terms in a U.S. history unit might include *imperialism, colonialism, diplomacy, commercial, treaty*, and *exploitation*. Have students work with partners or in cooperative groups to complete word family trees for these target words. Students can use any appropriate resource, including their textbooks, a thesaurus, a dictionary, or other vocabulary-rich sources to produce a word family tree such as the one in Figure 6.7. This activity also involves students in brainstorming, as they determine what kinds of people might use the word and devise sentences for those contexts. Students may also brainstorm possible mnemonic clues to help them remember the meaning of the word.

Step 3. **Allow time for students to share their word family trees.** They might discover that other students were able to identify related words that they overlooked, discovered additional possible synonyms, and identified other useful contexts in which the word might make an appearance.

Step 4. **Integrate consideration of word origin as a regular routine in classroom learning.** Students should be encouraged to raise questions of their own about possible word backgrounds and to consult sources other than abridged dictionaries to enrich their vocabulary understanding. Word family trees involve students in developing thorough rather than superficial understandings of important vocabulary. Students come to see the organic nature of vocabulary, as word meanings have grown and changed over the years, and they begin to identify useful word roots and notice connections among words derived from similar origins. Students are also more likely to remember the new words and feel confident in using them when they write and talk.

Summary

The important role of vocabulary and conceptual knowledge in comprehending text has been recognized by educators for some time. Researchers in the last decade have

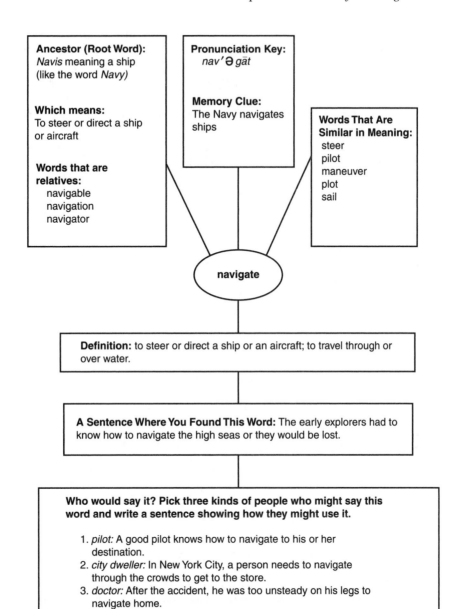

Ancestor (Root Word):
Navis meaning a ship
(like the word *Navy*)

Which means:
To steer or direct a ship
or aircraft

**Words that are
relatives:**
navigable
navigation
navigator

Pronunciation Key:
nav′ ə gāt

Memory Clue:
The Navy navigates
ships

**Words That Are
Similar in Meaning:**
steer
pilot
maneuver
plot
sail

navigate

Definition: to steer or direct a ship or an aircraft; to travel through or over water.

A Sentence Where You Found This Word: The early explorers had to know how to navigate the high seas or they would be lost.

Who would say it? Pick three kinds of people who might say this word and write a sentence showing how they might use it.

1. *pilot:* A good pilot knows how to navigate to his or her destination.
2. *city dweller:* In New York City, a person needs to navigate through the crowds to get to the store.
3. *doctor:* After the accident, he was too unsteady on his legs to navigate home.

FIGURE 6.7 *Word Family for* Navigate

pointed the way to more effective instruction in this area. Recent investigations involving the richness of context in natural text, the usefulness of text, the level to which a person knows a word, and the size and growth of vocabulary and concepts help educators to understand that the acquisition of a full, rich, and functional vocabulary involves the complex process of relating words to ideas.

Experts in the field of language development agree that the main vehicle for instruction should be encouraging students to read widely. Selected words, however, should be chosen for extended, rich instruction. This instruction should also focus on helping students become independent learners, encouraging students to become actively involved in the processing of selected words, providing multiple opportunities to use words, and guiding students to develop a good attitude about learning words outside the classroom. Learning strategies such as list-group-label, possible sentences, and concept mapping are useful to teachers at all levels; along with wide reading, these strategies help students to learn unfamiliar words by associating words to be learned with ideas and words they already know.

Extending Learning

Reviewing the Talking Points

Revisit the talking points at the beginning of this chapter. Answer the questions now that you have read the chapter, and compare your prereading and postreading responses.

Revisiting the Vignette

The opening vignette featured a good experience with figuring out the meanings of unknown words. Your experiences with vocabulary study during your middle school years may have included being given a word list on Monday, looking up words in the dictionary, writing them in sentences, and taking a test on Friday. Reflect back on your perceptions of vocabulary instruction and make some assertions as to what is different about today's demand for vocabulary development.

1. How have insights about vocabulary instruction changed in comparison to your own middle school experience?
2. What suggestions from the chapter would work best for your particular subject area?
3. How does the idea of context play an important role in the design of vocabulary instruction?

Terms to Remember and Use

listening vocabulary	context	morphology
morphemes	incremental learning	systematic instruction
metalinguistic	polysemous	possible sentences
antonyms	synonyms	tier 1, 2, 3 words
concept map	word family trees	important words

Write a series of sentences that meaningfully connect pairs of the above key terms. Your sentences should refer to ideas and concepts related to the literacy of middle school students.

Modifying Instruction for English Language Learners

Huckin, Haynes, and Coady (1995) suggested that vocabulary instruction for English language learners would ideally combine direct teaching of words with incidental learning fostered by multiple opportunities to encounter novel words in authentic and motivating texts. In addition, research shows the desirability of enhancing the value of incidental exposure by teaching ELLs strategies for inferring the meanings of newly encountered and unfamiliar words (Carlo et al., 2004). Teaching practices that reflect these findings and those discussed in previous sections can help ELLs to develop vocabulary more effectively. The following strategies can be included in classroom instruction to set a stage or to provide better learning opportunities for ELLs.

- Make it clear to students that unfamiliar words should be treated differently depending on their importance for understanding the key message in a given context. For ELLs, the percentage of unknown words can be very frustrating. To avoid unnecessary stress and anxiety, teachers need to clarify three choices that students have when facing these words: consult a dictionary or someone else; figure them out on their own as long as the answers make sense, regardless of what the real answers are; or completely ignore or skip the words. In helping students to make such decisions, strategies for determining key words and less important words have to be introduced.
- Encourage inferring word meaning by using grammar knowledge, contextual clues, and cognate knowledge as well as aids such as dictionaries and glossaries. Although morphology knowledge plays a crucial role in inferring unknown words, it is by no means the only knowledge that can assist students in figuring out meaning. Sometimes syntax knowledge, for instance, facilitates identification of important clues. Despite the argument that ELLs lack full command of English grammar (Stoller & Grabe, 1995), some ELLs who have studied English for several years in their native countries are more aware of many grammatical characteristics of English than their native English-speaking counterparts. To make this effort more effective, teachers can create learning activities that train students to use inferring strategies and check the correctness of inference. This can also be an opportunity to rectify students' incorrect concepts.
- Provide learning opportunities that combine listening, speaking/pronouncing, reading, and writing so that knowledge of new words can be reinforced in multiple ways and under various circumstances. Use of multiple senses and increasing of the chances of encountering the same words can help ELLs retain the words that they learn about.
- Use visuals when teaching important new words to create in students' minds images that correspond to the concepts being taught. This approach helps students to transcend language barriers and associate meaning with the form of words.
- Introduce origin of key words when teaching polysemous words. Students may use association to better understand different meanings of the word and find it easier to both distinguish those meanings and connect one to another.
- Emphasize the concept embedded in a word rather than its form or surface meaning. A good way to realize this as well as to expand the range of words is to organize new words around a theme. Specifically, teachers may use a passage that connects several important words around the same topic or subject for instruction,

or they can expand students' vocabulary by introducing other words in a word family after elaborating on the key word.

- Motivate students to engage in wide reading outside of the classroom by allowing them to select reading materials that interest them. Proper guidance is necessary, including clearly communicated objectives, rules, and expected reading outcomes. Small-group discussion and periodic sharing with more peers (for example, the whole class) should be encouraged in an effort to promote cooperative learning and broaden students' vocabulary and knowledge scope.

Beyond the Book

- Interview a middle school core subject area teacher to determine how he or she uses vocabulary instruction in content delivery.
- Meet with fellow content-area teachers and explore various ways in which you would implement strategies from this chapter or how you would modify some of those that you already use.
- Select a portion of a core subject-area text and analyze the language in terms of the morphological demands placed on the student.
- Peruse a content area textbook and decide which words are Tier 1, 2, or 3 words. Select the most important words for explicit instruction.
- Conduct an Internet search on Isabel Beck and/or Margaret McKeown. They have been involved with research on vocabulary for many years. Make a list of accomplishments in vocabulary acquisition.

References

Allen, J. (1999). *Words, Words, Words: Teaching Vocabulary in Grades 4–12.* York, ME: Stenhouse Publishers.

Beck, I. L., & McKeown, M. G., (1990). The acquisition of vocabulary. In P. D. Pearson (Ed.), *Handbook of Reading Research,* 2nd ed., (pp. 789–814). White Plains, NY: Longman.

Beck, I. L., McKeown, M. G., & Kucan, L. (2002). *Bringing Words to Life: Robust Vocabulary Instruction.* New York: Guilford Press.

Blachowicz, C. L. (1986). Making connections: Alternatives to the vocabulary notebook. *Journal of Reading, 29*(7), 643–649.

Buehl, D. (1999). Word family trees: Heritage sheds insight into words' meaning and use. *Wisconsin Education Association Council News & Views, 35*(2), 14.

Carlo M., August D., McLaughlin B., Snow C., Dressler C., Lippman D., Lively, T., & White C. (2004). Closing the gap: Addressing the vocabulary needs of English-language learners in bilingual and mainstream classrooms. *Reading Research Quarterly, 39*(2), 188–215.

Chase, A. C., & Duffelmeyer, F. A. (1990). VOCAB-LIT: Integrating vocabulary study and literature study. *Journal of Reading, 34*(3), 188–193.

Gonzalez, O. (1999). Building vocabulary: Dictionary consultation and the ESL student. *Journal of Adolescent and Adult Literacy, 43*(3), 264–270.

Graves, M. F., & Prenn, M. C. (1986). Costs and benefits of various methods of teaching vocabulary. *Journal of Reading, 29*(7), 596–602.

Graves, M. F., & Slater, W. H. (1987, April). *The development of reading vocabularies in rural disadvantaged students, inner-city disadvantaged students, and middle-class suburban students.* Paper presented at the meeting of the American Educational Research Association, Washington, DC.

Guthrie, J. T., & Wigfield, A. (Eds.). (1997). *Reading Engagement: Motivating Readers Through Integrated Instruction.* Newark, DE: International Reading Association.

Harmon, J. M. (2000). Assessing and supporting independent word learning strategies of middle school students. *Journal of Adolescent and Adult Literacy, 43*(6), 518–527.

Harris, A. J., & Sipay, E. R. (1990). *How to Increase Reading Ability: A Guide to Developmental and Remedial Methods* (9th ed.). New York: Longman.

Hill, M. (1998). Reaching struggling readers. In K. Beers & B. Samuels (Eds.), *Into Focus: Understanding and Creating Middle School Readers* (pp. 81–104). Norwood, MA: Christopher-Gordon.

Huckin, T., Haynes, M., & Coady, J. (1995). *Second Language Reading and Vocabulary Learning*. Norwood, NJ: Ablex.

Irvin, J. L. (2001). *Reading Strategies in the Social Studies Classroom*. Austin, TX: Holt, Rinehart & Winston.

Kibby, M. W. (1995). The organization and teaching of things and the words that signify them. *Journal of Adolescent and Adult Literacy, 39*(3), 208–224.

Laflame, J. G. (1997). The effect of multiple exposure vocabulary method and the target reading/writing strategy on test scores. *Journal of Adolescent and Adult Literacy, 40*(5), 372–381.

McKeown, M. (1993). Creating definitions for young word learners. *Reading Research Quarterly, 28*(1), 16–33.

Miller, G. A., & Gildea, P. M. (1987). How children learn words. *Scientific American, 257*(3), 94–99.

Moats, L. C. (2001). Overcoming the language gap. *American Educator, 25*(5), 8–9.

Moore, D. W., & Moore, S. A. (1992). Possible sentences. In E. K. Dishner, T. W. Bean, J. E. Readence, & D. W. Moore (Eds.), *Reading in the Content Areas: Improving Classroom Instruction*, 3rd ed., (pp. 196–202). Dubuque, IA: Kendall-Hunt.

Nagy, W., & Herman, P. A. (1987). Breadth and depth of vocabulary knowledge: Implications for acquisition and instruction. In M. G. McKeown & M. E. Curtis (Eds.), *The Nature of Vocabulary Acquisition* (pp. 19–36). Hillsdale, NJ: Lawrence Erlbaum Associates.

Nagy, W. E., Herman, P. A., & Anderson, R. C. (1985). Learning words from context. *Reading Research Quarterly, 20*(2), 233–253.

Nagy, W. E., & Scott, J. A. (2000). Vocabulary processes. In M. L. Kamil, P. B. Mosenthal, P. D. Pearson, & R. Barr (Eds.), *Handbook of Reading Research*, Volume III (pp. 269–284). Mahwah, NJ: Lawrence Erlbaum Associates.

Nagy, W. E., Winsor, P., Osborn, J., & O'Flahavan, (1994). Structural analysis: Some guidelines for instruction. In J. Lehr & J. Osborn (Eds.), *Reading, Language, and Literacy* (pp. 45–58). Hillsdale, NJ: Lawrence Erlbaum Associates.

Nist, S. L., & Olejnik, S. (1995). The role of context and dictionary definitions on varying levels of word knowledge. *Reading Research Quarterly, 30*(2), 172–193.

Paribakht, T. S., & Wesche, M. (1997). Vocabulary enhancement activities and reading for meaning in second language acquisition. In J. Coady & T. Huckin (Eds.), *Second Language Vocabulary Acquisition* (pp. 174–208). Cambridge, UK: Cambridge University Press.

Schatz, E. K., & Baldwin, R. S. (1986). Context clues are unreliable predictors of word meanings. *Reading Research Quarterly, 21*(4), 439–453.

Scott, J. A., & Nagy, W. E. (1997). Understanding the definitions of unfamiliar words. *Reading Research Quarterly, 32*(2), 184–200.

Stahl, S. A. (1990). *Beyond the Instrumentalist Hypothesis: Some Relationships Between Word Meanings and Comprehension* (Tech. Rep. No. 505). Champaign, IL: Center for the Study of Reading.

Stoller, F., & Grabe, W. (1995). Implications for L2 vocabulary acquisition and instruction from L1 vocabulary research. In T. Huckin, M. Haynes, & J. Coady (Eds.), *Second Language Reading and Vocabulary Learning* (pp. 24–45). Norwood, NJ: Ablex.

Taba, H. (1967). *Teacher's Handbook for Elementary Social Studies*. Reading, MA: Addison-Wesley.

7

Using Prior Knowledge

Talking Points _____

- Why is prior knowledge so important in reading comprehension?
- How can teachers assess students' prior knowledge, especially if students hold significant misconceptions about a topic?
- What literacy strategies can teachers use to activate students' prior knowledge and to prepare students for reading?

Brandie is a B student and completes her assignments faithfully, but her heart lies on the soccer field. She goes to her social studies class where they are studying the ancient Chinese. She learns about dynasties, the Yangtze Valley, millet, and jade. While she completes her graphic organizer, comparing and contrasting Chinese and Japanese history, she does not see how this topic relates to her life. She finishes her assignments, passes the test, and promptly forgets what she learned.

At least Brandie is able to complete the assignments. Scott, on the other hand, struggles to get through assignments. He knows that completing assignments is essential to passing a class. He has an afterschool tutor who helps him, but they only manage to complete the assignment—they rarely get to talk about what it means to him. He often wonders what high school will be like if he has to work so hard in middle school.

Both Brandie and Scott are having difficulty making connections. As a result, much of the schoolwork they are doing does not seem meaningful to them, and at times, their learning is stymied. Both students are apparently victims of being sent into reading assignments cold, without the benefit of advance activities that can assist them in discovering how their prior knowledge can be linked to the new content. The strategies that we present in this chapter, as well as those in Chapters 8 and 9, are designed to assist students in the maximum use and extension of their prior knowledge. Strategies for accessing and extending prior knowledge are also presented in this chapter.

The Role of Prior Knowledge in Reading

Anyone who has worked with computers knows that some computer manuals are written better than others. Some manuals are written in a user-friendly fashion, but unfortunately, many are not. It is surprising, however, that there are individuals who can make sense out of even the most poorly written manuals. These people usually already possess a vast knowledge of computers. That is, their schema on this subject is substantial, and this enables them to use their knowledge to compensate for the deficiencies of the text. Prior knowledge is one of the most important ingredients of comprehension.

If a person already knows something about a topic such as computers, that person need only locate new ideas while reading. The more a person knows about a topic, the less he or she needs information from the page. On the other hand, the reader who knows little about a topic is forced to rely more heavily on the text, using word recognition to build meaning, sentence by sentence. The lack of prior knowledge inhibits comprehension, and the "extent of knowledge influences the quality of understanding" (McKeown, Beck, Sinatra, & Loxterman, 1992, p. 79).

Generally, such an overreliance on text inhibits efficient reading. On the other hand, if readers rely too heavily on what they know without paying close enough attention to the text, they make reckless predictions or draw unsubstantiated conclusions about the meaning of what they read. A balanced interaction between the mind of the reader and the coherence in the text leads to a meaningful construction of an author's message. The more students know about the world, about text structure, and about a large number of concepts, the more knowledge they have available to them to use in understanding and remembering new information. However, unless learners can access their knowledge and apply it to new learning, it is useless.

Activating Prior Knowledge

Reading educators have recognized the value of background experience for many years. As they study the relationship between what readers know and how well they understand print, more precise facets of schema have emerged. Prior knowledge is all the information and all of the experience a reader has in memory. Topical knowledge, however, relates to the information a reader has on a particular topic, but readers must activate much more than what they know about a topic to have a successful reading experience. Knowledge about social interaction helps readers to understand characters, events in history, or the basic motivation of human beings. Knowledge of text structure helps readers to predict what will happen next and confirms their understandings. The metacognitive skill of monitoring comprehension, discussed earlier in this book, is another important aspect of reading to comprehend. Finally, domain knowledge—the use of language and vocabulary as well as writing styles that characterize each separate academic discipline—is essential. The more students know about earth/space vocabulary and how astronomers think and interact with their content, for example, the more domain knowledge of astronomy an individual reader can apply when trying to make sense of the earth/space science textbook. All of these types of knowledge and skill come into play during reading. All learning revolves around the condition that new information must be associated in some way with what is already known.

Teachers often spend the bulk of their lesson planning figuring out what they will do with students after the reading has been completed. Yet the research on prior knowledge clearly indicates that more explicit instruction needs to be undertaken to send students into reading assignments. Frontloading activities, those classroom strategies that prepare students for reading, might be the most important variable in student success with content. Helping students to activate and use their prior knowledge is one crucial role of the teacher; another is to diagnose what students do and do not know and to determine what misconceptions they hold. The prereading strategies that we suggest in this chapter can serve this diagnostic function so that instruction can be adjusted accordingly.

The act of reading can be likened to a trip to an art museum. People with a limited appreciation for art might wander quickly and aimlessly through the galleries, glancing at paintings and moving on to the next ones. For the artistically uninformed, the museum experience might give them a superficial overview of the great works of art, or it might only reinforce their misconceptions about artworks. An art student, by contrast, would likely spend a good deal of time studying and analyzing a painting because prior knowledge would compel the student to view the painting in more detail. The breadth and depth of prior knowledge on a topic partially determine how meaningful an encounter with print or any other medium will be. The extent and quality of prior knowledge will also determine how new or totally unfamiliar information is assimilated.

Frontloading by teachers helps students to activate relevant prior knowledge, which provides an opportunity for teachers to judge whether that knowledge is sufficient for comprehension of the text. In some instances, teachers will discover the need to build background where little exists. Many students are not particularly adept at drawing on their prior knowledge, especially in school settings, unless teachers help them to activate what they know. Students may possess relevant information about a topic to be studied but might not realize that what they know can be applied to what they are to learn. Time invested *before* reading will reduce the amount of time frustrated teachers must spend *after* reading by circumventing the need to explain to students what was not understood in a text assignment.

Prereading strategies are designed to stimulate cognitive functioning. The affective dimension, however, should not be ignored (Frager, 1993). Classroom discussions are often a part of prereading strategies, and too many students choose not to participate. Teachers need to recognize that there is a certain element of risk involved whenever students volunteer what they know or do not know about a particular topic. Teachers must create a climate of acceptance and safety for this risk taking. Interest is also an important affective dimension. Prereading activities often create student interest by asking students to predict, raise their own questions, or otherwise become involved in the material to be read. As interest in a subject increases, so does motivation and confidence toward the reading task.

Assessing the Knowledge Base of Students

How does a teacher determine how much students know? Most of the time, this assessment takes place during instruction, often during the prereading phase. For example, the first step of many prereading activities is to have students brainstorm a topic. After the initial brainstorming session, the teacher might determine that the students lack the prior knowledge and vocabulary required to comprehend the text and subsequently adjust instruction to build background information before reading.

Misconceptions

Not all prior knowledge is helpful. Students come to classrooms with extensive prior knowledge about many topics, but that knowledge often consists of naive impressions, erroneous explanations, stereotypes, or misconceptions of the world. These misconceptions can hinder the learning of new information. Science misconceptions are especially tenacious, as many students remain strongly committed to their flawed preconceptions even though these ideas about the world are not consistent with scientific thinking taught during science lessons. Students hold on to these mistaken beliefs, despite both instruction and information in their textbooks to the contrary, because their personal explanations seem logical on the basis of their previous experiences.

Researchers investigating effective strategies for correcting misconceptions generally have concluded that teacher-mediated discussions help to correct student thinking. Drawing on research on how the brain functions during reading, Sousa (2005) identified three ways in which a learner's schema can be modified during reading. First, readers might merely add new information without really changing their ideas about something. Second, readers might "tune" their previous understandings by altering what they formerly believed so that it is now consistent with their new learning. Third, readers might need to restructure their beliefs totally and replace their existing ideas with a new schema. Correcting misconceptions would generally fall into this third category of learning.

Successful strategies frequently involve the use of a graphic or visual display so that students can be an active part of the deconstruction of knowledge. A person's schema—that is, his or her collection of knowledge, attitudes, and beliefs—acts as a filter for new information, asking the question, "Does this make sense?". Learning consists of modifying, extending, and integrating new information into existing knowledge.

Prereading Strategies

Prereading strategies help students to activate what they know about a topic and anticipate what they will read or encounter. Buehl (2001) suggested three rules for choosing strategies.

1. What the students are learning is more important than which strategy is used.

2. The focus should be on what the students are thinking rather than on merely following the steps of a strategy.
3. Strategies should be tailored to match student needs and teacher goals.

Prereading strategies direct students' attention to the major ideas in the reading and introduce how information is structured in a text. Teachers can also use prereading strategies to point out how a text or lecture is organized, to teach unfamiliar vocabulary or concepts, and to provide the student with a purpose for reading or listening.

Students reading narrative texts are generally familiar with story structure and can readily identify characters, setting, and plot. Expository text, by contrast, does not always have such a clearly identified structure, and the topic might be unfamiliar to students. Knowledge of the structure of the text helps students to determine the most important information. For example, if students read a social studies text that compares two ancient civilizations, they can be directed to compare and contrast certain characteristics such as religion, politics, and economics. The teacher could help students further by reminding them to be sensitive to signal words such as *conversely, on the contrary,* or *like* to help differentiate between the two civilizations.

The prereading strategies that we describe in the remainder of the chapter are separated into three categories: building background knowledge when the students know little about a topic, activating prior knowledge when the students know something about a topic, and organizing knowledge when the students know a great deal about a topic.

Building Background Knowledge When Students Know Little About a Topic

Educators generally agree that background experiences and information are important in the learning process. A student who was raised in a rural town will

likely have a difficult time understanding the subway system in New York City. Kindergarten teachers in one small rural town in north Florida organize trips to a mall in a nearby city so that the children can ride the elevators and escalators—their small town has no two-story buildings. Personal experiences, of course, are best for facilitating learning, but reading offers the great advantage of providing vicarious experiences for students.

Students must, however, have some prior knowledge to assimilate new information; otherwise, the reading is meaningless. If teachers perceive that students know little or nothing about a topic to be studied, then prereading strategies become even more important in building the necessary information to relate to the unknown topic. Teachers who begin with a positive attitude about what a student might know and then use analogies and numerous examples to tie new information to existing prior knowledge facilitate making connections for student learning. It seems obvious, then, when teaching an adolescent to read that instruction should begin with familiar topics. The following strategies can be used when students know very little about a topic: predicting and confirming activity and visual prediction guide.

Predicting and Confirming Activity

Based on Beyer's (1971) inquiry model, the Predicting and Confirming Activity (PACA) strategy, like most prereading strategies, uses student predictions to set a purpose for reading; this process is what most good readers do naturally. The PACA strategy allows students to make predictions about a topic based on some initial information provided by the teacher, even if the students have little prior knowledge. Given additional information, they can revise their predictions (or hypotheses) and pose them as questions for further reading.

A social studies teacher, for example, is planning a lesson on postcolonial Africa. As a case study, the students will be reading a passage about the Hausa people of Nigeria. The teacher surmises that students will probably have little prior knowledge of the culture or geographical location of the Hausa and might harbor misconceptions about African society. The teacher introduces this activity with a short explanation that the Hausa people live in Nigeria and shows students where this country is located in Africa.

Step 1. **The teacher poses a general question.** One such question might be, "What is life like for the Hausa people?".

Step 2. **The teacher provides initial information.** The teacher divides the class into small groups for discussion and provides them with a list of terms associated with the Hausa and poses the general question, "On the basis of the words commonly associated with the Hausa, what is life like for the Hausa people?" Word lists, similar to the one that follows, are frequently located at the end of a section or chapter in content-area textbooks. The teacher can add ten to fifteen additional words to the list.

rainy season	merchant	desert
migration	multicultural	farm
Koran	debtor	servant
walled town	Ibo	dry season
mosque	drought	sheep
prophet	oil	unstable government
ethnic strife	God	yams
military	prohibition	clay oven
world markets	mother	aunt

Step 3. **Students meet in small groups to write predictions.** After the small-group discussions, the teacher again poses the question, "What is life like for the Hausa people?" to elicit predictions from the students. The teacher writes these statements on the chalkboard and asks students to cite the word or words that caused them to make each prediction. The teacher might also wish to record group responses using categories such as religion, politics, economics, and history. Some typical responses are as follows:

- The Hausa people are Moslem.
- They have a low level of technology.
- The Hausa people have an agricultural economy.
- They live under a military government.

Step 4. **The teacher presents new information at this time.** Pictures that are normally found in content textbooks are a good resource, but this additional information could be a video or story.

Step 5. **Students and teacher revise or modify statements.** On the basis of the new information, students, assisted by the teacher, revise their predictions by confirming or rejecting their original hypotheses. For example, a picture of three Hausa people on motorcycles who are wearing sunglasses would help students to understand the need to modify some of their original predictions. This picture might also elicit a new prediction about the extent to which the Hausa people engage in trade with other countries. Likewise, a picture of a Hausa community in the rapidly growing Nigerian city of Lagos might cause students to predict changes from a rural to an urban lifestyle. A picture of a mosque might confirm students' earlier prediction that the Hausa people are Moslem.

Step 6. **Students then read the selection in the textbook, using their predictions as a purpose for reading.** The teacher encourages students to keep their predictions in mind while reading. Writing predictions on the chalkboard for easy reference is often helpful.

Step 7. **The teacher helps students to revise their predictions on the basis of the reading.** For example, suppose students made a prediction, based on the word list, that the Hausa people have a low level of technology, and the textbook described advanced techniques of farming used by the Hausa. The teacher would then help students to revise these statements to reflect the new information. These statements, thus revised, may be used for further research or as an impetus for writing. Such revisions also counteract possible misconceptions, in this case about the technological sophistication of other cultures.

Although students might know little specific information about a topic such as life in Nigeria, they have an extensive knowledge base about cultures. PACA starts with a familiar knowledge base and builds background about a topic. Students can then use this new information to extend their understanding of culture in general.

PACA can be used with a variety of topics for which teachers need to build background information. Teachers have found this strategy to be a good way to help students relate to the vocabulary and concepts in a text before asking them to use this information. In addition, making and revising predictions on the basis of a limited amount of information is an excellent way to introduce students to formal reasoning in a gradual way. Accepting the premise that knowledge is tentative and can be revised on the basis of new information is a first step for students toward more abstract reasoning.

Visual Prediction Guide

Visual information such as charts, tables, graphs, and pictures is found abundantly in content-area textbooks and often ignored or only casually used by students and teachers. A quick flip through a new textbook reveals that publishers are now emphasizing visual displays as a major source of important content. To accommodate the space demands of visuals, publishers may adopt an either/or policy: Information will be presented either in words or in visuals but not in both forms. As a result, Ogle (2000) argued, visual literacy strategies are becoming a necessary part of content learning. However, the "development of visual literacy typically receives limited attention in . . . content area texts" (Rakes, Rakes, & Smith, 1995, p. 46).

Struggling readers in particular have difficulty visualizing ideas that are presented in text. The Information Age has certainly bombarded students with visual images. Some observers worry that the beautifully illustrated texts, television, the Internet, CD-ROMs, and so forth might have taken away a student's need (and perhaps ability) to visualize. Others might argue that young people think in visual images. Whatever the case, proficient readers visualize as they read; struggling readers generally have difficulty forming mental pictures. Irvin (2001) developed the following sequence to assist students in using visual information to comprehend text.

Step 1. **Preview the text, noting the visual information that is presented.** This information may be in the form of charts, diagrams, pictures, or illustrations.

Step 2. **Ask how the visual information relates to the text or why the author(s) included this information.** It is important that students create a link between the text and the visual. For example, have students place a transparency on a textbook page and draw arrows between the text and the corresponding visual.

Step 3.   **Generate questions raised by the visual aid.** Students should list two or three questions that arise from this visual aid.

Step 4.   **Read the text.**

Step 5.   **Go back and review visual aids in the text.** Students should evaluate whether the visual accurately displays the most important ideas in the text.

The visual prediction guide can, of course, be modified to suit the needs of students and their purposes for reading. Based on Rakes, Rakes, and Smith's (1995) levels of interaction, the teacher could do the following:

- Simply direct students to notice the visual information.
- Provide study questions based on the visual information.
- Have students evaluate how well the visual information helps them to understand the text better, or have students sketch their own understanding of the concepts in the text.

In addition, questions can direct students' understanding of how this concept fits with information presented before and after the text. A slightly different arrangement of this strategy would be used for other forms of visual information, such as charts, diagrams, maps, or photographs.

Some educators suggest that after reading, students be asked to draw the visual from memory. This works particularly well for diagrams that are explained in the text. The act of creating a graphic helps students to process it better and connect to the information presented in the text. In addition, this activity can certainly be used to assess how well students understood the text.

Student-created graphics can be extended through group work by having students explain their graphics to other students. They benefit from hearing and seeing the various perspectives of other students. Without employing competition such as "Who's graphic is the best?" students can be guided to give feedback on other students' graphics. Giving and soliciting feedback helps them to process the ideas in the text more deeply and become better consumers of displays of visual information.

Not all text has visual information that is placed strategically or is well explained in the caption and connected to the text. If this is the case, having students evaluate or redraw graphics can be useful. Also, because of time constraints, a teacher cannot give equal attention to every visual display in the text. But in cases in which the visual information helps students to better understand the ideas presented in the text, this strategy can be most helpful.

Most students, but especially struggling readers, can benefit from learning how to attend to and use the visual displays that accompany most texts. A teacher might wish to take a more- or less-structured approach to building background information using this visual data. For example, a history teacher might direct students' attention to the textbook photo depicting Hadrian's Wall in northern England and ask students to speculate about why the Romans would find it necessary to construct such an awesome project and ask whether they thought that such a barrier would be very effective. The answers to these questions can serve as a study guide while they read. Or the teacher might wish to use visual information to facilitate students' predictions about the content of the chapter. These predictions could set a purpose for reading and could be checked for accuracy after the reading has been completed.

The visual reading guide is a vehicle that students can use to organize their thoughts before reading or studying a topic. Especially for students who lack the necessary prior knowledge about a topic, study questions can help students to see important aspects of the content before reading. Later, while reading, during discussion, and when completing assignments, students can use this acquired information to begin to formulate generalizations about the content being studied.

Activating Knowledge When Students Know Something about a Topic

Students often know something about a topic, and reading will be more meaningful if that prior knowledge is activated before they read. Also, as was mentioned earlier, misconceptions about a topic can hinder students' understanding of a selection. When teachers perceive that students know something about a topic, the following strategies can be used to help students share information and activate what they already know before reading: a prereading plan and anticipation guides.

A PreReading Plan (PReP)

Langer (1981) developed a PreReading Plan (PReP) to help readers use what they know to understand new ideas. She also advocated using the technique as an assessment tool to determine how much students understand about the topic to be studied or whether they have any misconceptions.

Step 1. **The teacher asks students to make a list of words they associate with a topic.** A social studies teacher might use the prompt "electoral college" to introduce a textbook passage on U.S. presidential elections. Students might then offer terms such as *vote, election, president, Constitution, Republican, states,* or *Al Gore*.

Step 2. **The teacher asks students to reflect on their reasons for making the associations.** A question such as "What made you think of that?" might help to elicit responses. Through this process, teachers can help students to become aware of what network of associations is available to them and how to make maximum educational use of these associations. Also, by discussing reasons why one word is associated with another, a teacher can help students to cluster and categorize their responses. The association "Al Gore" might have occurred to some students because they remember that Gore won the popular vote in the 2000 presidential election but lost the electoral college vote, although they might not be sure how that process works.

Step 3. **After some organizational patterns have developed, the teacher asks the students to elaborate on and clarify their initial responses.** If students associate "states" with "electoral college," the students' rationale might be "because the winner of a state receives its electoral votes." In Step 3, the teacher could explore this statement further by asking how the electoral votes are determined for each state.

Students, either individually or as a class, may be asked to use these patterned associations to write statements or perhaps a paragraph about the topic. The value of this activity is to encourage students to think beyond their initial response, integrate their thoughts with the thoughts of others, and organize their information before reading about the topic.

Anticipation Guides

The purpose of anticipation guides is to highlight mismatches between what students may know and believe and what is presented in the text. The anticipation guide was first developed by Herber (1978), who suggested that comprehension can be enhanced if students make predictions about concepts covered in the text. The steps involved in this strategy are illustrated by an example that was developed to introduce a story dealing with the Holocaust.

Step 1. **The teacher identifies the major concepts and supporting details in the reading selection, lecture, or film.** In this text, the major concept is the Holocaust.

Step 2. **The teacher elicits the students' experiences and beliefs that relate to the major concept(s) that were previously identified.** The teacher could ask students to write down all the words they associate with the concept of the Holocaust.

Step 3. **The teacher creates statements reflecting beliefs concerning the topic, which may contradict or modify the beliefs of the students.** Some statements that are consistent with the students' experiential background and with the concepts presented in the material or lesson should be included. Three to five statements are usually adequate. In the example in Figure 7.1 students would be asked to place an *A* next to the statements they agree with and a *D* next to those with which they disagree.

Step 4. **The teacher arranges the statements on a sheet of paper, overhead transparency, or chalkboard.** The students respond positively or negatively

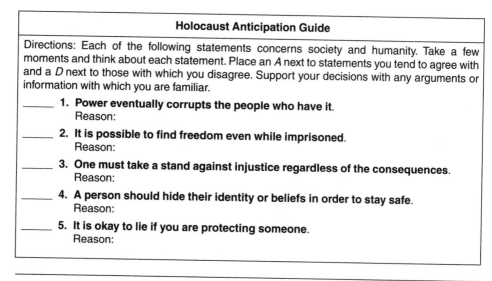

FIGURE 7.1 *Anticipation Guide*

to each statement on an individual basis. Students should record their justifications for each response in writing so that they will have a reference point for discussion.

Step 5. **The teacher engages students in a prereading discussion by asking for a hand count of responses to the five statements on the Holocaust.** Students can then share the justifications for their responses. This phase of the activity can also be undertaken in small groups.

Step 6. **Read the selection.** In this example, students would read the novel, *Daniel's Story* by Carol Matas (1993), a story about a young boy living in prewar Germany whose family is taken to the concentration camps.

Step 7. **The teacher engages students in a postreading discussion that compares their reactions to the statements before and after the reading.** This discussion may take place either in small groups or as a class activity.

Duffelmeyer (1994) maintained that effective statements convey a sense of the major ideas that students will encounter, activate and draw on students' prior experiences, are general rather than specific, and challenge students' beliefs. The anticipation guide is an excellent method for promoting active reading, encouraging expectations about meaning, and prompting students to modify erroneous beliefs. Middle school students particularly enjoy talking about value issues. As they move from the influence of their families to the influence of their peer groups, it is important for students to have a forum for stating their opinions and considering the opinions of others. Additionally, when students can identify with the value issues that are involved in a story or passage, they tend to comprehend better on literal as well as higher levels of understanding because the information is more meaningful to them.

Organizing Knowledge When Students Know a Great Deal about a Topic

Teachers might wonder whether precious class time is wisely spent on a prereading strategy if students already know a great deal about a topic. Yet prereading strategies can be especially advantageous when students are dealing with a large amount of information, such as a science unit on aquatic life. Under these circumstances, prereading strategies help students to organize the information before beginning their study. For example, the teacher might use a blue marker to construct a graphic organizer or semantic map with students at the beginning of a unit. As students learn new concepts, they fill in the new information with a red marker. Students and teacher are always gratified to see the organizer or map become more filled with red than blue. This practice is also a reminder that new information must be connected to what learners already know.

The graphic organizer and the semantic map are appropriate for all types of instructional settings and all age levels. These two strategies can be used to strengthen vocabulary, as prereading or prewriting activities; to organize information during reading; or to create a study guide after reading. In this section, these strategies are discussed as prereading strategies with application, of course, during and after reading.

Graphic Representations and Organizers

The value of graphic representations or organizers, also known as structured overview or advanced organizers, has been recognized by educators since Ausubel (1968) first conducted his work on conceptual development. Graphic organizers can introduce concepts and illustrate the nature of the relationships among these concepts. Moore and Readance (1984) found that the use of graphic organizers seems to have a positive effect on vocabulary learning, more mature learners obtain greater benefit from the use of graphic organizers, students perform better when they produce a graphic organizer after reading (instead of being presented with a complete organizer before reading), and teachers report that they are more confident as teachers when they use graphic organizers. The level of student involvement in the construction of the organizer is also a significant factor. Other research (Groller, Kender, & Honeyman, 1991) on advanced organizers suggested that "students need to use metacognitive strategies in order to use advance organizers effectively" (p. 470). Students need to be taught how "to use, monitor, and evaluate their use of advance organizers in order to use these to their best advantage" (p. 473).

In Chapter 5, we suggested there are primarily six types of organizational structures in textbooks: problem and solution, description, comparison and contrast, sequence, proposition and support, and cause and effect relationships. The structure of the graphic should reflect the structure of the text it represents. Graphic organizers have been used more extensively with expository text than with narrative, story-type material.

For example, students in a seventh-grade social studies class may be investigating the impact of command economy. As a prereading activity, the teacher and students collaborated on creating a tentative graphic organizer on the chalkboard, detailing possible reasons why a government might favor a command economy and its effects on the people. Students already had some prior knowledge on the topic, having discussed economy structures earlier in the year. As students read a passage describing the command economy of the USSR, they create their own comparative graphic organizer, recording pertinent information from the text related to the positive outcomes of a command economy as well as the disadvantages for the people. When students have completed their graphic organizers, the teacher solicits a comparison between the brainstorming graphic organizer on the chalkboard and the personal graphic organizers created by the students. What new information appeared in the text that was not known by the students before reading? Did the students offer information the text did not mention? Did the text contradict any student information (in other words, did the students suggest misconceptions or wrong information during the initial brainstorming phase)? As a final phase, students write a summary of the article, using their graphic organizers as a prompt as shown in Figure 7.2.

Cloze Graphic Organizers

One advantage of graphic organizers is that they visually represent the structure of text. Readers are more likely to comprehend new material through a cloze graphic organizer because some of the information is intentionally left out. If

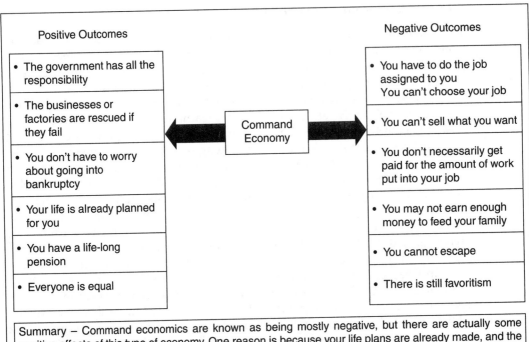

Positive Outcomes

- The government has all the responsibility
- The businesses or factories are rescued if they fail
- You don't have to worry about going into bankruptcy
- Your life is already planned for you
- You have a life-long pension
- Everyone is equal

Command Economy

Negative Outcomes

- You have to do the job assigned to you
  You can't choose your job
- You can't sell what you want
- You don't necessarily get paid for the amount of work put into your job
- You may not earn enough money to feed your family
- You cannot escape
- There is still favoritism

Summary – Command economics are known as being mostly negative, but there are actually some positive effects of this type of economy. One reason is because your life plans are already made, and the pressure is not on you to decide. Another is the government gets all the responsibility, and the businesses and/or factories are rescued if they are failing. Also, the unemployment rate is low because your job is the one you will always have.

Even though there are many positives, there are most likely more negatives. For starters, there is almost always a lack of supplies. All workers are unfairly paid because the quality of your work doesn't matter. In the shops the prices are too high. There is a lot of pollution, but strict government rules. People are assigned jobs, and can't leave the country.

FIGURE 7.2   *Comparative Map on the Outcomes of a Command Economy*

students were assigned a section in their physical science textbooks about simple machines, the teacher could present the graphic organizer in Figure 7.3, discuss the organization of the text, and direct students to fill in the organizer either during reading or directly after reading. By using graphic organizers in this way, students become actively involved in reading and more aware of text structure.

Semantic or Concept Mapping

Concept maps are diagrams that help students to see how words or ideas are related to one another. Circles and lines are used to show relationships between concepts.

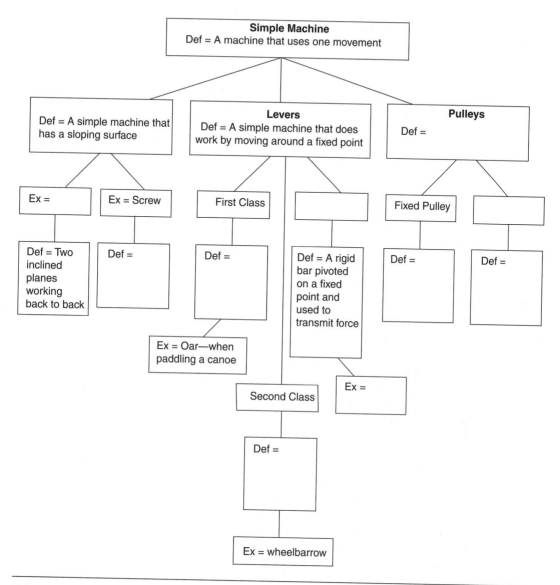

FIGURE 7.3 *Cloze Graphic Organizer of Simple Machines*

Mapping helps students to learn how to think critically because they must receive, organize, and evaluate information so that it makes sense to them. The map becomes a graphic display of main points, subcategories, and supporting details.

Figure 7.4 is an example of a map used before reading to help social studies students organize their ideas about freedom and provide an aid to writing. To elicit useful associations about freedom as a prereading activity, the teacher asked students to construct a concept map that included their associations for the word

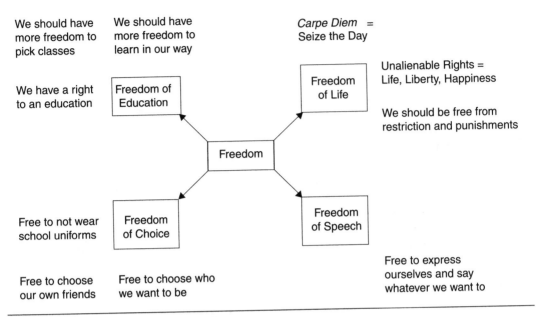

FIGURE 7.4   *Concept Map before Reading*

freedom. Jay's map (Figure 7.5) included connections to freedom granted as a nation as well as an individual at home and at school.

The teacher then asked students to read an article that discussed the increased amount of freedom teens are entrusted with today, a viewpoint ignored by most students as they constructed their prereading maps. The article argued that while teens need freedom to help develop a sense of autonomy, there is a line between space to make productive choices and the dangers associated with too much freedom. Jay's concept map (Figure 7.5) after reading the article demonstrates his enhanced understanding of the topic of freedom.

The teacher then used both maps as a springboard for writing. Students who usually had difficulty knowing what to write used the maps to provide the information for their essays. Even struggling learners were able to produce written responses using their concept maps as prompts. Semantic mapping can be used as a classroom activity before, during, and after a reading assignment. As a prereading strategy, semantic mapping activates prior knowledge, serves as a springboard for discussion, and helps readers organize a wealth of information as they sort through what they have learned from a text.

Summary

Prior knowledge is the sum of all experiences and information held in the readers' mind. Reading is an interaction between the mind of the reader and the cues given in

Acceptable Use	Unacceptable Use
Opportunity to learn Opportunity to learn about things you want Free to make mistakes in a safe and positive environment	Can't infringe upon someone else's learning Learning about topics that make other people uncomfortable Making fun of someone who makes a mistake—like laughing when someone reads a word wrong

Acceptable Use	Unacceptable Use
Inalienable rights—life, liberty, and happiness You have to think about your freedom and how it fits in with the rest of society You have to police yourself Some restrictions protect us—like curfew	Your actions shouldn't take away somebody else's rights to life liberty, and happiness Things like murder, robbery, illegal drugs—these all take away life

Freedom of Education

Freedom of Life

Freedom

Freedom of Choice

Freedom of Speech

Acceptable Use	Unacceptable Use
We are not restricted to the same thing all the time We can make decisions based on our own beliefs We don't have to conform to others We can think about our decisions and change them—like picking friends—some might end up being a bad influence	Cant always use freedom as an excuse to get our way Bad choices happen and you aren't free to ignore the consequences There is no such thing as complete freedom because we live with other people Ex. Choose to speed and someone can get hurt

Acceptable Use	Unacceptable Use
Free to express ourselves Free to say what we want Free to listen to the music we want Free to draw and paint what we want	If our expression takes away from others then it is not okay Speech that doesn't consider others is wrong—like how people in the U.S. used rude words to refer to black people We shouldn't advertise and encourage things that can hurt people—like smoking and drinking

FIGURE 7.5 *Concept Map after Reading*

the text. Thus, to a large extent, the scope and depth of a reader's prior knowledge determine the quality of the reading experience. Activities involving prior knowledge can be grouped into three categories: those that build knowledge related to a topic where little or none existed before, those that activate and build on existing prior knowledge, and those that help to organize large amounts of information. By building, activating, and organizing prior knowledge before reading, a teacher can enable students to bring the most to, and thus get the most from, their reading experiences.

Extending Learning

Reviewing the Talking Points

Revisit the talking points at the beginning of this chapter. Answer the questions now that you have read the chapter, and compare your prereading and postreading responses.

Revisiting the Vignette

1. In the opening vignette, there is a glimpse into the thought processes of students as they deal with homework and a curriculum to which they cannot always relate. Thinking back to your own experiences with homework as a middle school student, what were some of the strategies that you used to complete the assigned tasks? Think back to those classes that you felt were relevant. What elements of those classes held your interest?
2. What are some ways of building students' prior knowledge before they read a piece of text? Why would frontloading a lesson be advantageous to any content teacher?
3. If prereading strategies stimulate cognitive functioning, how can teachers best help students incorporate them into their interactions with texts?

Terms to Remember and Use

prediction	coherence	prior knowledge	topical knowledge
frontloading	affective dimension	brainstorm	graphic display
narrative	expository	signal words	PACA
anticipation guides	PReP	semantic map	text structure

Write a series of sentences that meaningfully connect pairs of the above key terms. Your sentences should refer to ideas and concepts related to the literacy of middle school students.

Modifying Instruction for English Language Learners

Although English language learners' prior knowledge about some topics is not necessarily less than that of their native English-speaking counterparts, ELLs need somewhat different ways to use what they already know to assist them with learning new content. The following practices are suggested in an effort to help teachers better provide assistance to students as they increase their prior knowledge and create their own strategies.

1. **Use visuals to activate ELLs' prior knowledge related to certain topics.** These visuals can be something associated with important or new vocabulary, themes of the texts, connections to previous topics, and so on. ELLs might have knowledge of a subject in their native languages and might only lack the English vocabulary to share this knowledge. Because much important information is presented primarily in words, the visual tools that are used for the general student population such as concept maps and a semantic map could be ineffective in helping some ELLs' understanding or associating. In this situation, the teacher might consider adapting the tools accordingly by replacing words with pictures.

2. **Connect the new lesson to what students previously learned from the class.** When the teacher presents new information in the context of known information, students can more easily integrate the new knowledge and comprehend it more effectively. Having students compare a new topic to a previous text and identify common structure, threads, features, and other comparable elements help them to connect the previous learning to learn the new content.

3. **Provide ELLs with a list of essential vocabulary a day or two before teaching a new lesson.** Ask the students to use a simplified English dictionary or bilingual dictionary to learn the meanings and to look for other resources that are relevant to the words. This practice helps ELLs to identify their prior knowledge about the topic from their native languages while assisting them in building prior knowledge in English.

4. **Use students' life experiences as an essential source of their prior knowledge.** This is a powerful motivating tool as well as an important inquiry approach. For example, before reading a story about traveling by airplane, the teacher might want to ask students to reflect on the times when they have ridden in an airplane. By using students' life experiences, the content becomes more real and comprehensible. In addition, the students feel more motivated when their experiences are talked about and their cultures and backgrounds are respected.

5. **Help ELLs to reflect on their native language acquisition processes.** ELLs may use some of the strategies and skills they have developed during first-language acquisition to facilitate their English learning. However, the teacher also has to watch for negative language transfer when students incorrectly apply rules from their first languages when using English. The students will benefit from reflecting on first-language acquisition and applying relevant metacognitive skills if their misconceptions about English and English learning can be identified and corrected before being perpetuated.

Beyond the Book

- Select an excerpt from a text and analyze what prior knowledge or information students will need to have for the selection to be meaningful.
- Select a text excerpt and create an anticipation guide from that selection.
- From this text selection, create a PACA and share it with a class member to determine whether he or she has sufficient schema to make meaning from it.
- Using this same text selection, create a concept map and share it with a classmate to demonstrate how the strategy aids in the articulation of important concepts.
- Examine a text selection from the texts used in your classes. Determine which activity for prereading best fits your text and utilize it in your classroom. Share your findings with your classmates.

- Using a PACA or an anticipation guide relies to some degree on some topical knowledge. How could a teacher ensure that there is enough topical knowledge with which to use the strategy? If students do not have the knowledge, how might a teacher accommodate that situation?
- If you were to use an anticipation guide, what considerations would you need to make to ensure that students could respond effectively?

References

Ausubel, D. R. (1968). *Educational Psychology: A Cognitive View*. New York: Holt, Rinehart & Winston.

Beyer, B. K. (1971). *Inquiry in the Social Studies Classroom*. Columbus, OH: Charles E. Merrill.

Buehl, D. (2001). *Classroom Strategies for Interactive Learning*. Newark, DE: International Reading Association.

Duffelmeyer, F. A. (1994). Effective anticipation guide statements for learning from expository prose. *Journal of Reading, 37*(6), 452–457.

Frager, A. M. (1993). Affective dimensions of content area reading. *Journal of Reading, 36*(8), 616–623.

Groller, K. L., Kender, J. P., & Honeyman, D. S. (1991). Does instruction on metacognitive strategies help high school students use advance organizers? *Journal of Reading, 34*(6), 470–475.

Herber, H. L. (1978). *Teaching Reading in Content Areas*. Englewood Cliffs, NJ: Prentice Hall.

Irvin, J. (2001). *Reading Strategies for the Social Studies Classroom*. Austin, TX: Holt, Rinehart & Winston.

Langer, J. A. (1981). From theory to practice: A prereading plan. *Journal of Reading, 25*(2), 152–157.

Matas, C. (1993). *Daniel's Story*. New York: Scholastic.

McKeown, M. G., Beck, I. L., Sinatra, G. M., & Loxterman, J. A. (1992). The contribution of prior knowledge and coherent text to comprehension. *Reading Research Quarterly, 27*(1), 79–93.

Moore, D. W., & Readence, J. E. (1984). A quantitative and qualitative review of graphic organizer research. *Journal of Educational Research, 78*(1), 11–17.

Ogle, D. (2000). Make it visual: A picture is worth a thousand words. In M. McLaughlin & M. Vogt (Eds.), *Creativity and Innovation in Content Area Teaching* (pp. 55–71). Norwood, MA: Christopher-Gordon.

Rakes, G. C., Rakes, T. A., & Smith, L. J. (1995). Using visuals to enhance secondary students' reading comprehension of expository texts. *Journal of Adolescent and Adult Literacy, 39*(1), 46–55.

Sousa, D. (2005). *How the Brain Learns to Read*. Thousand Oaks, CA: Corwin Press.

8

Comprehending Text

- What comprehension strategies do proficient readers use when they read?
- How can teachers organize instruction to improve their students' comprehension?
- What literacy strategies are effective for building student comprehension of content materials?

Johanna snatched the fishing magazine away from her father to read the latest article on grouper fishing in the Gulf of Mexico. She and her dad went fishing every day they could when there were were calm seas, good weather, and low winds. The featured article was on saving the grouper population for generations to come; it discussed the restrictions put on commercial and recreational fishermen.

She thought it was pretty interesting that all grouper fish were born as females and that some of them changed to males upon maturity. She also knew that the ecosystem of the grass flats was important to the survival of the grouper population. Developers were building huge housing tracts along the coast and she worried that the increased boat traffic would damage the grass flats. She was very concerned.

The article discussed the restrictions on commercial versus recreational fishermen. She knew some families that relied on commercial fishing of grouper for their income and, indeed, she enjoyed eating a grouper sandwich ordered in a restaurant. But, what was commerical fishing doing to the grouper population? As she read the article, she was trying to think about the pros and cons of the restrictions on both commercial and recreational fishermen. She also had questions that the article did not cover. She sat back and visualized fishing for grouper with her kids.

In this scenario, Johanna demonstrated an impressive array of comprehension strategies characteristic of proficient readers. Our point here is not that Johanna is a typical young adolescent reader but that middle school teachers will readily recognize the handful of voracious readers with strong interests who devour everything they can obtain in their areas of interest. In addition, students may read more difficult text if they are interested in the topic discussed.

Proficient readers such as Johanna make connections between what they already know and new material. These connections tap into past experiences, which help them to understand new information and establish their interest and motivation for reading a specific text. Proficient readers pose questions to themselves as they read because they are curious and they realize that questioning helps them to sort through information and make sense of it. Proficient readers visualize as they read, using their imaginations to help them picture in their minds what an author represents in prose. Proficient readers are able to differentiate key ideas and information from details so that they are not overwhelmed by a mass of facts. Instead they target main themes and salient details. Proficient readers make inferences as they read between the lines, which deepens their appreciation of the information that is detailed in a text. As a result, proficient readers are able to make generalizations and draw conclusions from a text. If they encounter problems while reading—unfamiliar vocabulary, perhaps, or references to information about which they know very little—they pause to determine whether to adjust their reading or to use additional strategies to make sense of the unclear passage.

Although proficient readers employ a variety of effective strategies to guide and enhance their comprehension, many adolescents fall short in their abilities to comprehend the texts that they are asked to read in content classrooms. (Refer to the full discussion on struggling readers in Chapter 4.) With new guidelines based on the *No Child Left Behind* legislation, teachers are pressured even more to ensure that students are able to comprehend grade-level texts. State standards and their accompanying high-stakes tests now guide curriculum, instruction, and assessment in reading, writing, mathematics, and the content areas. In particular, students are expected to demonstrate their abilities to read, write, and reason to meet standards in social studies, science, math, and other content areas.

Current literacy standards tend to regard reading as an interactive and constructive process (see discussion in Chapter 2). For example, in the Reading/Language Arts Content Standards for the state of California, eighth-grade students are expected to use information from a variety of consumer, workplace, and public documents to explain a situation or decision and to solve a problem. Point-of-view essays and various types of formal reading require students to evaluate and analyze ideas (California Department of Education, 1999). Improving reading comprehension of adolescents, then, involves teaching effective reading strategies and incorporating them into the ongoing routine of learning the course content. In this chapter, a model for comprehension is presented, guidelines for instruction are suggested, and strategies for teaching comprehension are explained.

Strategies Strong Readers Use: A Comprehension Model

Many students approach school reading assignments as something to get through, rather than something to absorb, integrate, synthesize, respond to, and extend. They might put in the time, their eyes might glance over the words, but they do

not learn or remember the information because they have not thought about it. When proficient readers are engaged in reading the text, they respond to the ideas in some way. They ask themselves questions, they organize the ideas, and they connect the ideas with what they already know. Strong readers keep track of whether things make sense to them and do something to "fix up" their comprehension if they do not understand. They might use the glossary, reread, read ahead, think about the topic, or ask someone. Figure 8.1, developed by Irvin (2001), shows these thinking processes in the center of the oval surrounded by the comprehension strategies that proficient readers use before, during, and after reading. These strategies can, of course, occur simultaneously as a person reads.

- **Activate background knowledge and set a purpose for reading.** Before reading, proficient readers activate what they know about a topic by looking at the table of contents, glossary, titles, captions, section headings, and graphics. If they are about to read a story, they may consider what they know about the setting or characters or look at any pictures that are available. They pause and make connections between the text and their experiences and prior knowledge. They might skim the structure of the text for main ideas and think about what they will be expected to do with the reading, such as taking a test, writing a report, explaining a concept to someone, or applying the information in a different setting.
- **Organize knowledge.** During and after reading, proficient readers summarize the major ideas and state them in their own words. They might skim the text and reread portions to create a concept map, write a summary, create an outline, make a list of the characters and major events, or take notes. It is the organization and reorganization of knowledge that helps students to understand, remember, and use the major concepts that are presented in the text.
- **Make inferences.** Making inferences involves connecting prior knowledge with what is on the page. Strong readers make numerous inferences throughout

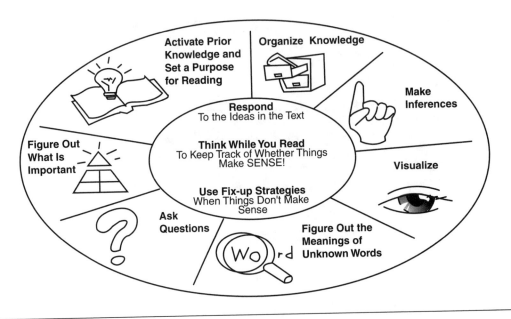

FIGURE 8.1   *Strategies Strong Readers Use: A Comprehension Model*

their reading; the accuracy of these inferences depends largely on the readers' background knowledge. It is this inference-making process that facilitates our understanding of any kind of text.

- **Visualize.** Students today are bombarded with visual information, whether from video games, television, product packaging, the ads that seem to be plastered everywhere, or the Internet. Students must analyze and interpret visual information they receive. Proficient readers can visualize the information that is presented in text whether it involves a particular setting or a description of some distant culture. Nonproficient readers do not seem to be able to use their imaginations to create pictures in their minds. Having students create concept maps, diagrams, charts, or other visual representations of the information assists students in creating these visual images. Verbal descriptions of student visualizations can help students as well.
- **Figure out the meanings of unknown words.** As students read increasingly complex text, they naturally encounter words that they do not know (referred to as "tier 2 words" in Chapter 6). Previewing text for key vocabulary and using context and morphology can help students to increase their vocabularies and comprehend the text. Chapter 6 presents a host of strategies to assist students in figuring out words they do not know.
- **Ask questions.** Before, during, and after reading, strong readers ask themselves questions such as "What do I know about this topic?" or "How does this event relate to the theme of the story?" or "What is the meaning of this concept in bold print?". These questions indicate that students are thinking about the reading and connecting the ideas in the text to their prior knowledge.

- **Figure out what is important.** One of the most common types of question on any standardized test is "finding the main idea." To comprehend text, readers must identify, remember, and summarize the major ideas presented in the text. Deciding what is important in the text should be tied to the purpose for reading. Taking notes from text, constructing a concept map, and creating an outline all involve identifying what is important in the text.

The application of these strategies depends on the purpose for reading. For example, when reading a novel, a reader might skip over a misunderstood passage or word and find that the story still makes sense; however, if studying for a test, the reader might consult a teacher for clarification. When students read to remember either a story or informational text, they must have some awareness of their own understanding. They must be alert to comprehension failure and call on their repertoire of strategies to fix the misunderstanding.

Central to these strategies is instruction in prior knowledge, text structure, and the context that enables students to comprehend text more proficiently. Struggling readers often become frustrated and give up when they do not understand. Teaching learning strategies and modeling when and how to use them gives students the essential tools to become independent readers.

Guidelines for Instruction

In the last decade, educators have made great strides toward the development of a theory of reading. Comprehension is now viewed as a much more complex process involving knowledge, experience, thinking, and teaching (Fielding & Pearson, 1994). The following guidelines for comprehension instruction can be helpful to educators in designing instruction.

1. **Focus on the process of comprehension and move toward independent learning.** The goal of instruction should be to improve students' abilities to comprehend text without the teacher's assistance. The emphasis during instruction should be on students' acquiring the ability to use comprehension strategies on their own. All too often, teachers are merely interested in the product, having students pass the test or exhibit the skill, rather than in the process, developing within students a true understanding of comprehension. In first presenting a strategy, it is best to use easy material so that students learn the process of the strategy. Then more and more difficult text can be introduced.

    Pearson and Dole (1988) suggested that teachers should model what they want their students to do and then provide guided practice opportunities in which teachers slowly and gradually turn the responsibility of completing the task over to students. (Refer to our discussion of the gradual release of responsibility in Chapter 2.) Students should then make application by actually transferring their learning to new reading materials. This scaffolding process assists students in using the strategy independently.

2. **Provide ample amounts of time for reading.** Students typically spend more time completing assignments than they do actually reading. Sustained silent reading programs are a vehicle during the busy and often fragmented school day to provide students with time to read. Silent reading provides students with practice in orchestrating skills and strategies with a variety of texts. In addition, more reading results in the acquisition of new knowledge that, in turn, helps students with future reading experiences (Fielding & Pearson, 1994).

   Teachers can improve the chances that students will increase their comprehension during silent reading by providing materials that are optimally difficult and opportunities for choice of materials and time for students to share their responses to reading with peers and adults. Reading easier material that is of high interest yet accessible to struggling readers can help students to develop fluency and confidence in reading. However, students should be encouraged to read increasingly complex, longer text containing unknown words so that they can increase their vocabulary and improve their ability to figure out the meanings of new words.

   Teachers, who discuss using strategies for figuring out unknown words before students read, help students became independent readers. In addition, students should have an opportunity to share what they have read after reading. In this way, students have an opportunity to practice what they have learned about the reading process.

3. **Provide opportunities to learn collaboratively and talk about reading.** Talking about one's understanding requires synthesis and elaboration. When students talk about their reading with each other, they learn about the strategies used by others to comprehend text.

   When I came to this word 'marginalize', I realized I didn't know what it meant, so I kept going in the passage. At the end of the section, I finally pieced together that 'marginalize' had something to do with actions that make people feel on the margins rather than in the middle of t hings.

   Members of this social studies cooperative group were able to share an effective strategy because the teacher had provided them with a structure to talk about reading. In addition, when students share their impressions, interpretations, and reactions to reading with others, the conversation elevates reading to an activity that is worthy of social interaction.

4. **Facilitate comprehension instruction before, during, and after reading.** The importance of building background information and activating prior knowledge before asking students to read is the focus of Chapter 7. Equally important is teaching students ways of being actively involved during reading, the subject of this chapter. Students should also be shown how to organize information after they read, which is especially necessary when students are studying or organizing information for later retrieval (the focus of Chapter 9).

5. **Think aloud.** Comprehension strategies can be illustrated and demonstrated by teachers sharing their own reasoning processes with students (Harvey &

Goudvis, 2000; Keene & Zimmermann, 1997). It is also helpful for students to verbalize their own thought processes with teachers and other students; "think alouds require a reader to stop periodically, reflect on how a text is being processed and understood, and relate orally to what reading strategies are being employed" (Baumann, Jones, & Seifert-Kessell, 1993, p. 3). Think-alouds can be beneficial for helping students to acquire word-learning strategies (Harmon, 2000), understand expository text structures (Gordon, 1990), and think at higher levels (Fawcett, 1993; Rosenshine & Meister, 1992). Think-alouds can also enhance students' comprehension of steps in solving mathematical problems. By listening in on the teacher's thinking process, students might find the mystery of using mathematical applications to be more accessible. Think-alouds can occur while students are working in pairs or small groups, and some teachers have used them to assess comprehension (Wade, 1990; Ward & Traweek, 1993).

6. **Reinforce and develop reading abilities through writing.** To express one's thoughts clearly in writing, one must have the ability to organize and relate information in an understandable manner. Proficient reading, like effective writing, involves building relationships between the text and the schema of the reader. Learning to read with comprehension, then, uses the same generative skills as learning to write.

   Students should be taught to read like writers (Gunther, 2000; Skeans, 2000). Effective writers are usually proficient readers as well; they tend to read more and produce more syntactically mature writing than struggling readers do. Writing instruction can generally enhance reading development. By pairing writing tasks with reading tasks, teachers reinforce reading through writing and writing through reading (Aihara, 1999; Bowman, 2000; Dickson, 1999). In addition, reinforcing reading and writing across the curriculum facilitates student literacy ability with a wide variety of texts (Lindsey, 1996). When students understand the value of writing as a process for reflection, they can improve their ability to reflect critically on issues that arise in content classes (Tierney & Shanahan, 1991).

7. **Assist students in using visual information to comprehend text.** Visual literacy involves the ability to interpret visual information such as pictures, charts, and diagrams in texts, as well as images displayed through electronic media such as the Internet or a CD-ROM. Lapp, Flood, and Ranck-Buhr (2000) suggested that our current definition of literacy must be expanded to include comprehending visual information. Researchers (Gambrell & Brooks-Jawitz, 1993; Purnell & Solman, 1991) found that pairing meaningful visual information with text assists students with comprehension and retention of information. Rakes, Rakes, and Smith (1995) suggested creating illustrations for embedded questions, using illustrations to summarize text, creating semantic maps, completing partial drawings or labeling drawings, tracing a text illustration, creating flowcharts, constructing maps, creating charts and graphs, creating icons that symbolize main ideas in text, solving

mathematics and science word problems, and using internal images as ways to help students pair text with visual images.

Hobbs (1998a, 1998b, 1999) advocated bringing the media into the classroom to assist students in analyzing the messages that are given through these media. She developed a system to help students understand media messages and become more critical consumers of advertising.

8. **Make assessment compatible with the kinds of learning encouraged.** Chapter 10 is devoted to assessment techniques that are compatible with instruction. When the assessment of comprehension becomes a seamless activity with instruction, students can document their growth in reading comprehension across a variety of texts. Assessment can be folded into instructional activities, placing the demand on students to demonstrate their understanding of content (Wiggins & McTighe, 2000). Answering higher-order questions and using analogies or reversals of outcomes give students a means of demonstrating that they can apply the information they have learned. Students move beyond a literal level of understanding and may even learn literal recall as an outgrowth of deeper engagement with the text.

Comprehension Strategies

The strategies that we present in the remaining pages of this chapter are consistent with the guidelines for instruction presented in this chapter and have been used successfully with middle school students. Strategies are presented in four categories: teacher-guided activities that facilitate comprehension before, during, and after reading; comprehension-monitoring activities; study guides; and graphic organizers.

Teacher-Guided Strategies

The strategies that we present provide teachers with the opportunity to model thinking processes and guide student thinking. All strategies have a before, during, and after reading component for facilitating comprehension.

Reciprocal Teaching

Reciprocal teaching (Palincsar & Brown, 1984, 1986) is a strategy for building reading comprehension that capitalizes on a reading apprenticeship model for learning. Every teacher can identify with the old adage that "to teach is to learn twice." Reciprocal teaching "is an instructional procedure originally designed to teach poor comprehenders how to approach text the way successful readers do" (Palincsar, Ransom, & Derber, 1989, p. 37). Teachers and students take turns talking to one another about the meaning of text. Reciprocal teaching provides the opportunity for both teacher guidance and modeling and eventual student independence. With this strategy, the adult and the students take turns leading the dialogue. The strategy models four essential components of comprehension: questioning, summarizing, clarifying, and predicting.

Step 1. **Teacher think-alouds are an excellent method for modeling the cognitive behavior involved in reading comprehension.** Periodically, teachers can share a piece of challenging text they are reading and model their own reasoning as they attempt to understand it. Students need opportunities to listen in as real readers struggle with real-world texts. These think-alouds underscore that proficient readers are constantly engaged in an active mission to make sense of what they read.

During a think-aloud, teachers make explicit reference to the four comprehension behaviors they are employing. For example, they might use questioning to talk their way through a passage. Why does the author tell me this? What seems to be the most important point or idea? Did I understand this correctly? Some questions will relate to salient details, but many of them should target understanding of the passage as a whole.

Next, teachers recap what they read by summarizing: "Basically this section is about. . . ." When modeling summarizing, teachers emphasize that a proficient reader hits the mental pause button every few paragraphs and paraphrases what was read to "make sure you got it." Emphasize that summarizing targets the main idea or gist of a passage and is not merely a litany of details.

Clarifying is the process of identifying aspects of the text that were not totally clear. A proficient reader might use a number of fix-up strategies to clarify: rereading, reading on until confusions are eventually resolved, zeroing in on difficult vocabulary, consulting with another reader, and so forth. Clarifying might also point out shortcomings in the text and focus on what an author could have done to make a passage more understandable.

Finally, a proficient reader is constantly thinking ahead, predicting where a passage might be going. Sometimes the predicting goes beyond a text, as a reader infers certain attitudes or beliefs on the part of an author. Predicting helps to develop a purpose for reading, as readers continue through a text to confirm or disprove their hunches about the material.

Step 2. **The teacher leads the students in using reciprocal teaching to problem solve their way through a piece of challenging classroom text.** Segments of the text can be displayed on an overhead transparency as the teacher models this process with the opening section. Then the teacher solicits student volunteers to generate questions, summarize sections, clarify meaning, and make predictions.

For example, students who are struggling with a life science textbook chapter that is packed with detailed information and unfamiliar vocabulary begin to obtain a feel for talking themselves through dense, challenging material. Here are some examples of useful questions.

- How are vertebrates different from invertebrates?
- What characteristics do all vertebrates share?
- What are some examples of vertebrates?
- Why does the author provide the information in this paragraph?

Students might focus on difficult vocabulary as they move through the clarification phase. Individuals are called on to summarize each section, and familiarity with textbook features might prompt students to use visuals as well as text information to make predictions about what will be discussed in the next part.

Step 3. **As students become practiced in reciprocal teaching, they can follow this procedure in cooperative groups.** Students trade off assuming the role of teacher in their groups as they lead their classmates through the four comprehension phases. The student teacher asks questions about a section and members of the group answer. The student teacher looks for anything that was confusing or not totally clear and comments as the group tries to resolve the problem. Finally, the student teacher summarizes the section and makes a prediction about what might be next. The group goes on to read the next portion of the text, and another student assumes the role of teacher.

Reciprocal teaching generally does not run smoothly the first time. Initially, teachers must spend time helping students to generate good questions, make predictions based on the text, and create summaries that are shortened versions of the text. But as students become more and more proficient and comfortable with the steps, reciprocal teaching can be a powerful tool for helping students to understand and internalize the comprehension process. This procedure can be used with individuals or groups.

Reciprocal teaching has been the object of much investigation (Brown & Palincsar, 1985; Palincsar, 1984) and is regarded by researchers as a highly effective method for teaching reading comprehension. Reciprocal teaching provides students with a window into the thinking of proficient readers as they problem solve their way toward meaning, and struggling readers are conditioned to approach reading as an active and strategic process. As a result, students learn behaviors that will help them to become more independent readers, capable of handling increasingly sophisticated material. Teachers have also reported that they experienced fewer behavior problems during reciprocal teaching because students were actively involved in the lesson and enjoyed playing the role of the teacher (Palincsar & Brown, 1984).

The K-W-L Plus Strategy

Developed by Ogle (1986), the K-W-L (Know, Want to Know, Learned) strategy provides an organization for students. This simple-to-use yet powerful procedure can be completed individually, in small groups, or with the entire class. Group discussions can help students to generate ideas and foster interest in the subject. This strategy is deceptively sophisticated, as it engages students in making connections to prior knowledge, self-questioning, determining the importance of information while reading, organizing learning, and summarizing. The following steps illustrate how this strategy might be used in an environmental science class that is studying the reintroduction of predators such as wolves into national parks and forests.

Step 1. **The teacher provides a chart in which students fill in the K column with what they know about a topic.** This step is, of course, designed to activate prior and topical knowledge and allow students to brainstorm ideas. After brainstorming as a class or small group, students fill in the column individually.

In our environmental science example, the teacher informs the students that they will be studying the impact of the reintroduction of predators and other species into wild areas. Students are asked to consider what they know about wolves and their reintroduction (see Figure 8.2).

Step 2. **Students categorize the information they have generated and anticipate categories of information they may find in the reading.** These categories serve as an impetus for further information and anticipation about the topic as well as a structure for the mapping and summarizing steps. Identifying categories that might emerge is helpful in providing a stimulus for beginning to organize information. These categories could be revised throughout the process. Categories about the reintroduction of wolves may be location, food, habits, and threats to survival.

Step 3. **The teacher leads a discussion to help students pull together information and formulate questions for reading.** The teacher might wish to write statements on the chalkboard; in this way, student knowledge can be shared. Although most students know that wolves had disappeared from most areas, some students may not have realized that the government is bringing them back in some parts of the country. Statements might be revised as the discussion continues.

K (What I Know)	W (What I Want to Learn)	L (What I Learned)
wolves were eliminated through hunting in many areas		
wolves threaten livestock such as cattle and sheep		
wolves fear humans		
wolves aren't really threatening to humans		
ranchers used poison carcasses to kill wolves		
wolves live in packs		
wolves are unpopular in many western states		
wolves are related to coyotes		
wolves keep the deer or elk population down		

FIGURE 8.2   *KWL Chart: K Column*

Step 4. **As a result of sharing and discussion, students then fill in the W column of the chart.** This step may be completed either individually or in a large group. One way to think about this column is to write down what one might want to know about a topic. These tentative questions help students to set a purpose for reading and focus their attention while they are reading. A sample chart may look like Figure 8.3.

Step 5. **Students read the selection.** The text should be divided into manageable units. Students should be encouraged to interrupt their reading after one or two paragraphs to determine whether any of their questions were answered or to make notes in the L column. As students have additional questions, they can add them to the W column. Students also use the text to confirm or reject items that were proposed for the K column. The text becomes a source to correct misinformation offered by the class during the brainstorming of knowledge phase.

Step 6. **Students fill in the L column of the chart, listing the things that they learned from the reading.** A completed chart might look like Figure 8.4. The primary value of this part of the activity is that information is shared among the students. Thus, this strategy activates and builds on the prior and topical knowledge of the individual and of the class as a whole. Students learn to see each other as sources of information, an experience that fosters the emotional well-being of the adolescents.

Step 7. **Mapping.** Students use the K-W-L worksheet to construct a semantic map (Carr & Ogle, 1987). Semantic maps help students to understand relationships among ideas. The categories that were established before reading can serve as the major headings of the map, and the information learned

K (What I Know)	W (What I Want to Learn)	L (What I Learned)
wolves were eliminated through hunting in many areas	How successful have the reintroductions been?	
wolves threaten livestock such as cattle and sheep	Are people still killing wolves?	
wolves fear humans	Do wolves present a danger to humans?	
wolves aren't really threatening to humans	What is the normal diet of a wolf in the wild?	
ranchers used poison carcasses to kill wolves	Do wolves mate for life?	
wolves live in packs	Won't wolves make national parks more dangerous for tourists?	
wolves are unpopular in many western states	What is a "lone wolf"?	
wolves are related to coyotes	What states now have wolves?	
wolves keep the deer or elk population down	How far do wolves travel once they have been reintroduced?	
	Is trapping of wolves still permitted?	

FIGURE 8.3   *KWL Chart: K-W Columns*

during reading can serve as supporting data for the map. A sample map of the reintroduction of wolves is presented in Figure 8.5.

Step 8. **Summarizing.** Students use the map to produce a summary. Preparing a written summary has been shown to improve comprehension (Brown & Day, 1983) because it helps students to distinguish between important ideas and background details. The categories on the map can be numbered and serve as topic sentences.

Sippola (1995) modified the K-W-L by adding a fourth column titled "What I still need to learn," which can serve as an impetus for further inquiry. The K-W-L Plus has been used successfully in high school classrooms and has been found to improve comprehension monitoring, enhance student awareness of content and how it is structured, and provide opportunities to summarize information (Carr & Ogle, 1987). It is a procedure that involves students in the learning process before, during, and after reading.

Questioning the Author

Questioning the Author (QtA) (Beck, McKeown, Hamilton, & Kucan, 1997) is a strategy that is especially appropriate for helping students cope with challenging content materials. QtA conditions students to think about what the author is saying, not

K	W	L
(What I Know)	**(What I Want to Learn)**	**(What I Learned)**
wolves were eliminated through hunting in many areas	How successful have the reintroductions been?	reappearance of wolves has generated much controversy
wolves threaten livestock such as cattle and sheep	Are people still killing wolves?	some are still hunted and killed
wolves fear humans	Do wolves present a danger to humans?	gray wolf was once one of the most widely distributed mammals on earth
wolves aren't really threatening to humans	What is the normal diet of a wolf in the wild?	wolves are highly intelligent, very loyal, and social
ranchers used poison carcasses to kill wolves	Do wolves mate for life?	wolves are feared because of stereotypes and fairy tales
wolves live in packs	Won't wolves make national parks more dangerous for tourists?	wolves have killed livestock and pets like dogs and cats
wolves are unpopular in many western states	What is a "lone wolf"?	wolves were reintroduced in north and west, Yellowstone National Park, Minnesota, Wisconsin, and Michigan
wolves are related to coyotes	What states now have wolves?	wolves have traveled 550 miles from home territory
wolves keep the deer or elk population down	How far do wolves travel once they have been reintroduced?	wolves eat a lot of rodents
	Is trapping of wolves still permitted?	wolves help with overpopulation of other species

FIGURE 8.4   *KWL Chart: K-W-L Columns*

what the "textbook states." Students have a tendency to consider their textbooks as having been anonymously written rather than being the work of authors who might not always have been successful in communicating their ideas to the reader. This becomes an especially critical issue when there is a mismatch between the text and the students, when the author assumes prior knowledge and a level of reading ability that may be uncharacteristic of many of the text's readers.

Step 1. **Establish the authorship of text materials to be read by students.** For example, a math teacher might ask: "Who is talking to you in this book?". Students then examine their math textbooks to identify the authors by name and locate any biographical information that provides insight into who these individuals are. Students are encouraged to consider the perspective these authors bring to the book: that of university professors, experts in the field, or classroom educators.

Step 2. **Model self-questioning as a think-aloud.** The teacher selects a passage from the textbook and models a self-questioning process that focuses on

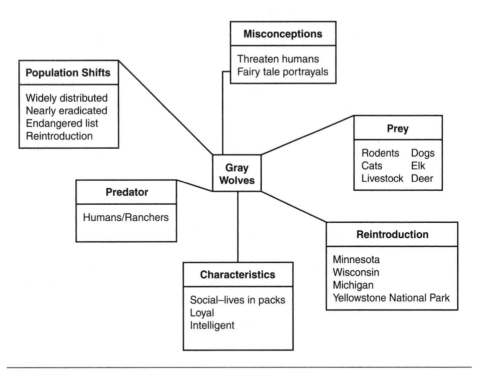

FIGURE 8.5   *Map from KWL*

what the authors expect from the readers and on whether any pitfalls to comprehension seem to be present. What do the authors expect students to know? What is not clear or easy to understand? What could the authors add or change to make this passage easier to understand? The math teacher might note that the author apparently believes that the reader knows the meanings of terms such as "expression," "whole number," and "variable" because these terms are used with no explanation or elaboration. The teacher might also note that the author should have continued discussing a sample problem because its solution was not apparent.

Although some textbooks clearly fall short, as is discussed in Chapter 5, the intent of the QtA process is not to condemn textbooks as poorly written; instead, the teacher emphasizes the dual responsibilities of readers and writers. Writers have a responsibility to communicate their ideas clearly to the audience they are targeting, and readers have the responsibility to make an effort to use their prior knowledge and clues offered by the author to make sense of a passage.

Step 3. **The teacher previews a section of the textbook that will be assigned for reading.** The teacher analyzes what is most important for students to understand from this passage and identifies segments that might prove challenging for students. The teacher then decides where students will pause in the text to discuss or clarify key points. For a QtA activity the teacher leads the discussion at predetermined breaks in the text. Students might read a paragraph or two before a discussion break, or the teacher might wish to follow a single pivotal sentence with discussion.

Beck and her colleagues (1997) advocated discussion that is focused on author queries, not the typical questions that are asked about specific information. The teacher generates questions related to the author's intentions: What is the author trying to say here? What is the author's message? Did the author explain this clearly? How does this connect with what the author has told us before? What does the author expect the reader to know already? Why do you think the author tells us this?

The teacher's role during QtA discussions is to model how a proficient reader endeavors to make sense of sometimes confusing or inadequate text. As the discussion about what the author is trying to communicate unfolds, the teacher is active in affirming key points offered by students, sometimes paraphrasing them, and turning students' attention to the text for clarification of specific issues. At times, gaps in the text might need to be augmented by the teacher's providing additional information.

Step 4. **As students become comfortable responding to QtA queries, the teacher can ask them to generate their own for a section of the textbook.** Working with a partner, students lightly pencil in an asterisk or use a sticky note in a couple of places in the text where they believe a reader should stop and ponder. Then they should select one or more questions from a list of author queries (which could be displayed as a classroom poster or provided to each student as a bookmark) that a reader might ask at each of these junctures. For added practice, teachers could pair sets of partners into groups of four and have them pose their queries to each other.

QtA discussions can be used to introduce selections that students will continue to read independently, perhaps as homework. These discussions are especially helpful when students need assistance coping with difficult but important segments of a chapter. QtA discussions are also valuable as a comprehension-building strategy for struggling readers. The strength of QtA discussions is derived from the modeling of appropriate problem-solving questions. Students are taught to be metacognitive readers who actively monitor their comprehension during reading.

Comprehension-Monitoring Activities

For students to become independent learners, they must monitor their own comprehension. The strategies that follow are designed to help students become more proficient in using metacognitive processes.

A Self-Monitoring Approach to Reading and Thinking (SMART)

A Self-Monitoring Approach to Reading and Thinking (SMART) is a strategy that helps students to identify what they do and do not understand in their reading. Vaughn and Estes (1986) described the steps that compose SMART. These steps are many, but they are simple and easy to use.

Step 1. **Students place a check mark in the margin if they understand what they are reading and place a question mark in the margin if they do not understand what they are reading.** A paper folded three times lengthwise with page numbers at the top makes a handy substitute for marking in the margins of the book. Sticky notes may also be used.

Step 2. **After each section of the assignment, students paraphrase the facts and ideas that they have understood. Students may look back at the text while they do this.**

Step 3. **After each section, students examine the ideas that they did not understand and then do the following.**

- Read the parts that were not understood. If they understand something now that was previously unclear, change the question mark to a check mark.
- If the idea remains unclear, try to specify what is causing the problem. Is it a word? a phrase? a relationship?
- Consider taking an action to help themselves understand (such as using the glossary, examining pictures or diagrams in the text, reviewing another part of the text) and try it. Again, if the strategy works, change the question mark to a check mark.
- Finally, try to clarify the ideas that still cause misunderstanding.

Step 4. **Have students study the entire assignment using the first three steps.** Students might find it useful to divide the assignment into sections. After studying the entire assignment, students should be instructed to do the following:

- Close the book and review the ideas that you understand. Some people do this by talking out loud to themselves.
- Look back at the book and refresh your memory for anything you left out.
- Reexamine the ideas that you do not understand. Think about those ideas. What could these ideas possibly mean? Is there anything else you could do to better understand?
- Close the book one last time and review what you do understand.

Students should be encouraged to think about information rather than memorize it. Students often ask for help without seeking a solution for themselves. By requiring them to specify what they do not understand (e.g., a word, a phrase, a relationship) and explain what they did to try to understand it, this strategy encourages students to solve problems independently whenever possible. Thus, SMART enables students to develop their metacognitive abilities and to have more control of their reading.

Paired Readings

Working under the assumption that two heads are better than one, Dansereau (1977) suggested paired readings as a means of helping students to learn and retain more of what they have learned.

Step 1. **Two students silently read a short segment of an assignment (about 600 words).** The student who finishes first can reread the material for the important points. After reading, both students put the material out of sight.

Step 2. **When both students have finished reading, the recaller orally retells what was read without referring back to the text.** One student (the recaller) recalls the information in the text and the other student (the listener) listens. During the retelling, the listener should interrupt the retelling to obtain clarification.

Step 3. **After the retelling, the listener should do two things: point out and correct any ideas that were summarized incorrectly and add any ideas that were not included in retelling that the listener thinks should have been included.** The two students work together to note as many ideas as possible.

Step 4. **Students should alternate roles after each segment.** Students tend to recall information better this way than if they worked alone. Students also enjoy working with a partner.

Students learn from each other's points of view and thinking strategies. To facilitate this learning, students should be encouraged to share their reasoning strategies with each other. Students understand material better because they have read the information in short segments and have spoken and listened to the information. One student might understand something that confuses the other. This activity strengthens students' metacognitive abilities while providing them with an opportunity to work cooperatively with others.

Study Guides

The purpose of a study guide is to lead students through a reading assignment and focus their attention on main points, thereby improving their metacognition. Study guides can motivate students by providing a structure for them, thus encouraging them to become active rather than passive readers. Group work seems to be especially effective when study guides are used.

Well-designed study guides are more than merely worksheets with an array of questions. The construction of a study guide takes time and effort. Teachers should first focus on the major points to be learned and the reading abilities to be practiced. Overcrowded print may confuse students; thus, the urge to overload students with information should be resisted. Teachers should try to make the study guide interesting. Students usually need to be talked through the study guide before they begin reading. As students become more and more proficient in the use of study guides, the teacher can make the study guides less detailed, thus releasing some of the responsibility to students as they are able to handle it. Chapter 4 presents the interactive reading guide as one type of study guide. The textbook activity guide provides another example of a study guide that may be helpful in leading students through difficult reading.

Textbook Activity Guide

The Textbook Activity Guide (TAG) facilitates the active involvement of students using content-area materials through cooperative activities. TAGs take time to construct, but students benefit from that time. The steps in constructing a TAG include selection of learning objectives and location of features in the text that best facilitate the mastery of those objectives. A sample TAG for an earth science text-book passage on freshwater pollution is presented in Figure 8.6.

Davey (1986) suggested that TAGs be used for only a limited amount of time at first (twenty minutes). She found that secondary school students benefited from using the TAG because it encouraged active involvement in textbook reading and assisted them in monitoring their comprehension of that reading. The teacher's role is to help students become independent learners. As students become better able to read expository text successfully and independently, the TAGs can be less structured. Some students have enjoyed making TAGs for other students.

FIGURE 8.6   *Textbook Activity Guide: Freshwater Pollution*

Strategy codes:

DP = Read and discuss with your partner
PP = Predict with your partner
WR = Each partner writes response on separate paper
Map = Complete the concept map
Skim = Read quickly for the purpose stated; discuss with your partner

Self-monitoring codes:
 _+_ I understand the information
 _/_   I'm not sure if I fully understand this information
 _?_ I do not understand this information. I need to restudy.

1. PP pp. 411–418—title and headings
   What do you think we will learn from this section?
   List at least eight things.

(continued)

2. DP p. 411—headings and first four paragraphs
   Consider the last sentence in the introduction: "Water pollution can affect surface water, groundwater, and even rain and results from both natural causes and human activities."
   What are some examples from the passage?
   What are some other examples that you can think of?

3. WR p. 412—table in Figure 10
   Why might it be helpful to know the source of a particular pollutant detected in a body of water?

4. Skim p. 413—last two paragraphs
   Purpose: Distinguish between "point source" and "nonpoint source" and connect to pollution

5. DP pp. 413–414
   Classify the following as point sources or nonpoint sources of water pollution.
   _____ salt used on icy roads
   _____ an open drain in a sink at a paint factory
   _____ a sanitary sewer pipe with a leak
   _____ fertilizer sprayed onto an orange grove

6. WR pp. 415–417
   a. Explain why people are often instructed to boil drinking water after a flood.
   b. To prevent water pollution, a factory proposes pumping its wastes into the ground instead of into a river. Would you support this change? Why or why not?

7. DP Map entire section, pp. 411–418
   Consider the sources of freshwater pollution, the kinds of pollutants, and examples. Fill in the blanks and add any missing sections.

Summary

Traditionally, reading has been viewed as a collection of discrete subskills, each of which could be tested and taught. Many modern educational theorists, however, have come to view reading as a whole that is greater than the sum of its parts. Reading is comprehension, and only by emphasizing the process of comprehension will we help students to acquire knowledge of what reading means.

Students must acquire a repertoire of learning strategies to help them deal effectively with problems in comprehension. Teachers can model, guide, and provide feedback, but students must learn how to apply these strategies to their own reading.

Extending Learning

Reviewing the Talking Points

Revisit the talking points at the beginning of this chapter. Answer the questions now that you have read the chapter and compare your prereading and postreading responses.

Revisiting the Vignette

In the opening vignette there is a description of a reader who is enthralled with the content and her engagement leads her to extended thinking about the topic of grouper fishing. Think back to your own experiences as a learner and remember a time when you were as engaged as Johanna was while reading. What was it about that material that interested you and guided you to learn more about it? Share with your classmates and determine what common features in those experiences lead to some generalizations about how to engage learners.

Terms to Remember and Use

visualize	inferences	comprehension failure	model
high interest	think-aloud	embedded questions	higher-order questions
reciprocal teaching	K-W-L Plus	SMART	study guides
TAG	QtA	paired readings	metacognition

Write a series of sentences that meaningfully connect pairs of the above key terms. Your sentences should refer to ideas and concepts related to the literacy of middle school students.

Modifying Instruction for English Language Learners

Many comprehension strategies have proven beneficial for helping students to understand various texts. However, some strategies designed for mainstream students need to be adapted for English language learners. Prior experiences, background knowledge, and cultural considerations are the primary factors that teachers should attend to when considering which strategies to use with ELLs. For example, Questioning the Author (QtA) may be a natural response for native English-speaking students during reading, but it could be viewed as disrespectful or threatening by students from cultures in which authority is highly regarded and authors are generally regarded as knowledgeable experts. In this case, teachers could word their prompting questions or clues differently to make them less obtrusive. When some comprehension strategies do not work for ELLs, teachers should discover whether the problems are related to particular learning habits, cultures, or thinking patterns.

ELLs benefit when teachers teach comprehension strategies explicitly. In most cases, students would not develop these strategies by themselves. Teachers have to articulate them even more explicitly for ELLs—with more emphasis on procedures and simpler, more understandable language. Labeling, defining, modeling, and explaining are the important steps in introducing a strategy or skill to ELLs. For example, after listing four facts about good eating habits and four opinions about what are good eating habits, students label one list as *facts* and the other list as *opinions*.

Creative use of student grouping can be another way to help promote learning and application of comprehension strategies. Teachers might consider pairing or grouping ELLs with more proficient readers (or native English speakers) for some reading activities. Besides teachers, peers who have better reading skills can also serve as excellent models through their demonstrations of some comprehending process and activities such as inferring and think-alouds. The same groups or pairs, however, should not be together for an extended period of time. Otherwise, it could lead to frustration of ELLs and boredom on the part of more proficient readers. A combination of comprehension strategy instruction, modeling, practice, and application is crucial. Moreover, corrective/formative feedback from the teachers is necessary for ELLs to learn the strategies and hone their reading skills. Finally, incorporating a review of the whole process would contribute to the overall effectiveness of comprehension instruction.

Beyond the Book

- Interview a middle school core subject teacher and pose questions about the kinds of strategies the teacher uses to help students with comprehension.
- Do an Internet search on one or more of the strategies listed in this chapter. Share pertinent background information with classmates to widen their knowledge base of the strategy's application.
- Interview a middle school student and determine whether the student can explain what strategies he or she uses to aid in comprehension. If the student is unable to articulate this, ask him or her to engage in a think-aloud while you transcribe or record what the student says. Share the results with classmates to gain insights into how this student copes with reading.
- Select a reading selection from a topic that you know little or nothing about. Record your own strategies as you try to make sense of the reading.
- Do an Internet search on the *No Child Left Behind* legislation to find out what implications the act has for content teachers to ensure that students increase their comprehension of grade-level text.
- Select one of the comprehension strategies listed in this chapter. Match it to a text selection and create the strategy based on that selection. Practice delivering the strategy either to some classmates or to one of the classes that you teach.
- Read a passage of a text that is somewhat familiar to you. Determine whether you can make inferences about topics or subtopics that relate to that reading and write them down. Then compare them to a classmate's inferences based on the same reading.
- Discuss with a classmate which of the strategies in the chapter might work best in certain content areas.

References

Aihara, K. (1999). The reading writing connection for struggling readers. *Reading Teacher 53*(3), 206–208.

Baumann, J. F., Jones, L. A., & Seifert-Kessell, N. (1993). *Monitoring Reading Comprehension by Thinking Aloud.* (Instructional Resource No. 1). Athens, GA: National Reading Research Center.

Beck, I., McKeown, M., Hamilton, R., & Kucan, L. (1997). *Questioning the Author: An Approach for Enhancing Student Engagement with Text.* Newark, DE: International Reading Association.

Bowman, C. A. (2000). Creating connection: Challenging the text and student writers. *English Journal, 89*(4), 78–84.

Brown, A. L., & Day, J. D. (1983). Macrorules for summarizing texts: The development of expertise. *Journal of Verbal Learning, 22*(1), 1–4.

Brown, A. L., & Palincsar, A. S. (1985). *Reciprocal Teaching of Comprehension Strategies: A Natural History of One Program for Enhancing Learning.* (Tech. Rep. No. 334). Champaign, IL: Center for the Study of Reading.

California Department of Education. (1999). *Reading/Language Arts Framework for California Public Schools.* Sacramento, CA: Author.

Carr, E., & Ogle, D. (1987). K-W-L Plus: A strategy for comprehension and summarization. *Journal of Reading, 30*(7), 626–631.

Dansereau, D. F. (1977). How to create and maintain a crummy mood. In D.F. Dansereau (Ed.), *Instructional packet: Techniques of college learning.* Ft. Worth, TX: Christian University.

Davey, B. (1986). Using textbook activity guides to help students learn from textbooks. *Journal of Reading, 29*(6), 489–494.

Dickson, S. (1999). Integrating reading and writing to teach compare-contrast text structure: A research-based methodology. *Reading and Writing Quarterly: Overcoming Learning Difficulties, 15*(1), 49–79.

Fawcett, G. (1993). Using students as think aloud models. *Reading Research and Instruction, 33*(2), 95–104.

Fielding, L. G., & Pearson, P. D. (1994). Reading comprehension: What works. *Educational Leadership, 51*(5), 62–67.

Gambrell, L. B., & Brooks-Jawitz, P. B. (1993). Mental imagery, text illustrations, and children's story comprehension and recall. *Reading Research Quarterly, 28*(3), 265–276.

Gordon, C. J. (1990). Modeling an expository text structure strategy in think alouds. *Reading Horizons, 31*(2), 149–167.

Gunther, M. A. (2000). Critical analysis of literature: Making the connection between reading and writing. *English Journal, 89*(4), 85–88.

Harmon, J. M. (2000). Assessing and supporting independent word learning strategies of middle school students. *Journal of Adolescent and Adult Literacy, 43*(6), 518–527.

Harvey, S., & Goudvis, A. (2000). *Strategies That Work: Teaching Comprehension to Enhance Understanding.* York, ME: Stenhouse Publishers.

Hobbs, R. (1998a). The seven great debates in the media literacy movement. *Journal of Communication, 48*(1), 16–32.

Hobbs, R. (1998b). The Simpsons meet Mark Twain: Analyzing popular media texts in the classroom. *English Journal, 87*(1), 49–52.

Hobbs, R. (1999). Media literacy: Teaching the humanities in a media age: The re-visioning project helps high school teachers analyze how language, visual images, editing, and composition can affect our interpretation of ideas. *Educational Leadership, 56*(5), 55–57.

Irvin, J. L. (2001). *Reading Strategies in the Social Studies Classroom.* Austin, TX: Holt, Rinehart & Winston.

Keene, E., & Zimmermann, S. (1997). *Mosaic of Thought: Teaching Comprehension in a Reader's Workshop.* Portsmouth, NH: Heinemann.

Lapp, D., Flood, J., & Ranck-Buhr, W. (2000). Visual literacy. In K. D. Wood & T. S. Dickinson (Eds.), *Promoting Literacy in Grades 4–9: A Handbook for Teachers and Administrators* (pp. 317–330). Boston: Allyn & Bacon.

Lindsey, M. (1996). Connections between reading and writing: What the experts say. *The Clearinghouse, 70*(2), 103–105.

Ogle, D. M. (1986). K-W-L: A teaching model that develops active reading of expository text. *The Reading Teacher, 39*(6), 564–570.

Palincsar, A. S. (1984). The quest for meaning from expository text: A teacher guided journey. In G. G. Duffy, L. R. Roehler, & J. Mason (Eds.), *Comprehension Instruction: Perspectives and Suggestions* (pp. 251–264). New York: Longman.

Palincsar, A. S., & Brown, A. L. (1984). Reciprocal teaching of comprehension-fostering and comprehension-monitoring activities. *Cognition and Instruction, 1*(2), 117–175.

Palincsar, A. S., & Brown, A. L. (1986). Interactive teaching to promote independent learning from text. *The Reading Teacher, 39*(8), 771–777.

Palincsar, A. S., Ransom, K., & Derber, S. (1989). Collaborative research and development of reciprocal teaching. *Educational Leadership, 46*(4), 37–41.

Pearson, P. D., & Dole, J. A. (1988). *Explicit Comprehension Instruction: A Review of Research and a New Conceptualization of Instruction* (Tech. Rep. No. 427). Champaign, IL: Center for the Study of Reading.

Purnell, K. N., & Solman, R. T. (1991). The influence of technical illustrations on students' comprehension in geography. *Reading Research Quarterly, 27*(3), 277–298.

Rakes, G. C., Rakes, T. A., & Smith, L. J. (1995). Using visuals to enhance secondary students' reading comprehension of expository texts. *Journal of Adolescent and Adult Literacy, 39*(1), 46–54.

Rosenshine, B., & Meister, C. (1992). The use of scaffolds for teaching higher-level cognitive strategies. *Educational Leadership, 49*(7), 26–33.

Sippola, A. E. (1995). K-W-L-S. *The Reading Teacher, 48*(6), 542–589.

Skeans, S. S. (2000). Reading . . . with pen in hand! *English Journal, 89*(4), 69–72.

Tierney, R. J., & Shanahan, T. (1991). Research on the reading-writing relationship: Interactions, transactions, and outcomes. In R. Barr, M. L. Kamil, P. Mosenthal, & P. D. Pearson (Eds.), *Handbook of Reading Research*, Vol. II (pp. 246–280). New York: Longman.

Vaughn, J. L., & Estes, T. H. (1986). *Reading and Reasoning Beyond the Primary Grades*. Boston: Allyn & Bacon.

Wade, S. E. (1990). Using think-alouds to assess comprehension. *The Reading Teacher, 43*(7), 442–451.

Ward, L., & Traweek, D. (1993). Application of a metacognitive strategy to assessment, intervention, and consultation: A think-aloud technique. *Journal of School Psychology, 31*(4), 469–485.

Wiggins, G., & McTighe, J. (2000). *Understanding by Design*. Alexandra, VA: Association of Supervision and Curriculum Development.

9

Using Study Strategies to Learn and Remember

Talking Points _____

- How is studying different from reading an assignment and completing homework?
- What role can teachers play in developing effective study habits in their students?
- How can teachers incorporate the teaching of study strategies into their ongoing classroom routines?

Studying in most classes means filling out the study sheet reviewed in class and glancing over it on the bus on the way to school, hoping that the items on the exam matched the items on the study guide. Then, Ms. Matthews came along. She expected students to study during the entire unit of study, not just at the end before the exam. After studying a topic, Ms. Matthews required students to construct a concept map—usually completed individually and then shared in small groups. Then, students had to take the information in the concept map and write a summary of key points or explain it to someone else.

Theresa, a student in Ms. Matthews class, at first resented the time taken to do all this summary work. But, she quickly learned that if you spend the time to learn and organize the material, studying for the exam is easy.

Teachers like Ms. Matthews can help their students see studying differently. Instead of cramming for an exam and forgetting the material, studying can serve the purpose of learning and actually remembering. Unlike reading for pleasure, most school reading tasks center on the acquisition of information, or reading to learn. Strategies for remembering—that is, studying—involve reading for meaning and much more. Readers who have a specific academic goal in mind must be able to choose among important ideas and organize these ideas to remember them. To achieve this organization, study strategies such as outlining, summarizing, underlining, and notetaking have been emphasized in high schools for many years. In this chapter, the importance of depth of processing, five generalizations about strategic learning, and strategies for teaching study strategies are presented, and examples are provided.

Depth of Processing

What do students do when they study? Students like Theresa would describe study behaviors that generally involve review, or what Buehl (1995) referred to as "studying by looking." To prepare for a test, for example, they would look over the chapter, look over their notes, look over their homework, or look over the study guide. In contrast, students whose study involves some sort of reformulation of the material practice "studying by doing." They recite in their own words, summarize, make flashcards, predict questions, use memory strategies, quiz each other with a partner, and so forth. They are engaged in a deeper processing of the material.

Students taking notes might merely copy an author's words or they might synthesize and summarize ideas into a graphic organizer. The former is a fairly passive task, whereas the latter indicates deep processing—an understanding of the major concepts presented in the text. Deep processing is facilitated by strategies such as chapter mapping that allow readers to connect ideas in the text to each other and to their prior knowledge. Although taking notes and underlining the text can be useful study strategies, it is best for students to employ such strategies as a means for understanding relationships between ideas.

Sousa (2001) made a distinction between *classroom review* (the teacher goes over key concepts and reminds students of what was learned) and *closure* (students themselves summarize what they have learned). Students might listen and recall information during a teacher review, but closure involves much deeper processing. When a social studies teacher reserves the last five minutes of a class period for asking students to summarize the causes of the American Revolution, the teacher is encouraging the class to sum up their learning before they leave for the day and to check their understanding and retention of important unit concepts. This study activity could take the form of a think-pair-share activity (Chapter 3) or a written entry in their notebooks.

Brown (1985) advised that for effective study, "effort must be coupled with strategic ingenuity" (p. 5). Some teachers use learning logs or journals to assist students in the metacognitive awareness that it takes to monitor understanding (Commander & Smith, 1996). These logs help students to evaluate their study and performance on tests, make their strategies for organizing material more public, and give teachers a starting point for discussing effective strategies for studying. Learning logs can thus assist students with the "how" of learning as well as the "what" and "why."

Whatever the task, students must actively engage in learning the material by organizing information, remembering, and demonstrating learning at a later time. Teachers can help students to identify the important ideas in a text by engaging students in a dialogue about how important ideas are selected and what relationship these ideas have to one another. Successful study occurs when students monitor their understanding of the important ideas in text and select a strategy that matches the task.

Identifying Important Ideas

Differentiating important ideas from background details is a necessary step if new material is to be understood, remembered, and then connected to one's own prior knowledge. Finding the main idea is an essential comprehension strategy; learners need to become skilled at determining the point of a passage. Many middle school students resemble our extraterrestrial in the supermarket (described in Chapter 2): They end their reading with a lot of details in mind, but they have not seen the big picture of a selection. Two strategies that guide students in mentally sorting what is essential from what is background are presented in the following sections: coding text and underlining or highlighting.

Text Coding

Text coding is a relatively simple procedure to help students become more involved in their reading, make decisions as they read, and clarify their own understanding. The strategy consists of a marking system that records the students' reactions to what is being read and prompts them to monitor their comprehension. As a variation for use with texts that cannot be marked, the teacher could provide students with small sticky notes, which can be affixed to the margin for writing text codes. In addition, Tovani (2000) recommended using double-entry diaries, a simple note-taking format that involves drawing a line down the center of a notebook page. The left side of the paper is reserved for phrases that are taken from the text; students use the right side to place the code and jot down thoughts they had at that point in the reading. Figure 9.1 presents a portion of a double

Quote from the Reading	My Thinking
"Immigrant workers trapped on the upper floors during the Triangle Shirtwaist fire jumped to certain deaths rather than remaining in the flaming factory." [page 221]	R—I am reminded of the 911 terrorist attacks at the World Trade Center, when people also leaped to their deaths to escape the fire. Thinking about 911 helps me understand this factory tragedy for these workers.

FIGURE 9.1   *Double Entry Diary*

entry diary used to respond to a U.S. history textbook passage on the rise of unions during industrialization.

Most students, especially those who struggle with reading assignments, do not understand that to comprehend text involves responding to it in some way. In fact, some struggling readers do not realize that thinking is necessary while one reads. Proficient readers integrate the information in the text with what they already know. They constantly make decisions or have a running conversation with themselves, such as the following.

- This point is important; this one is a supporting detail.
- This seems like an example to help me understand the text.
- I already knew that. This is something new.
- This is a summary statement, must be a major concept.
- I don't understand this explanation.
- This concept map must be here for a reason, probably to illustrate the important ideas.

Text coding is designed to help students have those conversations while they read. It also provides a system for "tracking" thinking. A text triggers a host of useful connections and associations for readers, but if students have no system for processing them, these insights might not be available when the students reflect back on the passage and decide how to make sense of it. Struggling readers in particular have difficulty harnessing their thinking as they negotiate the terrain of a challenging text. As a result, they might conclude their reading with only a hazy outline of disjointed facts. Text coding should be introduced gradually and can be simplified and changed when needed.

Step 1. **Introduce students to text coding with think-alouds.** The teacher selects a short piece of text that presents a challenge and enlarges it so that it can be projected on an overhead transparency. The teacher observes that even excellent readers occasionally encounter problematic texts. Short pieces that contain confusing segments, ambiguities, unfamiliar vocabulary, or technical subject matter make excellent choices for these think-alouds. As the students follow along, the teacher reads the passage aloud, pausing periodically to illustrate what he or she is thinking. The following strategies should be included during this modeling.

- Making predictions: "I think this author is going to talk about . . . "
- Making connections: "This reminds me of . . . "
- Creating images: "I can picture what the author is describing . . . "
- Posing questions: "I wonder (why, how, what, who, where, etc.) . . . ?"
- Clarifying and fixing lack of understanding: "This does not make sense to me. I think I should try . . . "
- Determining importance: "This is important because . . . "

Teacher think-alouds underscore that comprehension involves active engagement with a text and constructing meaning by connecting information provided by an author with a reader's prior knowledge and expectations. After students have experienced several teacher think-alouds, they can practice the process themselves with partners as they tackle potentially difficult class material. The partners take turns reading a segment aloud, pausing to share their thinking and strategies as they go along.

Step 2. **Read the text and respond using symbols.** Coding a text involves two elements: highlighting or marking a spot in a paragraph and then jotting a symbol in the margin to indicate the kind of thinking that was elicited at this point. An endless set of symbols can be used to help students focus on the text. The following are examples of symbols that could be used to code text (Buehl, 2001):

R—"This reminds me of . . ." to signify a connection to background knowledge or experiences
V—"I can picture this as a visual image" to signify visualizing
E—"This makes me feel . . ." to signify an emotional response to the text
Q—"I wonder . . ." to signify a question that occurred during reading
I—"I think that . . ." to signify making an inference, such as a prediction or an interpretation
*—"This is important . . ." to signify main ideas or important information
?—"I don't understand this . . ." to signify a segment that is confusing or does not make sense

Students are not normally allowed to write in textbooks. One alternative is to have students fold a sheet of paper lengthwise. Students can write the coding symbols at the top and use this sheet for note taking. Text passages and page numbers are written on the left side, and the code and student comments are written on the right side. Other teachers use pads of sticky notes with the symbols written on them or use notes of different colors to mark passages in the text. The symbols that are chosen for text coding depend on the purpose for reading and type of text. Some additional codes are listed:

➤   I knew this
++   Main idea
SD   Supporting detail
Ex   Example

Step 3. **Use symbols to organize notes from the reading.** Have students meet with partners or in small groups to share their text coding. For example, students can indicate how various passages reminded them of things they already knew, they can describe what they visualized during a particular section, or they can identify parts of the text that confused them. Students applying the codes listed earlier can compare what they thought were the most important points, the details, or the examples presented in the text. The discussion can help students to understand how to find the main idea in passages and the supporting information. They can then organize these main ideas in the form of notes.

Taking notes from text is an important skill for writing a report or making a presentation. The Cornell or divided-page note-taking system is a popular system that is used in many middle and high schools (Pauk, 2005). In this system, the important points are listed on the left side of the paper, and the details are listed on the right. In this example, the page might look like Figure 9.2. This information can easily be translated into a concept map or a graphic organizer to help students see the relationships among ideas. This strategy is most effective when it is used with a

Key Point	*Details*
Influences of steam power	1. A new source of energy. 2. Factories use steam, which allows them to operate without waterpower.
History of steam power	1. 1700s in Europe, James Watt. 2. American Oliver Evans developed a more powerful steam engine.
How steam power works	1. Boiler fuel is burned to heat water and produce steam. 2. Cylinder steam is built up to push piston up and down. 3. Condenser increases power by pulling steam out of cylinder and speeds up the piston.

FIGURE 9.2   *Cornell Notetaking System*

Source: From *Reading Strategies and the Social Studies Classroom*, by J. L. Irvin, 2001, Austin, TX: Holt, Rinehart & Winston.

prereading strategy that activates what students know about a topic before reading or a postreading strategy such as creating a concept map or graphic organizer.

Teachers should feel free to change the symbols depending on the purpose for having students read a selection. For example, if students are reading a proposition and support essay, the following symbols might be used:

A   Agree with this statement
D   Disagree with this statement
*   Important, I need to think about this statement

Text coding allows a reader to return to a piece and recapture thinking that was useful for developing comprehension. This technique provides students with a system to verbalize their problem solving through difficult texts and encourages them to attempt fix-up strategies rather than giving up or accepting partial comprehension of a passage. In addition, students become conditioned to make decisions about what is most important when reading a passage.

Underlining or Highlighting

Underlining or highlighting is the most popular technique used to study text. Text marking requires that readers understand what is most important or worth remembering, although underlining has not been shown to be any more effective than any other study technique. The major benefit of highlighting or underlining, it seems, comes from rereading and from the decision about what to mark. Selecting key ideas from a text takes a certain amount of deep processing.Unfortunately, this highly used strategy is also one of the most abused; students really struggle with making intelligent decisions about what to mark and what to overlook. Think about your experiences as a college student. Buying used books was a significant way to reduce expenses for many students. If you were not careful, however, you might arrive home with books that had been previously owned by sufferers of "yellow marker syndrome" (Buehl, 1997). This malady is easily recognizable: Whole passages of text are randomly colored yellow, the legacy of a confused student with a highlighter pen. The reader apparently could not discriminate between important and unimportant information.

Step 1.   **Modeling text marking.** Santa, Havens, and Harrison (1996) suggested that it is helpful to students for teachers to model the process by marking an overhead with text, talking aloud about what is important in a passage, highlighting key ideas, putting an asterisk by main points, and making up study questions. Simpson and Nist (1990) suggested that making marginal comments and using personal coding systems or annotations are effective study strategies that facilitate the remembering of important points more than just underlining. The annotation system includes surveying or previewing material, reading carefully, thinking about ideas presented in the text, and annotating key ideas in the margins.

Step 2. **Read the text and underline or highlight.** Provide students with content material that they can mark and use the following guidelines (Buehl, 1997).

- Quickly read the section before doing any marking.
- Reread, marking only key words and phrases, not entire sentences or paragraphs.
- Mark essential information not supporting details.
- Annotate in the margins or on the text (number items, jot brief comments or questions, use abbreviations).
- Highlight relationships between facts (cause and effect, compare and contrast, proposition and support, problem and solution, concept and definition).
- Color code information using different markers (yellow for main ideas, pink for important secondary information, etc.).
- Be highly selective! (No more than 20 percent of a text should be marked.)

Step 3. **Reinforce the strategy with practice.** Periodically provide students with opportunities to mark what they read. Supplementary materials that are photocopied for each student are excellent sources for this practice. The teacher might also wish to give students transparencies of chapter sections occasionally or photocopies from the textbook for marking. Old textbooks that are no longer used in class are also a great resource for marking practice. Students can work in cooperative groups of two or three to mark an overhead transparency of a text selection. Each group then projects its transparency for the class and explains its decisions on what deserved highlighting and what did not. One variation of this strategy is to assign each section of a chapter to a different cooperative group within the class. Each group marks its transparencies for its section and during the unit has the responsibility for teaching that section to the entire class, using its transparency on the overhead projector. Another variation is to give students blank transparencies and washable markers. The students can place the transparency on the textbook page, mark it, and clip it to the page. When they have completed studying the information, they wash off their markings and start on the next chapter.

When developing these activities, cue students into the key relationships in the information. For example, students can annotate in the margins: + (alike) or - (different) for compare-and-contrast relationships. For a cause-and-effect passage, they might write "cause" in the appropriate spot in the margin and then number each of the effects that is subsequently discussed. Identifying important information is central to all study strategies. Simpson and Nist (2000) suggested four categories of strategic learning: question generation and answer explanation, text summarization, student-generated elaborations, and organizing strategies. These categories follow naturally from the generalizations about strategic learning that are presented next.

Generalizations about Strategic Learning

Extensive reviews of the literature on study strategies fail to confirm that any one study strategy is superior to another (Anderson & Ambruster, 1984; Nist & Simpson, 2000; Simpson & Nist, 2000). Rather, strategies that are effective embody the cognitive and metacognitive processes necessary for students to learn and remember information (Mayer, 1996). Simpson and Nist (2000) developed five generalizations about strategic learning. Although these researchers worked primarily with college students, these generalizations are applicable to middle school study strategies and are discussed in the following section.

1. Task understanding is critical to strategic learning.
2. Beliefs about learning influence how students read and study.
3. High quality instruction is essential.
4. Cognitive and metacognitive processing should be the instructional focus.
5. It is important to teach a variety of research-based strategies.

Task Understanding Is Critical to Strategic Learning

The tasks for which students read to remember are familiar to students and teachers alike. These tasks such as multiple-choice or essay exams, research papers, book reports, class presentations, or speeches, are called criterion tasks. The degree of knowledge students have about the criterion task is an important variable in the effectiveness of time spent studying. "When the criterion task is made explicit to the students before they read the text, students will learn more from studying than when the criterion task remains vague" (Anderson & Armbruster, 1984, p. 658). If students are to study effectively and efficiently, they must have enough information

about the task at hand so they can adjust their studying accordingly. "Academic tasks are not only specific to a content area, but also specific to an instructor and a setting" (Simpson & Nist, 2000, p. 530).

When students prepare for essay and completion exams rather than multiple-choice and true-false tests, they generally perform better on all types of tests. When studying for objective tests (multiple-choice and true-false), students engage in more random note-taking and underlining. Studying for an essay exam prompts students to focus on the understanding of major points. An understanding of the major concepts in the text and their relationships to each other seems to aid students in their overall recall of the text. Clearly, "different study activities involve students in very different thinking patterns and also lead to different kinds of learning" (Langer, 1986, p. 406). In addition, academic tasks are specific to a content area, to an instructor, and to a setting. "It appears that students' understanding of a particular task is an important determinant of whether students select and employ appropriate strategies" and that task identification must precede strategy selection (Simpson & Nist, 2000, p. 530).

An analogy might be found in the preparation that coaches undertake when getting their teams ready for competition. Coaches use practice time to approximate game conditions so that players will feel comfortable performing under the pressure of an actual competition. Effective coaching instruction includes scouting information on exactly what to expect from the opposition during the competition. A clear goal for teachers is to remove as much of the mystery about a task as possible so that students know exactly how to use their time to prepare effectively.

Beliefs about Learning Influence How Students Read and Study

In Chapter 2, we suggested that the more students know about how people learn, the more empowered they will be with regard to their own learning. Students' beliefs about how knowledge is constructed, particularly within a discipline, play an important role in how they interpret a task and how they select a strategy (Hofer, 1998; Simpson & Nist, 2000). For example, students who believe that effort will influence learning will adopt a much more aggressive approach to studying than students who regard performance on criterion tasks as primarily a result of luck or ability. Students who feel that they "just aren't good in math" or that those who excel in math do not have to study but can merely rely on their natural talents might be less likely to undertake strategies that could maximize their learning in pre-algebra.

High-Quality Instruction Is Essential

Most educators will agree that study strategies are essential to success in school. Yet it appears that middle school teachers do not teach study strategies consistently because they believe that elementary teachers are responsible for teaching all learning strategies, see themselves as content experts rather than study skill teachers, or feel the constraints and pressure of covering a prescribed content (Jackson &

Cunningham, 1994). Simpson and Nist (2000) suggested that high-quality instruction includes the following.

- A substantial amount of time committed to instruction
- Declarative knowledge (what is the strategy), procedural knowledge (the steps or processes involved in a strategy), and conditional knowledge (why, where, and when to select and apply a strategy as well as how to evaluate its effectiveness)
- Instruction within a specific content area and situation—strategies taught in isolation appear to have little transfer value
- Strategy instruction that is explicit, direct, and occurs over a sustained period

The purpose of instruction in study strategies is to foster independent learning. Content teachers are the most capable of teaching study strategies because they can best explain the criterion task and help students to adjust their studying accordingly. Content teachers have the academic knowledge necessary to identify important concepts to be learned and to develop the relevant background information to help students see the relationships among concepts. Additionally, content teachers are most familiar with the text and its organization and can most effectively guide students through it.

Cognitive and Metacognitive Processing Should Be the Instructional Focus

A study strategy program should include both instruction in the strategies and instruction in the cognitive and metacognitive processes that help students to know when and how to apply strategies. The teaching of the mechanics of a study strategy sometimes overshadows the all-important processes that underlie this technique and may inhibit the transfer of a study strategy to a new situation.

For example, although the two-column format is an excellent system for taking notes, students must still contend with the essential underlying thinking if their notes are to be effective learning aids. They must determine what is important and worthy of inclusion, perceive connections among important information, clarify confusions, flesh out concepts with understandable examples, and become adept at summarizing key ideas into manageable notes. Merely copying information from the chalkboard or an overhead transparency into the two-column format is not the same as recording thoughtful and useful notes.

It Is Important to Teach a Variety of Research-Based Strategies

In an extensive review of the literature, Simpson and Nist (2000) found four research-based and classroom-tested strategies that are useful for students:

- Question generation and answer explanation
- Text summarization

- Student-generated elaborations
- Organizing strategies

Question Generation and Answer Explanation

Answering questions after reading is a common practice in schools. Often, students do not receive much instruction in how to answer these questions. In addition, developing self-questioning habits for readers is vital for improving reading comprehension. Keene and Zimmermann (1997) observed that proficient readers spontaneously generate questions before, during, and after reading—to clarify meaning; to speculate about what the text may contain next; to determine the author's intent, style, content, or format; to locate specific answers; to consider rhetorical questions inspired by a text; and to focus attention on important components of the text. Proficient readers realize that many intriguing questions are not answered explicitly in the text, necessitating an interpretation on the part of the reader. Proficient readers are able to determine whether they can derive an answer from a text or whether they need to infer an answer, using their background knowledge or other text (Keene & Zimmermann, 1997, p. 119).

Questioning the author (Beck, McKeown, Hamilton, & Kucan, 1997) is an excellent study strategy that helps students with question generation and answer explanations; it is explained in Chapter 8. The question-answer relationship strategy is also highly effective in developing questioning abilities in readers.

Question-Answer Relationships

Raphael (1981, 1982, 1984, 1986; Raphael & Pearson, 1985) developed the Question-Answer Relationship (QAR) to assist students with using information from the text and from their prior knowledge to answer questions. The four types of questions are shown in Figure 9.3.

QAR instruction begins with students' classifying various types of questions according to how they can be answered. Teachers then model the thinking processes that are required in answering these questions and provide practice opportunities. "Students learn to consider information both in the text as well as information from their experiential background" (Helfeldt & Henk, 1990, p. 510).

Struggling readers, in particular, can benefit from experience with QAR. Often, these students become frustrated with responding to questions that elicit inferential thinking and may give up when they "can't find the answer," or they might merely write down something in order to hand in a completed assignment. Tovani (2000) offered a four-step formula for walking students through inferential thinking. First, students are prompted to ask "I wonder" questions as they read. This step reinforces that authors do not directly state everything they wish to communicate and that readers must become involved in the process of creating meaning. Second, students examine the text for important clues about what an author is leaving unsaid. Making an inference begins with a search for textual evidence. Third, students think about what they know that connects to information in the

In-the-Book Questions	In-My-Head Questions
Right There Questions The answer is in the text. The words used to make up the question and words used to answer the question are found in the same sentence.	*Author and You Questions*  The answer is not in the story. You need to think about what you already know, what the author tells you, and how it fits together.
Think and Search  The answer is in the selection, but you need to put together different pieces of information to find it. The answer comes from different places in the selection.	*On My Own*  The answer is not in the text. You can answer the question without even reading the text. The answer is based solely on your own experiences and knowledge.

FIGURE 9.3 *Question-Answer Relationship*

Source: From Santa, C., Havens, L., & Valdes, B. (2004). *Project CRISS: Creating Independence through Student-Owned Strategies* (3rd ed.). Dubuque, IA: Kendall/Hunt.

text. Fourth, students return to their "I wonder" question to ascertain whether they can now generate possible answers.

Text Summarization

Students tend to have a very difficult time summarizing what they have read. Student summaries often consist of a string of disconnected snippets of information or segments of a story, while major themes or main ideas are overlooked. Summarizing entails the ability of readers to retell what they have read, in their own words. In addition, synthesizing, which combines summarizing with the reader's perspective, is involved in this sophisticated process. When proficient readers talk about a piece of meaningful text—a discussion about an article in the newspaper, for example, or a book club chat about a novel—they do not merely repeat what the text said, instead they offer their personal "take" on a selection.

- "That's not the way I read it."
- "This is what I think the author was getting at."

- "I think the character acted this way because . . ."
- "This is my understanding of this passage."

Synthesizing can be modeled for students by using an analogy, such as cooking. Chefs read recipes and assemble ingredients to make something, such as a cake. But the recipes do not always lead to exactly the same results, because each person adds a personal touch to the process. Some cooks turn out to be great chefs because of their abilities to bring their own ideas and experiences into the mix as they work from a recipe. Proficient readers are assembling their own thinking as they read, taking the elements of a text and combining them with their own background knowledge and experiences to create thoughts, ideas, and understandings. Synthesizing is the process of deriving insight from reading.

Asking students to write about what they have read, to express their thinking in their own words, is an important step in teaching them to summarize. Writing helps students to realize what they have learned, and it provides them with a visual record of their thinking. Writing also gives students the opportunity to continue to refine their thinking as they revisit their thoughts on paper and revise what they have written to clarify and expand their understanding. In addition, outlining strategies help students to "separate the wheat from the chaff."

Power Notes

Outlining is a familiar method for organizing and summarizing information. Yet the process of outlining can be difficult for students because they must think through the logical relationships in the text before beginning the outline. This task requires analysis and synthesis, and many students struggle with distinguishing attributes, examples, and other details from main ideas. Power notes (also referred to as power thinking) provide a systematic way to help students organize information for their reading, writing, and studying (Santa, Havens, & Valdes, 2004).

Step 1. **Model power notes.** Power notes are a streamlined form of outlining and are relatively easy to introduce to students. Unlike traditional outlining, which involves teaching roman numerals and alphabetic keys, the power notes system is straightforward. Main ideas or categories are assigned a power 1 rating. Details, examples, or attributes are assigned ratings of power 2, 3, or 4. Start by modeling power notes with categories that are familiar to the students. Discuss how the powers relate to each other: Power 2s offer examples or elaboration of power 1s, power 3s provide examples or elaboration of power 2s, and so on. Indenting helps to establish how the powers relate to each other, as demonstrated in the following musical instruments example.

     1. Stringed instruments
        2. Usually played with a bow
           3. Violin

3. Viola
3. Cello
3. Classical string bass
2. Usually plucked
   3. Guitar
   3. Banjo
   3. Jazz string bass
1. Brass instruments
   2. Played with valves
      3. Trumpet
      3. French horn
      3. Tuba
   2. Played with slide
      3. Trombone
1. Reed instruments
   2. Played with single reed
      3. Clarinet
      3. Saxophone
   2. Played with double reed
      3. Oboe
      3. Bassoon
1. Percussion instruments
   2. Struck with a stick
      3. Snare drum
      3. Gong
      3. Triangle
   2. Struck together
      3. Cymbals

Step 2. **Guided practice.** Provide students with opportunities to use power notes to categorize information and explore relationships. For example, select a number of power 1, 2, and 3 terms from a unit of study and write them on separate index cards. Distribute sets of cards to students working in cooperative groups and give them the task of arranging the cards according to powers and corresponding relationships. This activity can serve as a review exercise. Students could be given blank cards to add power 4 information to power 3 cards, or add other items to the outline.

Step 3. **Taking power notes from text.** When students understand the concept of power notes, this strategy can be assigned as a study activity to outline sections of a text. Power notes can also be an effective way to help students organize their writing. A simple 1-2-2-2 outline (a main idea and three supporting details) can help students construct a well-organized paragraph. Students can further elaborate each point by adding power 3 and 4 details to flesh out their writing.

Power notes contribute to students' awareness of text structure as they read and write. Students learn to read actively, to distinguish main ideas from details as they study, and to take coherent notes from textbooks or classroom presentations. All of these skills are necessary for summarization of text.

Summarizing

Writing a summary is a complex activity that involves condensing information to the main ideas and reporting the gist or essence of text. Students must remember the most important ideas and omit the unimportant or irrelevant details. Paraphrasing and condensing information are two important skills in writing a good summary. In addition, sensitivity to text structure is necessary to identify the most important ideas. The activities that are involved in summarizing (identifying main ideas, paraphrasing, condensing information, and sensitivity to text structure) are important metacognitive skills and, when internalized by the student, naturally lead to more thoughtful reading.

Summarizing information from text is a valuable study technique that is often neglected in content areas (Vacca & Vacca, 2005). In the past decade, the effectiveness of summarizing as a learning strategy and a study skill is well documented. Just as with answering essay questions, the process of summarizing facilitates learning and metacognitive abilities, and the product is useful in recalling information for a later criterion task.

Writing summaries forces learners to use in-depth processing for the more important ideas in the text. Composing a summary is a complex task that requires considerable skill. Researchers have documented clear developmental trends in summarizing (Brown & Day, 1983; Brown, Day, & Jones, 1983; Paris, Wasik, & Turner, 1991; Winograd, 1984). That is, older and more proficient readers summarize better than younger and less skilled readers do. More capable summary writers planned before they wrote, used text structure as an aid in selecting and generalizing, recorded important information in their own words, and monitored the text to evaluate their own accuracy.

Effective summary writing is one of the abilities that differentiates proficient readers from struggling readers, and learning to summarize can improve poor readers' comprehension (Brown & Day, 1983). Teaching students to summarize can facilitate learning by helping readers clarify the meaning and significance of text. Self-directed summarization can be an excellent comprehension-monitoring activity (Hidi & Anderson, 1986). Struggling readers, however, do not readily engage in self-directed summarization (Palincsar & Brown, 1983). So although summary writing is a complex activity, it can be taught, and the teaching of summarizing improves comprehension and recall of information.

Summary writing is difficult for students to learn, so initial attempts to teach summary writing should be as simple as possible. Hidi and Anderson (1986) suggested the following guidelines for teaching students to write good summaries.

- Use brief passages at first, and begin with the more familiar narrative text.

- Texts should be well organized, with vocabulary and content that are familiar to students.
- Text should be in view when students write summaries. This reduces the burden of remembering information and focuses on the skill of summarizing. As students become more proficient in summarizing, the text can be taken away.
- Initial summaries should be just slightly shorter than the original text, which may involve a retelling of a story with the deletion of only the most trivial details.
- Initial summaries should be more like journal entries in which the main focus is on content, not on the mechanics of writing. Once students become more proficient at writing summaries, they can be shared with other students and the teacher. Peer-editing groups are a good way to help students revise and perfect their summaries before publication or grading (pp. 487–491).

Students should have enough practice summarizing orally that they can easily and confidently summarize aloud before being asked to compose written summaries. It is important for students to see and hear the teacher summarizing. Teachers can summarize the day's activities, a story that has been read aloud, or current events. Students can be asked to summarize mathematics and science lessons or to give brief oral or written accounts of books they have read. Partner shares are an especially good way for students to practice verbalizing their summarizing. Students who are not fluent writers can use tape recorders to record their summaries.

Daily classroom activity provides numerous opportunities for teachers to model and students to practice summarizing. Teachers must model what they want students to be able to do. Research clearly indicates that summarizing is an important metacognitive and comprehension skill that deserves systematic attention in the content areas.

Student-Generated Elaborations

When students themselves create study materials, they are engaging in a deeper processing of information. For example, students preparing for an exam might review a study guide provided by the teacher, or they might collaborate with classmates to predict possible test questions. The students predicting questions are in a sense creating their own potential exams as they analyze the material to determine importance, seek connections, and consider how their learning might be evaluated. Students with the study guide might be preoccupied with memorizing of basic information.

Student-generated elaborations may take a variety of forms. Students may attempt to supply examples of ideas they are studying, they may brainstorm analogous relationships among new material and something familiar, and they may develop their own interpretations of what the material means. Many of the strategies in this chapter represent student-generated elaborations.

Elaborative Interrogations

Pressley, Symons, McDaniel, Snyder, and Turnure (1988) argued that teaching students to ask "why" questions has a significant payoff in reading comprehension. Their elaborative interrogation technique conditions students to ask why certain ideas may be true and to look for relationships among pieces of information. Some why questions will be answered by explicit statements in a text, but students will frequently discover that they must infer answers or even hypothesize possible reasons.

Typically, students focus on the what of new information: what it is, what happened, what the steps are, and so on. Many textbooks do a poor job of communicating the why aspects of new material: why this is significant, why this happened, why these steps matter, why a certain conclusion may be warranted. The elaborative interrogation procedure asks students to search for why connections in the material they are studying.

Teachers can model this process with students by providing a short text on the overhead transparency or by calling attention to a brief passage (perhaps a paragraph or two) in the textbook. Then the teacher can ask a series of why questions about the material. Students will realize that many of these questions are "in my head" or "on my own" QARs. (See the section on question-answer relationships earlier in this chapter.)

Teachers should caution students that authors assume that readers will fill in many of these gaps with their own knowledge and experiences and that proficient readers speculate about possible answers to these why questions. For example, students might read the following passage on the aftermath of World War I in a social studies textbook:

> The war ended abruptly for American industries, which were geared to operating at full capacity to produce military supplies. Demobilization caused the demand for wartime production to drop off, and factories were not ready for the change. In addition, the huge influx of 4 million soldiers into the workplace caused serious social and economic strains. Women who had taken on factory jobs during the war were now forced out of their positions, and many African Americans likewise lost their recently assumed jobs in America's industry.

Elaborative interrogation questions on this passage might include the following: Why would the end of the war affect factories' ability to operate at full capacity? Why would demobilization cause the demand for wartime products to drop off? Why were factories not ready for demobilization? Why would the returning soldiers cause strains in American society? Why did women take on factory jobs during the war? Why would women lose their jobs? Why would African Americans lose their jobs?

Some of the answers to these questions might seem obvious, but others require an inference and a presumed knowledge base. Articulating clearly defined answers to all of these questions is not necessarily as beneficial as the actual asking of the questions. Students who pose questions like these as they study are endeavoring to elaborate on their understandings by connecting information within the text to their prior knowledge.

Organizing Strategies

Many of the strategies presented in this chapter help students to organize material for study. Organizing strategies induces students to perceive the interconnectiveness of information, to separate main ideas from supporting details, and to look for relationships among ideas. Visual displays of information are especially effective as organizing strategies. This section describes the use of graphic representations as a study technique.

Graphic Representations

Graphic representations can assume a variety of forms. Some graphic representations are designed to show ideas in a hierarchical fashion (graphic organizers, structured overviews, and pyramids). Others show the relationships and relative importance among concepts, words, or ideas (networks, concept maps, and word maps). All of these graphic representations help students to put information into a manageable format, show relationships, and increase the involvement of the reader through modeling and displaying graphic illustrations, story structure charts, and so forth (Valerio & Readence, 2000). In a review of research on graphic organizers, Robinson (1998) concluded that the "true purpose of the graphic organizers is to organize, rather than to simply list concept information" (p. 99).

Anderson-Inman and Zeitz (1993) suggested that electronic methods of constructing a graphic organizer help students to represent their visions of how a knowledge domain is structured and foster reflection of how concepts interrelate. Several graphic representations are presented in Chapters 6, 8, and 9, but chapter mapping is discussed in this section because it is a powerful tool to help students comprehend and remember the important ideas in a text or lecture. Mapping helps students to understand the important relationships in the text by providing them with a visual outline of the logical connections between key ideas. Comparing a preinstructional map with a postinstructional map can help students connect prior knowledge with learned information (Avery, Baker, & Gross, 1997). This strategy helps students to become more active readers or listeners, facilitating deep processing. Mapping can also help students to organize difficult or poorly written texts. Figure 9.4 shows an example of a chapter map from a history textbook.

Mapping adds a visual dimension to the concepts presented in a text and thus can enhance comprehension and recall of information. Two or three students can work together to produce a more complete map. Discussion about what should be included and what should not helps students to understand the process of distinguishing between important and unimportant information. Otherwise, some students might create chapter maps that feature only a mishmash of facts. Power notes can easily be extended to chapter mapping. The center of the map is reserved for the topic that is being developed. Only power 1 ideas can emanate from the center. Each power 1 idea is further defined with power 2s. Power 3s elaborate the power 2s on the map. (See the discussion of power notes earlier in this chapter.) Figure 9.5 shows an example of a chapter map made for a science textbook unit on waves using power notes.

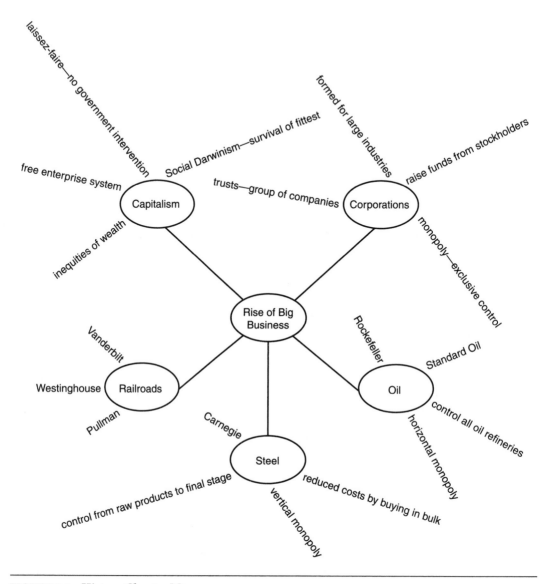

FIGURE 9.4 *History Chapter Map*

Many teachers find graphic representations invaluable in helping students to activate and organize what they know and relate that knowledge to new learning. In fact, social studies teachers have successfully used maps to aid in decision making for many years (Howard, 2001). Graphic organizers serve as maps for where students have been and what they have learned, and this powerful technique is flexible enough to adapt to a variety of subject material.

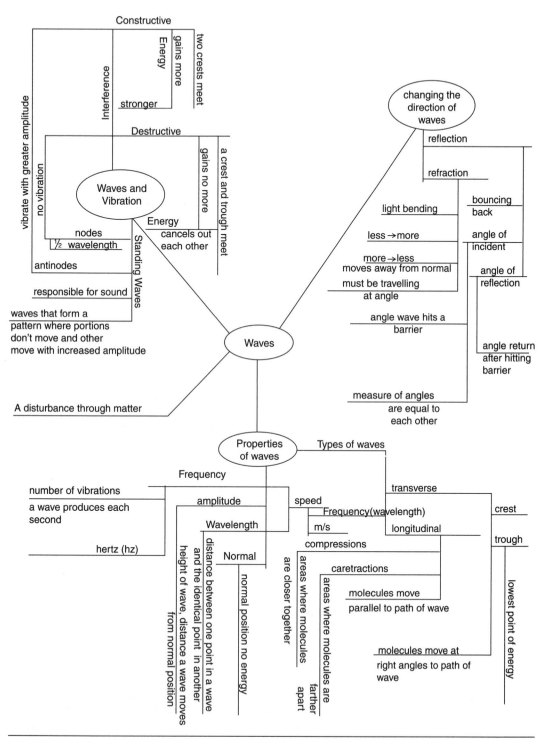

FIGURE 9.5 *Chapter Map*

Summary

Students read to pass tests, write reports, do presentations, create projects, and complete assignments. That is, students are reading for a purpose, often a purpose that has been defined by someone else. Study strategies enable students to meet these purposes and to learn and remember the material they read. To study effectively, of course, students must know what to study. The teacher must carefully define the criterion task that students will be expected to perform after studying. Beyond this, students must learn how to study effectively and efficiently. Students must learn how to grasp a main idea, how to summarize information, and how to interrelate or synthesize information. They must learn how to check their comprehension and how to adjust their reading rates to the demands of the task. In short, students must learn how to achieve a deep understanding of the material they are to study. Study strategies serve as the means to this end.

Extending Learning

Reviewing the Talking Points

Revisit the talking points at the beginning of this chapter. Answer the questions now that you have read the chapter and compare your prereading and postreading responses.

Revisiting the Vignette

In the opening vignette, we visit the angst that some students experience when they are confronted with the "unknowns"of a test. How do you prepare for tests or other forms of assessments? How is this similar to or different from how you prepared for exams as a middle school student? What are some of the strategies from this chapter that you incorporate into your own scheme for studying?

Terms to Remember and Use

study by doing	closure review	text coding	main idea
supporting detail	text marking	task understanding	criterion tasks
declarative knowledge	QAR	question generation	concept maps
student-generated elaborations	power notes	organizing strategies	graphic representations

Write a series of sentences that meaningfully connect pairs of the above key terms. Your sentences should refer to ideas and concepts related to the literacy of middle school students.

Modifying Instruction for English Language Learners

To help English language learners, teachers can create an outline of the text topic using simple syntax and vocabulary. Key concepts and essential technical vocabulary should also be highlighted at the beginning so that they know what to focus on while reading. Teaching students to use outlines and graphic organizers helps ELLs to grasp the overall structure and main ideas before engaging in reading the details of the text. Students also need to be encouraged to summarize what they have read, paragraph by paragraph or section by section.

Furthermore, it can be helpful for teachers to ask ELLs to identify places in the text where they have trouble understanding. Timely assistance can be offered when teachers are aware of specific difficulties rather than getting a general statement of failure to make sense of the text. Is it a language problem resulting from unfamiliarity with the vocabulary or an information processing difficulty in which the student knows the word but is still unable to comprehend? The former can be solved by having students learn the new vocabulary. The latter may reveal inadequate knowledge in one or more areas, for example, background information, sentence structure, text structure, or context.

Finally, taking note of vocabulary through reading can be a good study habit that helps to improve ELLs' reading ability in the long run. There are several types of vocabulary that students can jot down in a small pocket notebook:

- Key words from a text
- Unfamiliar but important words
- Words of interest
- Words that they have difficulty learning or mastering

Of course, there are more categories that individual ELL students might find useful. No matter what words they decide to write down in the vocabulary notebook, it is advisable that students indicate where they encounter the words and the meanings of the words in the particular contexts. Because vocabulary is a huge barrier for ELL language learning, especially in reading, this strategy can help students to accumulate a working vocabulary, which in turn contributes to each aspect of their language development.

Beyond the Book

- Interview a middle school student to find out whether the student can clearly articulate how he or she prepares for an exam or other assessment. Try to determine whether the student understands what the "performance" might be.
- Model a power notes session for a small group or a class. Determine whether the notes acccurately reflect what you want the students to learn from that text selection.
- Find a text selection from your content area and get together with a colleague. Design a graphic representation of the selection and determine whether the graphic is accurate and detailed enough to be useful.
- Exercise summarization skills by reading a short passage to a class, a small group, or a classmate. Ask your listeners to summarize what you read, and then change roles as you continue to read through the selection.
- Analyze the five steps for strategic teaching. Determine whether you experience these in any of your current classes, either as a student or as a teacher. Recreate a lesson that you taught or were taught, and determine where these strategies could be employed.
- Examine the questions at the end of a chapter of text. Try to classify them on the basis of Figure 9.3 to determine whether the questions offer variety and whether they stimulate thinking.
- Select an excerpt from a text. Write a summary of that excerpt as a model and then give it to a classmate or a student and compare and contrast the two products.

References

Anderson, T. H., & Armbruster, B. B. (1984). Studying. In P. D. Pearson, M. L. Kamil, & P. Mosenthal (Eds.), *Handbook of Reading Research* (pp. 657–680). New York: Longman.

Anderson-Inman, L., & Zeitz, L. (1993). Computer-based concept mapping: Active studying for active learners. *The Computing Teacher, 21*(1), 6–8, 10–11.

Avery, P. G., Baker, J., & Gross, S. H. (1997). "Mapping" learning at the secondary level. *The Clearinghouse, 70*(5), 279–285.

Beck, I., McKeown, M., Hamilton, R., & Kucan, L. (1997). *Questioning the Author: An Approach for Enhancing Student Engagement with Text.* Newark, DE: International Reading Association.

Brown, A. L. (1985). *Teaching Students to Think as They Read: Implications for Curriculum Reform* (Reading Education Rep. No. 58). Champaign, IL: Center for the Study of Reading, University of Illinois at Urbana–Champaign.

Brown, A. L., & Day, J. D. (1983). Macrorules for summarizing texts: The development of expertise. *Journal of Verbal Learning and Verbal Behavior, 22*(1), 1–14.

Brown, A. L., Day, J. D., & Jones, R. S. (1983). The development of plans for summarizing texts. *Child Development, 54*(4), 968–979.

Buehl, D. (2001). The A-B-Cs of coding text. *Wisconsin Education Association Council News and Views, 2*(1), 13.

Buehl, D. (1997). Yellow marker syndrome: Highlighting of text is a skill. *Wisconsin Education Association Council News and Views, 32*(11), 13.

Buehl, D. (1995). *Classroom Strategies for Interactive Learning.* Schofield, WI: Wisconsin State Reading Association.

Commander, N. E., & Smith, B. D. (1996). Learning logs: A tool for cognitive monitoring. *Journal of Reading, 39*(6), 446–453.

Helfeldt, J. P., & Henk, W. A. (1990). Reciprocal question-answer relationships: An instructional technique for at-risk readers. *Journal of Reading, 33*(7), 509–515.

Hidi, S., & Anderson, V. (1986). Producing written summaries: Task demands, cognitive operations, and implications for instruction. *Review of Educational Research, 56*(4), 473–493.

Hofer, B. K. (1998, April). *Personal Epistemology in Context: Student Interpretations of Instructional Practice.* Paper presented at the annual meeting of the American Educational Research Association, San Diego, CA.

Howard, J. (2001). Graphic representations as tools for decision-making. *Social Education, 65*(4), 220–223.

Jackson, F. R., & Cunningham, J. W. (1994). Investigating secondary content teachers' and preservice teachers' conceptions of study strategy instruction. *Reading Research and Instruction, 34*(2), 111–135.

Keene, E., & Zimmermann, S. (1997). *Mosaic of Thought: Teaching Comprehension in a Reader's Workshop.* Portsmouth, NH: Heinemann.

Langer, J. A. (1986). Learning through writing: Study skills in the content areas. *Journal of Reading, 29*(5), 400–406.

Mayer, R. E. (1996). Learning strategies for making sense out of expository text: The SOI model for guiding three cognitive processes in knowledge construction. *Educational Psychology Review, 8*(4), 357–371.

Nist, S. L., & Simpson, M. L. (2000). College studying. In M. L. Kamil, P. B. Mosenthal, P. D. Pearson, & R. Barr, *Handbook of Reading Research*, Vol. III (pp. 645–666), Mahwah, NJ: Lawrence Erlbaum Associates.

Palincsar, A. S., & Brown, A. L. (1983). *Reciprocal Teaching of Comprehension-Monitoring Activities* (Tech. Rep. No. 269). Champaign, IL: Center for the Study of Reading.

Paris, S. G., Wasik, B. A., & Turner, J. (1991). The development of strategic readers. In R. Barr, M. L. Kamil, P. B. Mosenthal, & P. D. Pearson (Eds.), *Handbook of Reading Research*, Vol. II (pp. 609–640). New York: Longman.

Pauk, W. (2005). *How to Study in College* (8th ed.). Boston: Houghton Mifflin.

Pressley, M., Symons, S., McDaniel, M., Snyder, B., & Turnure, J. (1988). Elaborative interrogation facilitates acquisition of confusing facts. *Journal of Education Psychology, 80*(3), 268–278.

Raphael, T. E. (1981). *The Effect of Metacognitive Awareness Training on Students' Question-Answering Strategies.* Unpublished doctoral dissertation, University of Illinois, Urbana-Champaign.

Raphael, T. E. (1982). Question-answering strategies for children. *The Reading Teacher, 36*(2), 186–191.

Raphael, T. E. (1984). Teaching learners about sources of information for answering comprehension questions. *Journal of Reading, 27*(4), 303.

Raphael, T. E. (1986). Teaching question-answer relationships, revisited. *The Reading Teacher, 39*(6), 516–522.

Raphael, T. E., & Pearson, P. D. (1985). Increasing students' awareness of sources of information for answering questions. *American Educational Research Journal, 22*(2), 217–235.

Robinson, D. H. (1998). Graphic organizers as aids to text learning. *Reading Research and Instruction, 37*(2), 85–106.

Santa, C., Havens, L., & Harrison, S. (1996). Teaching secondary science through reading, writing, studying, and problem-solving. In D. Lapp, J. Flood, & N. Farnan (Eds.), *Content Area Reading and Learning* (pp. 137–151). Englewood Cliffs, NJ: Prentice Hall.

Santa, C., Havens, L., & Valdes, B. (2004). *Project CRISS: Creating Independence Through Student-Owned Strategies* (3rd ed). Dubuque, IA: Kendall/Hunt.

Simpson, M. L., & Nist, S. L. (1990). Textbook annotation: An effective and efficient study strategy for college students. *Journal of Reading, 34*(2), 122–129.

Simpson, M. L., & Nist, S. L. (2000). An update on strategic learning: It's more than textbook reading strategies. *Journal of Adolescent and Adult Literacy, 43*(6), 528–541.

Sousa, D. (2001). *How the Brain Learns* (2nd ed.). Thousand Oaks, CA: Corwin Press.

Tovani, C. (2000). *I Read It, but I Don't Get It: Comprehension Strategies for Adolescent Readers.* Portland, ME: Stenhouse.

Vacca, R. T., & Vacca, J. L. (2005). *Content Area Reading: Literacy and Learning Across the Curriculum* (8th ed). Boston: Allyn & Bacon.

Valerio, P. C., & Readence, J. E. (2000). Promoting independent study strategies in the classrooms of the twenty-first century. In K. D. Wood & T. S. Dickinson (Eds.), *Promoting Literacy in Grades 4–9: A Handbook for Teachers and Administrators* (pp. 331–343). Boston: Allyn & Bacon.

Winograd, P. (1984). Strategic difficulties in summarizing texts. *Reading Research Quarterly, 19*(4), 404–425.

10

Assessment That Guides Instruction

Nancy Dean and Jeannette Schiffbauer
University of Florida

Talking Points _____

- What do classroom teachers need to know about standardized testing?
- How can teachers devise high-quality assessments that provide them with useful information about their students and their instruction?
- What advantages can authentic assessments offer teachers and students?

Mr. Taylor knew that to engage students in learning, they had to have some choice over what they studied and be involved in the self-evaluation process. He decided to use an inquiry project approach to their study of environments. First, they studied the concept of environments in several contexts, listed the attributes of an environment, and then explored several examples as a class. He engaged the class in listing several types of environments on the board. The next day, students were to chose an environment to study based on the attributes listed the previous day and select a small group to work with. They were to compile the information through reading, interviewing people, and Internet searches. Next, they were to construct a concept map of all of the information they gathered and then create a PowerPoint presentation to present to the class.

Before they started, however, the class agreed upon a rubric of how the project would be evaluated. They tested out the rubric by scoring three projects completed by last year's class so they understood how they would be graded on the project. In addition to the project and the rubric, students would complete an examination on various aspects of the concept of environments. So, they would receive an individual grade for their exams and a group grade for their projects.

Too many teachers use assessment only as an evaluation rather than as an opportunity to give feedback to students to help them improve their work. The purpose of assessment is twofold: to provide teachers with the knowledge they need to plan instruction and support student learning and to provide students with the knowledge they need to "become more reflective, active, and purposeful learners [and] includes providing teachers with knowledge about how best to improve and support learning for their students and self-knowledge for learners that will allow them to become reflective, active, and purposeful learners" (Brozo & Simpson, 1999, p. 96).

Teachers need information that helps them to create experiences to facilitate student learning. Assessment provides the vehicle for teachers to modify and refine their teaching practices. Through assessment, teachers can determine what students have or have not accomplished so that classroom activities can be tailored to ensure student success. In addition, assessment can help teachers, administrators, and guidance counselors to talk with students and their parents about what the student has accomplished and the steps necessary to achieve future goals.

In this chapter, we first define assessment in general terms and present some characteristics of high-quality assessment. In the following parts of the chapter, we explore classroom-based assessment and describe ways in which teachers can incorporate authentic assessment into their classroom instruction. The goal of this chapter is for educators to understand assessment and to use it to inform instruction. Specifically, we want educators to do the following.

- Understand the characteristics of quality assessment
- Be able to describe the process and purposes of authentic assessment
- Design effective, authentic assessment
- Create and use rubrics that meet specific student needs and assignments

Characteristics of High-Quality Assessments

High-quality assessments must be multifaceted and meaningful. Assessments should include multiple texts, formats, and evaluators. Specifically, high-quality assessments should include the following characteristics.

1. **Assessments must have both formative (ongoing) and summative (final) components.** Formative assessments are used frequently so that teachers can evaluate the effectiveness of their instruction and make adaptations to ensure student learning. Additionally, students should be made aware of any problems so that they can make necessary changes in their strategies. Formative assessments can help students to learn to self-monitor and self-evaluate so that they can take charge of their learning. Summative assessments (including standardized and high-stakes tests) can be used as one measure of programs and of student progress. Most educators agree that summative assessments should not be the only measure of student achievement.

2. **Students need multiple kinds of assessments.** Individual student assessments such as teacher anecdotal records, traditional multiple-choice and essay tests, portfolios, and teacher-student conferences are helpful types of assessment. In addition, assessment should involve students working in groups or pairs. Cooperative groups, performances, graphic presentations and PowerPoint presentations can be used to demonstrate students' collaborative work.

3. **Assessments should be fair and equitable.** Rubrics provide a way to connect requirements to assessments. Because rubrics help students to understand at the onset what is expected of them, students are more likely to feel that the assessment is fair and equitable. Rubrics give a range of scores, which are aligned with specific characteristics of the activity. Also, rubrics outline requirements for students and can guide the students as they complete assignments. In schools and classrooms where teachers use rubrics as evidence of achievement, both teachers and students are more likely to hold clear expectations for learning.

4. **People other than teachers should be included in the assessment process.** When the whole learning community shares the responsibility of assessment, students ultimately benefit. This community includes teachers, students, parents, administrators, school board members, and elected officials. The first step to broaden the base for assessors should be to include other students. Students can gain experience sharing their work with peers with whom they feel comfortable. The next steps can be to involve other teachers, administrators, and school staff, and then to involve parents and other community members, including local politicians and businesspeople. Students are often more motivated by the presence of outside evaluators. An added benefit to portfolios and exhibitions is the parents' connection with the process.

    Of course, assessments are more valuable when criteria are constructed by the students as one of the first steps in any project. These rubrics can form the basis for all assessments and can provide a common understanding and vocabulary that make assessments more powerful. When outside community members and parents agree to be members of a review board, the rubrics often make the community members feel more comfortable and knowledgeable in their roles as assessors.

5. **High-quality assessment uses multiple types of texts, incorporates a variety of strategies and processes, and allows for a variety of responses.** Students should be reading a variety of texts, including the traditional published forms such as short stories, novels, biographies, autobiographies, poetry, and textbooks as well as newspapers, magazines, journals, atlases, government documents, and journals. In addition, students need to know how to read and interact with a variety of media, including film, television, and radio. These media require special instruction to help students understand the different underlying structures of text. Also, as each day passes, computer technology and the Internet require additional specialized skills and strategies for critical reading, writing, and thinking. Teachers need assessment that continues to help them tailor their instruction for achieving student proficiencies in using these multiple texts. Assessment that encourages divergent and creative thinking and uses a variety of responses (written, oral, graphic, multimedia, individual, and group) will best serve students and teachers.

6. **Students should be involved in constructing assessments.** One way of helping students to understand the structure of tests and learn what is important in the academic content is to show them how to construct tests. A starting point in the process of helping students to construct assessments is explaining Bloom's

taxonomy and the kinds of questions and activities associated with each level. You can begin by giving the students question stems and having them complete questions for each level of the taxonomy. For example, for a unit using maps, graphs, and charts, the question stems for *synthesis* might be "Construct a chart to show_____." These stems would help students to understand the different levels of questioning and how to form their own questions.

Using High-Stakes Tests and Other Standardized Tests

Although the debate about the effective use of high-stakes tests and other standardized tests continues, a question remains in the minds of most teachers: What is my role? Teachers' responsibilities here are varied and complex. Teachers must help students to perform well, help parents and students to understand the tests, and effect changes in assessment as needed.

1. **Helping students to perform well on the tests.** Research and common sense support the assumption that attempting to teach the test in isolation does not improve student test scores. After working in schools in Florida, California, and Texas, Langer (2000) identified six features of classroom instruction that improved student test performance.

   - Teaching skills with a variety of approaches
   - Integrating test preparation into all instruction

- Making connections across instruction, curriculum, and life
- Teaching learning and test-taking strategies explicitly
- Encouraging creative thinking
- Fostering collaboration

This research supports the basic premises of this text and helps teachers to define their roles as instructional leaders in their schools. Good classroom instructional practices based on a solid curriculum help students achieve on tests and, more important, learn.

2. **Helping students and parents to understand the tests.** When teachers and administrators are well informed about the construction of different forms of assessment, they can help parents to read and interpret the test results on a level that is least threatening to their self-esteem.

- Teachers should become thoroughly familiar with the tests and how the results are reported. For example, some parents might not understand the differences between percents and percentiles.
- Parents and students need to know and understand test scores. For example, if John scored a 312 on reading, what level of mastery is that and how does John compare with other students?
- Parents and students should know exactly what sections of the test students passed or failed. They also need to know the specific connection among scores on the high-stakes tests, retention, and graduation.

3. **Effecting change in assessment.** Teachers must wrestle with ethical issues of high-stakes testing and determine their own personal stance. Some education reformers argue that the tests "correlate highly with socioeconomic status" and that the predictable scores invite the "stigmatizing of low-scoring schools and communities" (Daniels & Bizar, 1998, p. 205). But, the goal of high-stakes testing is to ensure that all students become proficient readers and writers.

The school administration also needs to be able to plan for the long-term education of each student and the whole student body. Standardized and high-stakes tests can give the teacher information about the students and school programs that the teacher cannot otherwise get. Naturally, teachers gain most of their knowledge about their students through working and learning with students on a daily basis. But most teachers cannot adequately compare their own students with students from other schools and other parts of the state or country. Standardized tests help teachers and administrators to compare their students with others because the tests are norm referenced and standardized on a state or national population.

In sharp contrast to the standardized high-stakes tests is the movement for authentic or curriculum-based assessment. Proponents of curriculum-based assessment believe that assessment should be "a social construction that is a continuous, recursive, and divergent process for sharing accountability, not assigning it" and a process that affords "students opportunities to engage with teachers, caregivers, and stakeholders in meaningful partnerships involving genuine decision making" (Tierney, 2000, p. 244). In the remainder of this chapter, we discuss curriculum-based assessment in detail.

Curriculum-Based Assessment

Curriculum-based assessment is any assessment that is drawn directly from specific course curricula rather than from state performance standards or nationally normed data. Curriculum-based assessment includes both traditional teacher assessment of student performance—such as grades determined by multiple-choice tests, essay exams, short answer quizzes, matching—and what is known as authentic assessment—assessment activities that reflect the actual learning.

Traditional Teacher Assessment: Grades

No discussion of assessment in the secondary school would be complete without an examination of grades. Grades remain an important factor in students' lives and success. Grades determine both promotion and graduation. Because grades are so important to students, it is imperative that teachers assign grades that are consistent and fair. The following are some guidelines for teachers to use in assigning grades.

1. **Clearly specify the basis for a course grade at the beginning of the term.** Teachers need to make clear what constitutes a student's grade (Brozo & Simpson, 1999). Students and parents need to know the value of class participation, the relative weight of tests and papers, and the importance of homework. If criteria for grades are clear, students can work toward personal goals with understanding and confidence.

2. **Clearly specify the requirements and expectations of each assignment.** Students need to understand what grades are based on before they begin an assignment. If expectations are clear, students are rarely surprised by their grades. Teachers can use rubrics, checklists, and assignment outlines to help students understand the expectations of each assignment. Figure 10.1 shows an example of a specific assignment outline. Examples of rubrics are provided in the following Authentic Assessment section.

3. **Include a variety of assignments when calculating grades.** Grades should reflect a student's learning; however, grades are sometimes viewed too narrowly as simply the average of test scores. For many students, tests do not adequately reflect learning. Students may panic and perform poorly on tests; tests might not be able to assess understanding of ideas and concepts; ELLs may struggle with the English of tests. For these reasons, teachers should include such assignments as essays, oral presentations, group work, and portfolios (see the next section) in students' grades. The resulting grades will more accurately reflect student learning.

Assignment Outline

Assignment: Write a coherent, focused research paper on a document of historical importance. Use at least 3 critical sources; use at least 2 that are *not* Internet sources. Use both textual support and references to the research. Be certain to document all ideas that are not yours.

Steps:
1. Read the document—several times.
2. Think about your focus. Focus on a major theme (balance of power, racial equality, etc.). Focus on some aspect of the document that interests you. Decide your focus before you start doing research.
3. Write a clear thesis statement.
4. Conduct research that relates to your thesis statement. Your research can support or negate your position.
5. Take notes—on the document and on your research.
6. Get organized: think, talk, make an outline.
7. Draft your paper. Be certain to cite ideas properly that are not your own. A paper of this sort should have 2–3 quotes from the document and 3–5 quotes from your research. Work the quotes in carefully. Introduce a quote, give the quote, then **comment about it**. Don't leave your reader hanging. Your job is to make the implicit, explicit.
8. Have someone read over your draft. Do not give it to someone who will just tell you it is great. Give it to someone who will ask questions, challenge you, and help you make it better.
9. Revise and produce your final copy. If you have questions about documentation, look in any standard guide to writing research papers. Use internal citations and a "works cited" page.

FIGURE 10.1 *Assignment Outline*

4. **Provide timely feedback to guide student learning.** Students cannot improve if they do not know what to address with each new assignment. Timely feedback will help students to identify their own shortcomings and work to improve performance.
5. **Include self and peer assessment in grades.** The responsibility for learning is ultimately the student's. Involving students in self and peer evaluation encourages them to look honestly at their work and set personal goals for improvement.

Authentic Assessment

The use of authentic assessment represents an effort to change assessment from a negative event, in which knowledge and people are measured, to a positive process, by which knowledge is applied and people are valued. With authentic assessment, the focus is on learning. Assessment is collaborative, involving multiple stakeholders, and is a natural part of the learning process (Darling-Hammond, Ancess, & Falk, 1995). The environment of authentic assessment is positive and has an instructional purpose. Authentic assessment leads to reflective instruction, which helps students to develop meaning.

Underlying Beliefs of Authentic Assessment

Effective educational practices do not begin with assessment. Instead, they begin with instructional commitment to student learning (Darling-Hammond et al., 1995). This focus leads naturally to authentic assessment, with its goal of guiding instruction. Authentic assessment closely mirrors the world outside of school, is an essential part of the classroom life, and at times becomes indistinguishable from instruction itself. It is performance-based and features such real-world activities as formal presentations, portfolios, and exhibitions. Furthermore, authentic assessment is collaborative. The teacher is not viewed as the exclusive judge of mastery. Instead, authentic assessment incorporates many judges and evaluators with many different viewpoints: self and peer assessment, parental assessment, and community review boards. The goal is to give the responsibility of learning back to the student, with the teacher and other community members functioning as advisors and coaches.

Authentic assessment focuses on the learning task itself. If educators want to find out how students are writing, for example, they must observe students and read the students' work during the many steps of the writing process. Fragments of the task will not yield valid conclusions. The goal of authentic assessment is to assess students' abilities to gain new information and skills in a context that can be easily translated and applied to the world outside the classroom.

With authentic assessment variety is expected (Darling-Hammond et al., 1995). Students are evaluated on individual work and group work; the process of learning is documented and considered in assessment; learning products are placed in context; and students are encouraged to delve into alternative media, such as film and computer research. In addition, students may often choose to demonstrate knowledge in ways compatible with individual interests and learning styles, focusing attention on successful completion of the learning task. Figure 10.2 highlights the differences between norm-referenced testing and authentic assessment.

Because authentic assessment is collaborative and learner centered, the focus is on mastery of skills and strategies in addition to specific content. Classroom conversations must center on student work, and assessment is designed to convey what has actually been learned. Assessment procedures have to communicate on several levels—to the public, to parents, to other concerned educators in the students' lives, to the teacher, and to the students themselves. To this end, teachers might ask the following questions to guide decisions about assessment procedures.

- Why are we testing or assessing?
- What information are we gathering?
- What is it we want students to be able to do?
- Why should students be expected to know and use this material?
- How will this information direct instruction?
- How will this information influence students to make decisions about their own learning?
- How can we communicate the information and instructional decisions to all of the stakeholders?

Norm-Referenced Testing	Authentic Assessment
Selected response of discrete items	Complex, holistic activities
Objective is to compare students	Objective is to evaluate individual students
End result important	Learning process important
Cannot study for	Study definitely helps
Limited focus	Comprehensive view of what students can do
Reliable results	Reliability varies
Usable for large comparisons	Usable for instructional decisions
Used for ranking or sorting	Used for finding strengths and weaknesses
Passive student involvement	Active student involvement
No self-assessment	Includes self-assessment
Not a real-world activity	Involves real-world activities

FIGURE 10.2   *Differences between Norm-Referenced Testing and Authentic Assessment*

Authentic assessment does not include sorting who can and cannot perform certain tasks. Instead, authentic assessment focuses on what and how students learn. Assessment then leads to instructional decisions naturally. The result is an environment of collaboration, inquiry, process, and pride in achievement. This environment is positive for all learners and allows students of all abilities to succeed and demonstrate what they have accomplished.

Authentic Assessment Design

Authentic assessment includes oral presentations, performances, portfolios of student work, solutions to problems and experiments, and debates. It also includes observations, interviews, graphics that demonstrate mastery, conferences, learning logs, response journals, and self-assessment. In short, any learning activity can be restructured as an authentic assessment of student work. It is important to remember that the activity must be meaningful, be carefully tied to instruction, and involve multiple checkpoints and evaluators. In addition, expectations (in the form of rubrics or checklists) must be clear to all stakeholders. Designing authentic assessment requires several steps.

Step 1. **Thinking about what processes, strategies, or skills students are expected to demonstrate.** The teacher identifies the content or concepts that will be used as a vehicle for the process or skill and formulates the objectives for the assessment.

Step 2. **Devising the actual performance task.** The teacher writes a complete description of the task, which includes the required resources and clear, specific directions that are consistent with the desired performance. Students can be invited to participate in the editing of the task description. Completing the editing on a transparency using the overhead projector with the class can be useful and motivating. The teacher can use the questions students ask to check the clarity of the task.

Step 3. **Developing the criteria and a scoring procedure.** Evaluators may use an analytic rubric, which awards points to each element of the performance, or a holistic rubric with criteria that evaluate the overall performance. A simple checklist may also be appropriate for certain tasks. The choice should be meaningful to students and should motivate them to demonstrate their abilities. Students should be involved in the construction of criteria and scoring procedures. Because the goal of authentic assessment is student learning, students should learn to judge their own work with consistent and fair criteria, processes that are best learned with practice.

Step 4. **The performance task itself and its evaluation by multiple evaluators.** The performance task and evaluation will allow students to show how well they can use the learning process.

To illustrate how authentic assessment works, we focus on four authentic assessments of student learning: technology to show mastery, visual demonstrations of mastery, oral demonstrations of mastery, and portfolios. For each type of assessment, we describe the assessment procedures in general, and then give a specific example, grounded in the curriculum—complete with rubrics, checklists, and illustrations. The intent is that these examples can serve as guides for the teacher's own authentic assessment development.

Technology to Show Mastery

As more and more schools acquire adequate technology, students can be provided with the experiences needed to be computer proficient. Preparing computer Power-Point presentations encourages students to use multiple sources of information, select effective presentation designs, organize and synthesize the information, and master a powerful tool with real-world applications, as shown in Figures 10.3 and 10.4.

Step 1: The processes and skills
Students will demonstrate understanding of

☐ The relationship of a great inventor to the times in which he/she lived
☐ The invention itself, its creation and use
☐ The skills of oral interpretation

Step 2: The task
Design and execute a PowerPoint presentation:

☐ Choose an inventor who interests you.
☐ Research the inventor's life and times.
☐ Select the inventor's most significant invention.
☐ Study the invention. Focus on how the invention works and its influence on modern civilization.
☐ Design a PowerPoint presentation with the following features:

1. Title slide
2. Minimum of two slides about the inventor and times
3. Minimum of six slides explaining the invention, using visual and auditory images from the Internet
4. Minimum of two illustrative slides (graphics, pictures, or video clips)

Step 3: Scoring criteria and procedures
Figure 10.4 is a suggested PowerPoint rubric. This rubric can be used for self, peer, and teacher evaluation. This activity also can be used successfully with outside evaluators: parents, other teachers, or administrators. PowerPoint presentations are well suited for parent nights and student exhibitions.

Step 4: The task and its evaluation
Students deliver their PowerPoint presentations. Evaluators use the rubric in Figure 10.4 to assess the presentations.

FIGURE 10.3   *Example: PowerPoint Great Inventor Presentation*

Rank each part of the presentation on a scale from 4–1, with 4 indicating *excellent*, 3 indicating *good*, 2 indicating *fair*, and 1 indicating *poor*.

The title slide was informative and attractive.

4   3   2   1

The slides about the inventor and his/her times were insightful, informative, and attractive.

4   3   2   1

The explanation of the invention showed insight into the importance of the invention, how the invention works, and the impact of the invention on civilization.

4   3   2   1

The visual images were integrated into the presentation and added to the understanding of the invention.

4   3   2   1

The auditory images were integrated into the presentation and added to the understanding of the invention.

4   3   2   1

The illustrative slides were well designed, integrated into the presentation, and added to the understanding of the invention.

FIGURE 10.4   *PowerPoint Rubric*

Visual Demonstrations of Mastery

Visual demonstrations of mastery include charts, clusters, illustrations, and sketches that demonstrate understanding of concepts or processes. Of special interest is the graphic map. The map encourages students to discover an organizational pattern and support the pattern with symbols and words. It combines creativity with intellectual rigor and helps struggling learners participate in the intellectual atmosphere of the classroom as shown in Figures 10.5 and 10.6.

Figure 10.7 shows an example of a student-drawn thematic map on the novel *The Lion, The Witch, and The Wardrobe*. Evaluators would use the rubric in Figure 10.6 to assess the student's thematic map.

Oral Demonstrations of Mastery

Oral demonstrations of mastery include oral reports, speeches, interviews, storytelling, retellings of literature, readers' theater, dramatizations, role-playing, and debates (See Figure 10.8.). Oral demonstrations allow students to show in creative and spirited ways what they have learned. Furthermore, performances create an atmosphere of excitement and enthusiasm for learning that many forms of assessment cannot accomplish. Students perform their scenes. Class members and the teacher use the performance rubric in Figure 10.9 to rate individual performers.

Step 1: The processes and skills
Students will demonstrate understanding of

- ☐ The main themes of a novel
- ☐ Thematic support and development in a novel
- ☐ Organization and support in discussing and writing about a theme
- ☐ Using textual support in discussing and writing about a theme

Step 2: The task

- ☐ Decide what you think is the most important theme of the novel.
- ☐ Construct a cluster with your theme in the center.
- ☐ With a partner, select a symbol for the theme and sketch it on a blank piece of paper.
- ☐ With your partner, design branches that support the central symbol for your map—you must include characters, events, and features of the setting.
- ☐ With your partner, find quotes to support your ideas and include them in your map.
- ☐ Individually, revise your map, integrating colors, symbols, and words, and creating a final product that is visually and intellectually meaningful.

Step 3: Scoring criteria and procedures

- ☐ Self-assessment: Use the following rubric to score your final product.
- ☐ Peer assessment: Use the following rubric to score your partner's final product.
- ☐ Teacher assessment: Use the following rubric to score the student's final product.

Step 4: The performance and evaluation.

FIGURE 10.5   *Example: Thematic Map of a Novel*

FIGURE 10.6   *Thematic Map Rubric*

Criteria	4	3	2	1
Theme	The theme is an important one and is stated clearly.	The theme is important but not stated clearly.	The theme is not a central theme in the novel.	The theme is so abstract and generic as to be meaningless (e.g., man vs. man).
Symbol	The symbol is clearly related to the theme and is visually interesting.	The symbol is clearly related to the theme but the visual representation needs more care and thought.	The symbol is related to the theme but not in a compelling manner. The work is visually sloppy and careless.	The symbol is not representative of the theme. The work is visually sloppy and careless.
Branches	Branches clearly support the central theme. Characters, events, and features of the setting are all included.	Branches clearly support the theme central. One element (characters, events, and features of the setting) is missing.	Most branches clearly support the central theme.	Branches do not clearly support the central theme.

Quotes	Quotes clearly support the branches. Quotes are varied and appropriate. Citations are clearly indicated.	Quotes clearly support the branches. Quotes are appropriate but limited. Citations are clearly indicated.	Quotes do not always clearly support the branches. Inadequate number of quotes. Citations may be unclear.	Few or no quotes. Placement of quotes seems random.
Organization	Clearly organized. Shows insight and coherence.	Clearly organized but lacks compelling insight.	Organization rough but workable. Some parts seem random.	Aimless and disorganized.
Visual quality	Uses colors, symbols, and words in an interesting way. Final product is visually and intellectually meaningful.	Uses colors, symbols, and words in an appropriate way. Final product is visually and intellectually adequate.	Use of colors, symbols, and words lacks thought and planning. Final product is visually and intellectually rough.	Intellectually and visually sloppy.

Portfolio Assessment

The portfolio is an authentic assessment tool that allows students full participation in the assessment process. A portfolio is a purposeful collection of student work over time that exhibits the student's efforts, progress, and accomplishments in a particular area. It demonstrates the development of both the class's curriculum and the student's achievement. A portfolio might take the form of a writing portfolio, showing the student's knowledge of the writing process and skill in different kinds of writing. A portfolio might be used to show development of knowledge in social studies or mathematics. A portfolio might demonstrate achievement in different forms of art. Regardless of subject matter, portfolio assessment focuses on learning as a process, students' knowledge of learning and the approaches used to accomplish a task, and assessment as a tool for learning. Portfolios show engagement and self-reflection and provide a snapshot of student learning.

Portfolios are not meant to be collections of every piece of work a student has completed. To be effective, portfolios must be selective and demonstrate the care and reflection the student used to put it together. It becomes a series of records of the student's performance. The decision making, the thought given to how each entry fits and what it shows about the individual's effort and progress, the evidence of personal goals and interests, and the testimony to growth and change are all part of a learning process for the student. Certain elements are common to most portfolio assessment.

FIGURE 10.7 *Thematic Map of The Lion, the Witch, and the Wardrobe*

Step 1: The processes and skills
Students will demonstrate understanding of

☐ The role of a particular incident in history
☐ The importance of the particular incident in history
☐ The relationship of this incident to modern times
☐ Drama techniques: volume, pacing, vocal expression, facial expression, and gesture

Step 2: The task

☐ Choose an incident in history that is pivotal: a turning point in the course of a civilization's development.
☐ Study and discuss the incident in a small group.
☐ Write a script dramatizing the incident. Your script should capture a complete scene and center around some conflict. Be certain your script brings out the importance of the incident in history.
☐ Practice performing the scene.
☐ Perform the scene for the class.

Step 3: Scoring criteria and procedures

Two rubrics are needed for this project: a rubric for the written script and a rubric for the performance. Remember to involve students in the construction of the rubric. Figure 11.9 is a suggested performance rubric. This rubric can be used for self, peer, and teacher evaluation. This activity also can be used successfully with outside evaluators: parents, other teachers, or administrators.

Step 4: The task and its evaluation.

FIGURE 10.8   *Example: Scripting and Performing a Pivotal Time in History*

Criteria	4 Exemplary	3 Accomplished	2 Developing	1 Beginning
Volume				
Pacing				
Vocal expression				
Facial expression				
Gesture				

FIGURE 10.9   *Performance Rubric*

- **Goal setting.** The teacher, together with the students, should set the goals of portfolio assessment. Goals should be clear and should be consistent with the goals of the class. Students with a voice in this process are more likely to see the assessment as a meaningful part of instruction.

- **Selection of entries.** The number and types of entries need to be determined at the start of the instructional process. Entries should include both drafts of finished works and the finished works themselves. Because the aim of authentic assessment is student self-knowledge and learning, students should have a voice in determining what sort of entries should be included in the portfolio. Teachers, of course, should retain veto power and keep students focused on the purpose of portfolio assessment.
- **Table of contents.** The final portfolio should contain a table of contents to facilitate grading by multiple scorers and to keep portfolios consistent with the stated goals.
- **Rubrics.** The portfolio should contain grading rubrics for individual assignments as well as for the portfolio itself.
- **Reflective piece.** The portfolio should contain a student-written essay demonstrating self-knowledge of the contents of the portfolio and the learning the portfolio represents. It is the key to a successful portfolio assessment. Students may evaluate individual pieces of the portfolio, justify the inclusion of a piece, and explain growth from one piece to another. The reflective piece pulls the portfolio together and gives it meaning.
- **Grading and presentation procedures.** Who will grade the portfolios? Will they be on display for others to examine and enjoy? Answers to these questions must be decided before the portfolio process begins.

Portfolios can be used to keep students and teachers informed about learning; they can also help parents, the school, or the school district to stay informed about student progress. Portfolios may be used for parent and student conferences, for planning the next steps of instruction, and as evidence that students are developing learning skills. Sharing the portfolio may be done student to student, student to teacher, student to parent, teacher to teacher, or teacher to supervisor.

Portfolios take many forms and have many purposes. Although it is impossible to give an example that works for all instructional purposes and for all classroom settings, Figures 10.10 and 10.11 are guidelines for a personal essay portfolio. These are examples only and may serve as a guide in developing your own portfolio assessment.

Managing the Grading Load

Most teachers agree that assessment is important. The problem teachers face is how to cope with the tremendous time and energy that grading demands. Although there are no easy answers, there are some ways to make grading more manageable. The following is a collection of suggestions, gathered from seasoned teachers, for making grading less time consuming for teachers yet informative for students.

Focus Grading

Rather than marking every error in a written assignment, focus on one element at a time. For example, you can grade for a particular answer or a particular concept. If

Step 1: The processes and skills
Students will demonstrate an understanding of the writing process, specifically:

- ☐ Topic selection
- ☐ Originality and freshness in writing
- ☐ Coherence
- ☐ Organization
- ☐ Development
- ☐ Focus
- ☐ Pacing
- ☐ Experimentation
- ☐ Voice
- ☐ Mechanics

Step 2: The task

- ☐ Help develop goals for the personal essay portfolio. Goals must be consistent with the skills needed for effective personal essay writing.
- ☐ Help decide what entries should be included in the personal essay portfolio. Not open for negotiation is the inclusion of multiple drafts of at least one essay, the essay you are most proud of, and the essay you think needs most improvement. We can negotiate the number of essays to include in the portfolio and which essays to include.
- ☐ Write a reflective piece explaining why you chose each entry: its strengths and weaknesses and any changes you would make to create a stronger piece of writing.
- ☐ Complete a table of contents, including all selections, reflective pieces, rubrics, and page numbers.

Step 3: Scoring criteria and procedures
The scorers for the portfolio can include teachers, parents, students, and community members. This should be decided early in the portfolio development process. Expectations should be clear and deadlines specified to all stake holders.

The portfolio should include rubrics for each portfolio entry and a general rubric for the entire portfolio. Students should help with the development and writing of the rubrics, giving them insight into and ownership of the expectations for each essay and the portfolio itself. Figure 10.11 is an example of a general personal essay rubric that can act as a guideline for the development of rubrics pertinent to specific assignments and curricula.

Step 4: The task and its evaluation
Students develop and compile their personal essay portfolio. Evaluators use rubrics (see Figure 10.11) to assess the portfolios.

FIGURE 10.10   *Example: Personal Essay Portfolio*

you are grading written compositions, you can grade for organization in one assignment, paragraph transitions in another assignment, writing conventions such as spelling the next, and so on. It is important to remember in assessing student work that the teacher is not the editor. The purpose of assessment is to inform instruction, not to weigh the teacher down unnecessarily.

Monday for Comments

Teachers spend countless hours writing comments on students' papers only to have students turn quickly to the grade at the end and then put the papers aside.

Grade	Qualities
A	The topic is handled thoughtfully, with insight and originality. The paper is coherent, organized around some central idea. Ideas are developed and supported, but not belabored. The beginning of the paper captures the reader's interest. The paper focuses on a single incident. The pacing is well considered and crafted. The ending is well integrated into the paper and captures the reader's interest. Experimentation is evident. The paper has a clear voice: uses diction detail, imagery, syntax, and tone in a distinctive manner. The paper is free of spelling and mechanical errors.
B	The topic is handled thoughtfully, with insight. The paper is coherent, organized around some central idea. Ideas are developed and supported, but not belabored. The beginning of the paper captures the reader's interest. The paper focuses on a single incident. The ending is integrated into the paper and keeps the reader's interest. There is an attempt at creating a clear voice: the paper uses diction detail, imagery, syntax, and tone in a somewhat distinctive manner. The paper is free of spelling and mechanical errors.
C	The topic is handled thoughtfully. The paper is coherent, organized around some central idea. The ideas are developed and supported with detail. The beginning of the paper captures the reader's interest. The paper focuses on a single incident. The ending is integrated into the paper and keeps the reader's interest. The paper has few spelling and mechanical errors.
D	I better not see any of these. These papers exhibit sloppy thinking, shallow ideas, and careless writing.

FIGURE 10.11   *The Personal Essay Rubric*

One suggestion is to establish a "Monday for comments" policy. If students turn in assignments on Monday, the teacher will write comments on their work. If students turn in assignments the next class day, there is no penalty, but the teacher will simply read the assignment and give it a grade. If the students value comments, they will turn their assignments in on Monday. If students do not care whether they get comments, they get an extra day to turn in their work, and the teacher saves the time and energy he or she would have spent in writing comments that are not valued.

Code Sheets

Rather than writing the same comments over and over again, teachers can memorize and use a code for common errors. It takes much less time to write a 4 than it

1. Word choice
2. Spelling
3. Run-on sentence
4. Sentence fragment
5. Punctuation
6. Pronoun-antecedent
7. Thesis or topic sentence problem
8. Thought not related to the thesis
9. Thought not clearly expressed
10. Needless repetition
11. Transition needed
12. Inadequate development and support

FIGURE 10.12   *Error Key*

does to write out *sentence fragment*. There are many possible codes. Figure 10.12 is one example. Teachers can use this code or use it as a starting point to develop a code that suits the purpose and content of their classes.

Alternative Evaluators

If the purpose of assessment is to enhance student learning, the teacher is no longer the sole arbiter of achievement. The teacher should evaluate some assignments, of course. However, students can learn from many evaluators. Parents can read and comment on an assignment. Community volunteers can read and comment on projects or class sets of assignments. Older students can give helpful feedback, as can peers. A panel of community members can evaluate major projects or displays. This feedback from alternative evaluators is invaluable to students; it helps them to understand the value of the adult community and gives them experience with different standards of judgment. It also saves the teacher time and energy he or she can then devote to planning and curriculum design.

Writing Conferences

Writing conferences, even conferences lasting five minutes or less, can be excellent assessment tools. Conferences should be personal, pointed, and positive. They support students' efforts to improve their writing. The best time for writing conferences is when students are involved in some phase of the writing process. The teacher can circulate around the room, quickly read a student's work, and provide immediate feedback and guidance. More formal conferences are also helpful. These conferences can take place while students are completing a reading assignment or while a classroom volunteer is supervising an activity. Writing conferences give students evaluative feedback that enables them to improve. At the same time, conferences save teachers the time it would take to write comparable comments on students' work.

Holistic Scoring with Rubrics

When teachers use holistic scoring, they simply assign a score, without comment, based on the rubric that accompanies the assignment. Holistic scoring with carefully designed rubrics saves teachers time and provides students with the feedback they need to improve. Students know the expectations for the assignment, and teachers evaluate assignments with clear criteria in mind. Students can also learn to score their own assignments using carefully formulated rubrics, and they can learn to construct and use rubrics themselves, thereby learning to isolate the criteria for achievement in a particular assignment.

Rubrics can be especially useful for informing students about their progress in developing specific skills or abilities. Buehl and Stumpf (2005) created a rubric for reading comprehension strategies that teachers can use to communicate to students the degree to which the students are demonstrating comprehension traits of a reader while engaged in classroom reading tasks (see Figure 10.13).

Summary

Standardized testing has a role in education as a means of ranking students and appears to hold students and teachers accountable. The curriculum-based assessment, however, has changed the environment of testing and learning to one of positive accomplishment with instructional purpose. Authentic assessment proposes that if educators want to find out how students are reading and writing, students must be observed while doing these activities. Performance assessment requires students to demonstrate their understanding of the process of reading and writing as well as the ability to read and write effectively. Performance assessment gives evidence of literary appreciation, wide reading, strategic interactive reading, and application to life. Portfolios are useful collections of student work that show evidence of effort and progress, personal goals and interests, growth, and change of a student. The most important aspect of the new assessment is the tie to instruction. Assessment becomes the means by which the teacher determines what new learning should be initiated or what learning needs reinforcement. Self-assessment is powerful because it involves students in their own learning. Teachers no longer dispense knowledge while students receive it. The environment of the new assessment creates a positive collaboration between teacher and student as a learning team.

Extending Learning

Reviewing the Talking Points

Revisit the talking points at the beginning of this chapter. Answer the questions now that you have read the chapter and compare your prereading and postreading responses.

Revisiting the Vignette

In the opening vignette Mr. Taylor combined individual and group assessments and gave students experience in creating, testing, and using a rubric for evaluation. Think back to

FIGURE 10.13 *Traits of a Reader Rubric*

Traits of a Reader Rubric.

The Traits of a Reader rubric can be used to monitor and assess key elements of students' reading comprehension and thinking. This scoring rubric is based on a five-point scale from emerging (1) to advanced competence (5). This Traits of a Reader rubric is a useful tool for tracking student progress over the course of a school year.

	MAKING CONNECTIONS	Score _____
5	Consciously draws upon a wealth of prior knowledge and experiences to make text-to-self, text-to-text, and text-to-world connections to create an understanding of text.	
3	Is increasingly able to identify relevant personal knowledge and experiences as a key comprehension strategy when prompted to do so.	
1	Does not recognize how personal knowledge and experiences can be tapped to make sense of text. Has difficulty matching relevant personal knowledge and experiences to the demands of understanding text.	

	SELF-QUESTIONING	Score _____
5	Approaches a text in an inquiring mode before, during, and after reading. Generates questions that may be clarifying, speculative, curious, critical or author-directed and assesses a text for possible answers.	
3	Is increasingly inclined to formulate significant questions before, during, and after reading when prompted to wonder about text.	
1	Is dependent on questions posed by others (author, teacher, etc.) to guide comprehension.	

	INFERENCING	Score _____
5	Consciously searches for implicit meanings through melding the author's information with relevant prior knowledge.	
3	Is increasingly able to gain implicit meaning from a text with prompting.	
1	Concentrates on explicit information; struggles with layers of implied meaning.	

	VISUALIZING	Score _____
5	Independently creates visual and sensory images through a sensitivity to the author's language cues, both literal and figurative, and through accessing relevant prior knowledge.	
3	Is increasingly able to create visual and sensory images with prompting.	
1	Concentrates on identifying words and does not generate visual and sensory images from text.	

	DETERMINING IMPORTANCE	Score _____
5	Decides upon key ideas and themes by identifying meaningful relationships of information within text.	
3	Is increasingly able to separate significant ideas and information from background details when prompted by activities such as graphic organizers.	
1	Is unable to distinguish major ideas/themes from background information within text.	

(continued)

SYNTHESIZING	Score _____
5	Creates an essence of text, including personal interpretations and conclusions about meaning, which can be accessed in future learning situations as new background knowledge.
3	Is increasingly able to summarize text and to reflect on its meaning with prompting.
1	Is unable to condense a text into a concise, meaningful summary.

USING FIX-UP STRATEGIES	Score _____
5	Assumes all text makes sense and confidently employs multiple strategies to achieve necessary comprehension.
3	Is increasingly able to monitor comprehension and use a variety of fix-up strategies with prompting.
1	Does not expect reading to be meaningful and/or feels helpless to correct any deficiencies in comprehension.

From Buehl, D. & Stumpf, S. (2005). Traits of a reader rubric. In *6–8 Literacy Notebook*, Madison, WI: Madison Metropolitan School District, 21–22.

your experiences in writing reports or completing projects when you were a middle school student. Recall any instances when you were able to receive feedback before finishing the project. Did you have a clear understanding of the task and the expectations? Did you know the criteria by which the teacher was going to evaluate or grade the work? If so, share your experiences with classmates. If not, retell just how you knew when a project or paper was complete and ready to be submitted.

Terms to Remember and Use

formative assessment	summative assessment	high-stakes tests
standardized tests	curriculum-based assessment	authentic assessment
portfolio assessment	writing conference	self-assessment

Write a series of sentences that meaningfully connect pairs of the above key terms. Your sentences should refer to ideas and concepts related to the literacy of middle school students.

Modifying Instruction for English Language Learners

Assessment plays a crucial role in determining the effectiveness of teaching as well as students' progress in learning. The assessment for English language learners is particularly important for several reasons (Hargett, 1998; Walqui, 1999). First, it helps teachers to identify ELLs' English proficiency levels so that teachers can make appropriate decisions concerning instruction, enrollment of ELLs in specialized language programs and placement in the right levels of the service. Second, assessment helps to monitor a student's progress in English language and other subject areas. Third, assessment results can be used in formative evaluation for improving the instructional programs. Finally, it provides information needed for deciding readiness of ELLs to exit special programs. The usefulness of any assessment to provide information for different audiences is dependent on wisely matching assessment strategies with the purpose and goal of conducting the assessment.

With *No Child Left Behind*, inclusion requirements for ELLs in large-scale standardized testing have been articulated and implemented in all fifty states. However, Abedi (2001) found that standardized testing fails to reflect ELLs' learning. Furthermore, many issues arise from accommodations for ELLs in those tests, validity of the test being the major problem. Performance-based assessment, which is closely associated with standards-based learning, has been advocated in an effort to fairly evaluate ELL learning progress. Despite criticism and challenges (Gordon, 1992; Winfield, 1995), the merits of using authentic assessment to address equity and cultural diversity shows promise. (Hancock, 1994; Lachat, 1998, 1999; Meisels, Dorfman, & Steele, 1995; Neill, 1995).

Although which assessment system is used is often beyond teachers' control, knowledge about attributes of effective instruction for ELL students could inform assessment for them (Anstrom, 1997). ELLs should be assessed for both content knowledge and language proficiency, and schools should make efforts to assess students' content knowledge and abilities in their native languages as well as in English whenever possible. It is important to remember that students' achievement may be underestimated when they have already learned concepts in their native languages but they have difficulty demonstrating their knowledge in English. A diversity of measures should be used to measure content knowledge and skills. For instance, observation could be a more useful method to evaluate ELLs' understanding of a concept when a criteria-reference test fails to reveal such knowledge. Knowledge of students' background, such as educational experience and parents' English and literacy levels, contributes to complete and accurate assessment.

At a classroom level, there are many strategies that teachers can use to provide more appropriate assessment for ELLs. In *The Guide to Performance Assessment for Linguistically Diverse Students*, Navarrete and Gustkee (1996) suggested the following specific techniques for assessing language minority students.

- Allowing extra time to complete or respond to the assessment tasks
- Designing administration procedures to match classroom instructional practices (e.g., cooperative small groups, individual conferencing, and assessing in the language of instruction)
- Simplifying directions in English and/or paraphrasing in the students' native language. Also providing additional clarifying information during and/or after administration of the assessment (e.g., synonyms for difficult words or phrases)
- Permitting students to use dictionaries or word lists
- Supporting assessment tasks in a contextualized manner by doing the following:
    i.   Incorporating familiar classroom material as a stimulus, such as brief quotations, charts, graphics, cartoons, and works of art
    ii. Including questions for small group discussion and individual writing
    iii. Mirroring learning processes with which students are familiar such as the writing process and reading conferencing activities.

Beyond the Book

- Discuss an upcoming or current assignment with a current middle school student. Try to determine whether the student has a clear understanding of the expectations of the teacher and an understanding of how students will be graded on their work.
- Interview a colleague about his or her assessment practices. Determine whether this teacher used rubrics, student conferences, or any other kind of formative assessments. Ask whether this person gives clear descriptions of how the assignments will be graded or evaluated.

- Do an Internet search on the "Six Traits of Writing" and scan through the rubrics. Determine if this will be useful for your own writing assignments.
- Meet with a classmate and share assignments. Become a critical friend to that classmate and discuss how the assignments will be assessed using formative and summative evaluations.
- Make an inquiry in your school as to who utilizes portfolios and student conferences. Ask them to share their criteria for portfolios and protocols for the student conferences. Share these with your classmates to determine how many variations your class can come up with.
- Do an Internet search on the term "assessment." Find an article that seems pertinent or informative and share it with your classmates to see how much has been written about this important issue.
- Think back to an assignment that you gave to a class or one that you were assigned in middle school. What changes could be made to make the task an authentic asessment?
- How can a teacher best ensure that students have a clear understanding of the tasks they are asked to do as well as clear expectations for how they will be evaluated? Discuss this with a colleague.

References

Abedi, J. (2001). *Assessment and Accommodations for English Language Learners: Issues and Recommendation. (CRESST Policy Brief 4, 2001 summer)*. Los Angeles: UCLA Center for the Study of Evaluation.

Anstrom (1997). *Academic Achievement for Secondary Language Minority Students: Standards, Measures and Promising Practices*. Washington, DC: National Clearinghouse for Bilingual Education.

Brozo, W. G. & Simpson, M. L. (1999). *Readers, Teachers, Learners: Expanding Literacy Across the Content Areas* (3rd ed.). Columbus, OH: Merrill.

Buehl, D. & Stumpf, S. (2005). Traits of a reader rubric. In *6–8 Literacy Notebook*, Madison, WI: Madison Metropolitan School District, 21–22.

Daniels, H., & Bizar, M. (1998). *Methods That Matter: Six Structures for Best Classroom Practice*. York, ME: Stenhouse.

Darling-Hammond, L., Ancess, J., & Falk, B. (1995). *Authentic Assessment in Action: Studies of Schools and Students at Work*. New York: Teachers College Press.

Gordon, E. W. (1992). *Implications of Diversity in Human Characteristics for Authentic Assessment*. Berkeley, CA: National Center for Research on Evaluation, Standards, and Student Testing (CRESST).

Hargett, G. (1998). *Assessment in ESL & Bilingual Education*. Portland, OR: Northwest Regional Educational Laboratory.

Hancock, C. R. (1994). Alternative assessment and second language study: What and why? *ERIC Digest*. Washington, DC: ERIC Clearinghouse on Language and Linguistics.

Lachat, M.A. (1998). *What Policymakers and School Administrators Need to Know About Assessment Reform and English Language Learners*. Providence, RI: Northeast and Islands Regional Educational Laboratory at Brown University.

Lachat, M.A. (1999). *Standards, Equity and Cultural Diversity*. Providence, RI: Northeast and Islands Regional Educational Laboratory at Brown University (LAB).

Langer, J. A. (2000). Excellence in English in middle and high school: How teachers professional lives support student achievement. *American Educational Research Journal, 37*(2), 397–439.

Lewis, C. S. (1950). *The Lion, the Witch, and the Wardrobe*. New York: HarperCollins.

Meisels, S. J., Dorfman, A., & Steele, D. (1995). Equity and excellence in group-administered performance-based assessments. In M. Nettles & A. Nettles (Eds.), *Equity and Excellence in Educational Testing and Assessment* (pp. 243–261). Boston: Kluwer Academic Publishers.

Neill, M. (1995). Some prerequisites for the establishment of equitable, inclusive multicultural assessment systems. In M. Nettles & A. Nettles (Eds.), *Equity and Excellence in Educational Testing and Assessment* (pp. 115–149). Boston: Kluwer Academic Publishers.

Tierney, R. J. (2000). Snippets: How will literacy be assessed in the next millennium? *Reading Research Quarterly, 35*(2), 244–250.

Walqui, A. (1999). Assessment of culturally and linguistically diverse students: Considerations for the 21st Century. In *Including Culturally and Linguistically Diverse Students in Standards-Based Reform: A Report on McREL's Diversity Roundtable I* (pp. 5–84). Aurora, CO: Mid-continent Research for Education and Learning (McREL).

Winfield, L. (1995). Performance-based assessments: Contributor or detractor to equity? In M. Nettles & A. Nettles (Eds.), *Equity and Excellence in Educational Testing and Assessment* (pp. 221–241). Boston: Kluwer Academic Publishers.

Index